The Greatest Thinkers

Weidenfeld and Nicolson London

The Greatest Thinkers

Edward de Bono

diagrams by Edward de Bono with George Daulby

Designed by George Daulby
for George Weidenfeld and Nicolson Ltd,
11 St John's Hill, London sw11

Art Editor: Tim Higgins
Layout: Soona Hodivala
House Editor: Hilary Lloyd Jones

isbn 0 297 77198 1

Printed in Great Britain by Morrison and Gibb Ltd,
London and Edinburgh
Filmset by Keyspools Ltd, Golborne, Lancs

Contributions by **Igor Aleksander**
Michael Berry
Peter Brent
Graham Davey
Len Doyal
James Fenton
Felipe Fernandez-Armesto
Christopher Frayling
Michael Grant
Pamela Gray
David Holloway
Jonathan Keates
Shirley Letwin
Kenneth Minogue
Robert Orr
William Page
John Paxton
Jonathan R. Pedder
Colin A. Ronan
David Sceats
Martin Seymour-Smith
Alan Sked

Contents

Introduction

There has never been anything more powerful than an idea in the mind of a single man

One man amongst the millions that have lived on this earth must seem pretty insignificant. An idea is intangible and insubstantial. Yet there has never been anything more powerful than an idea in the mind of a single man. Einstein was a man who ate like other men, washed his face like other men and needed to sleep like them. Yet with the thinking of his mind we have been able to tap the ultimate source of energy in nature. There is no type of energy more fundamental than the fusion energy in the hydrogen bomb, for it is the same energy as the sun itself uses. Hopefully we shall soon be able to use it for peaceful purposes. Marx was a very ordinary Victorian with such Victorian habits as fathering a child by his chambermaid, yet from the activity of his mind came an ideology which is probably the most powerful in the world today and determines the lives, in detail, of half the world's population. Every day of our lives is made by the rising of the sun. Before Copernicus people used to think of the sun as moving around the earth; after Copernicus they knew that the sun was still and it was the earth that rotated around it. Darwin's idea of evolution was very simple in hindsight and it was not even worked out thoroughly, yet that single idea at once gave man a plausible story for his very origins.

That simple idea, which might have occurred to many people, is enough to qualify Darwin amongst the greatest thinkers. Pavlov made the simple observation that if a bell was rung before his dogs were fed then the sound of the bell would make them salivate. From that simple experiment has developed the possibility of controlling the thinking and behaviour of humans without their knowledge or consent. Columbus was a sailor with a larger streak of stubbornness than most others, but to him fell the honour of discovering just about half the world, and a half that has become the most powerful. Sooner or later it would have been discovered by someone or other, but in fact it was discovered by Columbus, for all practical purposes.

It is not easy to define a great thinker and even more difficult to define the greatest thinkers. A thinker cannot be separated from the effects of his thinking. No doubt there have been immensely powerful minds whose thoughts were never published or if published were ignored. There are certainly such minds which have not been included in this book. The greatness of the thinker is, for the purposes of this book, assessed by the effect of his thought on society. Perhaps the title of the book should have been 'The Greatest Thinkers in Society', since it is the role of the thinker in society that has determined the assessment of greatness. The book is not meant to be a Hall of Fame for those with the most powerful minds or the most profound thoughts. There is no award of merit for abstraction or subtlety of thinking. The effect on society is what matters.

The thinking of Jesus, in the form of Christianity, has dominated civilization ever since. The thinking of St Augustine set the tone of both the Catholic Church, and even more so of the Protestant Churches, with its emphasis on original sin and the need for grace from God for salvation. The thinking of Plato and Aristotle has dominated the thinking of the Western world: Platonic thinking with the search for the ultimate truth beneath surface appearances; Aristotle with the truths hidden in language. For over two thousand years the thinking system of Aristotle, as re-packaged by St Thomas Aquinas, was the only one approved by Western logicians. The cultural and thinking climate today is very strongly influenced by Rousseau, Freud and Sartre in direct and indirect ways. In some cases the thinker included in this book provided a sort of switch-point or change of direction. This was so with James or Nietzsche, who would not qualify in terms of the profundity of their thoughts but who provided definite switch-points away from the traditional line of thinking: one towards pragmatism and the other towards the rule of supermen. Sometimes, as in the case of Malthus, a quite ordinary thinker by paying attention to a new area has started an important line of thinking. Finally there are the thinkers who have really solved problems: Newton, Clerk Maxwell, Einstein.

It will be easy to criticize the selection of thinkers on the ground that they did not merit inclusion or by their inclusion have excluded others more worthy. For instance it could be argued that in the field of economics Adam Smith was more fundamental a thinker than Keynes. Nevertheless in the days of Smith economics was a descriptive science, since commerce had its own momentum, whereas in the days of Keynes, and subsequently, the lives of millions have been affected directly by economic policy. It would be absurd to compare the thinking of Columbus, Bacon or Malthus with that of the giants like Clerk Maxwell, Euclid or St Thomas Aquinas. Yet in their way the thinking of these men had as much effect.

Quite often a thinker has been *lucky*, in so far as publicity has ascribed to him a role which he may not really have merited. The treatment of Bacon as the father of the scientific method is such a case. But the direction of his thinking, if not the quality of his ideas, justifies the claim. Copernicus was not the first to claim that the sun was the centre of the earth's orbit but he did start the switch-over in thinking towards accepting this. He was lucky to have his ideas backed up by

9

The ripeness of an idea is rarely the direct consequence of the thinking of the thinker himself

such a capable team as Johannes Kepler and Tycho Brahe. Rousseau was lucky to be idolized by the French Revolution and by the Romantics under Byron, otherwise his writings would never have had the effect they did. Luther was extremely fortunate in having the political backing of the German princes, otherwise his fate would have been that of any other dissenting cleric. Darwin was lucky to find a materialistic world gasping for an explanation of man that did not include God. Luck with reception, luck with political backing, the ripeness of an idea are rarely the direct consequences of the thinking of the thinker himself, and so it must seem unfair to acclaim an idea because it has been lucky in its reception. But 'effectiveness' depends on a contribution from the thinker and a contribution from the state of society.

There are not many philosophers in this book. That may seem surprising, because most books of this sort are written by philosophers and usually start off with a string of Greek philosophers such as Thales, Parmenides, Pythagoras, Heraclitus, Anaximander, Socrates and so on. The exclusion of such heavy-weight philosophers as Leibniz, Spinoza, Hegel, Russell and Wittgenstein will surprise many. And yet philosophy was something of an 'in-game' for 'in-players', and had little effect on society. Wittgenstein has had a huge influence on other philosophers, but much less effect on society than Keynes, Sartre or Wiener. What has tended to happen in philosophy is that one philosopher has constructed a way of looking at the world and set up his school of followers and then another philosopher has disagreed with him and set up the opposite school. In this way philosophical heat is generated but not always very much light. The distinction between Realists and Nominalists, and between Rationalists and Empiricists, has not seemed as important to other people as it has to philosophers because in practical terms it has always seemed that both parties were right in all except their rejection of the other party.

This argument against the inclusion of too many philosophers in favour of the thinkers with a more practical impact could be turned around to challenge the exclusion of some obvious men of action. Edward Jenner by his conquest of smallpox probably had more practical effect on the world than many thinkers. Great scientists like Pasteur and Planck and Faraday have also exerted a strong influence. Engineers of genius like Brunel, Archimedes and the Wright brothers have helped to change the face of society. Marconi turned Clerk Maxwell's theories into practical telecommunications. Then there were the generals like Napoleon and Alexander the Great. Can thinking be divorced from literature:

should not Dante, Shakespeare and Goethe have their place? What about men of unquestioned genius like Leonardo da Vinci? It is difficult to give a sound logical foundation for the exclusion of any of these. On the whole the emphasis has been on those thinkers who by the expression of pure thinking have shaped our civilization. I would not be prepared to argue this point, except to say that any such list must be personal and based on a complex of aesthetic and unexpressed reasons.

The book is essentially about the influence of thinkers on Western civilization. This is not strictly true, because the effect of thinkers like Jesus and Marx has been as great or greater outside the West than within it. Jesus himself lived in the Middle East, and there would be as much justification for including Mohammed, who would certainly qualify in terms of his effect on society. But that effect was exerted in the Middle East, whereas the effect of Jesus was exerted directly in the West. There is no doubt that Western civilization owes an unrecognized debt to the Arab civilization for the basis of scientific knowledge and also most mathematical knowledge. In addition it was through the continued interest of the Arab civilizations that the wisdom of the Greeks reached Europe. There have been great thinkers in Islam and in the Far East. Geography alone has been the excuse for not including them here. There is the single strange inclusion of Confucius, which is logically unjustified except that by contrast his thinking illustrates the road which Western thinking did *not* take.

There are many important aspects of society which have been formed gradually by a succession of thinkers. Some individuals have made contributions large enough to qualify their thinking as 'personal' rather than 'team-effort', but there remains a distinction between the idea that takes place in the mind of one man and the idea that is built up gradually by many minds. This has been the case with such important areas as politics, the legal system, statistics, computer information processing and aesthetics in general.

It is almost impossible to write in an unbiased manner. Without wishing it so, a point is made by a subtle distribution of emphasis, by ignoring some detail and exaggerating another, by dismissing one thing with a curt adjective and praising another with a value adjective, by creating certain links and connections and failing to notice others. Had I myself written all the individual biographies of the greatest thinkers, those biographies would have reflected my opinion of that thinker's contribution rather than the contribution itself. Instead, each biography has been written by an outside contributor in the hope that he can be more objective. In this way the book can be used as a collection of individual accounts of the greatest thinkers rather than support for my own point of view. The reader is put into the same position as myself with regard to these accounts.

The comment pieces which group the thinkers look directly at the thinking itself. The purpose of each of these pieces is to examine some aspect of thinking as it is illustrated by the thinkers under discussion. In the biographical pieces the emphasis is on the thinkers as people. In the comment pieces the emphasis is on the phenomenon we call thinking.

The book actually provides three opportunities for the reader to look at the thinking of the greatest thinkers. The first opportunity is in the visual representation of the thinking that precedes each biography. These drawings are my own, in collaboration with a graphic designer. Then there is the biography written by a contributor. Finally, in the linking piece, there is usually another look at the thinking. This structure is deliberate because it is not easy to grasp the essence of the thinker's contribution from one reading or one point of view.

In many instances it is fascinating to speculate as to what might have happened if a particular influence had been absent or if an alternative point of view had prevailed. What would Christendom have been like if Pelagius with his doctrine of positive self-help had triumphed over St Augustine with his emphasis on the predestination of man? If Aristotle had not existed or been re-packaged by St Thomas Aquinas, what would our logical system have been like? If Euclid had not set the fashion for axiomatic system building, might our philosophers have occupied themselves with more practical matters? In the absence of Plato would there have been less search for Platonic truth and less of the material effectiveness we take for granted? Would our thinking have been more like that of the East or would it have been totally different? The speculations are endless. What is fascinating is to appreciate in how definite and deliberate a manner our thinking style was formed by the ideas of these greatest of thinkers. There is nothing *inevitable*. At many points our culture or concepts could have taken off in entirely different directions: as different as the alternative approaches of Moses, Confucius and Plato.

At many points our culture or concepts could have taken off in entirely different directions

Moses

Moses acted as the loudspeaker who broadcast God's will as a tight set of laws that established a people and a religion. His contribution was very much more than that of a passive communication channel for he had to weld the detail of the law and the lives of the people together. Moreover he had to do it in a way that would survive his personal authority.

?13th century BC

Of all the kings, prophets and patriarchs of the Bible, it is Moses who has most often captured the imagination of painters, poets and musicians. Solomon may be more magnificent, Jacob more human in terms of his amazing combination of cunning and sheer good luck, David a figure of more obvious bravado and panache, but in the end Western art has inevitably turned, for the expression of some of its profoundest concerns, to the agonized, solitary lawgiver of Sinai.

This timeless concept of a man alone both in his capacity as leader and in his role as visionary has successfully resisted either verbal or visual categorization. Poetry, for example, has created for us the picture of baffled and sickened old age that animates the *Moïse* of the French Romantic writer Alfred de Vigny, while music has made of Moses both the craggy, monolithic protagonist of Rossini's epic opera *Mose in Egitto* and the rejected prophet-cum-artist of Arnold Schoenberg's music drama *Moses und Aron*. But perhaps the most disparate perspectives are offered by painting and sculpture, where Michelangelo's grim-visaged, leonine giant jostles Rembrandt's sad-eyed mystic, and Tintoretto's shadowy magician makes a striking contrast to Botticelli's workaday shepherd. Where was there ever, we may find ourselves asking, a real Moses?

All that is known of the historical figure can be found in the opening books of the Old Testament, and even here the divisions between fact and legend are so hopelessly blurred as to make us accept all the more readily the definition of Moses's life as a 'saga' fraught with heroic grandeur and passion, sudden reverses and miraculous triumphs. The story of the infant Moses being found in the bulrushes by Pharaoh's daughter is surely no more than legend, but it is significant that he should have been adopted by the Egyptian princess, given what is just as likely to be an Egyptian as a Hebrew name, and brought up in the highly sophisticated milieu of the royal court.

A change of dynasties had recently taken place, the Pharaoh Ahmose I (*c.* 1570–46 BC) having successfully overthrown the hated foreign rule of the Hyksos, a motley array of shepherds and charioteers who had surged into Egypt at the beginning of the second millennium BC. In a burst of nationalism, Ahmose and his successors of the Eighteenth and Nineteenth Dynasties began a policy of oppression towards the Hebrews settled around the former royal capital of Avaris in the Nile delta. This attempt to mould the Hebrews into a permanent slave labour force was combined with an effort to regulate their growth as an immigrant population, culminating in the widespread slaughter of male children from which Moses himself so narrowly escaped.

In his historic role as a lawgiver, Moses cannot fail to have

benefited from an Egyptian court education. Egypt during the thirteenth century BC was reviving itself after years of decadence, and the vigorous rule of such Pharaohs as Seti I and Rameses II triumphantly re-established the social and religious structures from which their predecessor, the weird, neurotic Akhenaton, had tried to break away. As a dominant Middle Eastern force, Egypt had maintained contact with such empires as those of the Hittites and the newly powerful Assyrians. The resultant atmosphere in which Moses grew to maturity was inevitably cosmopolitan, as is shown in the detail of surviving reliefs and wall-paintings. This atmosphere, as we shall see, will have had its effect on the formation of the so-called Mosaic tradition.

The crucial event in Moses's early life — the vision of God in the Burning Bush — followed his first challenge to Pharaonic oppression. His situation at this point uncannily resembles those of certain nineteenth-century revolutionaries: rejected by his own people, themselves sullenly resigned to their servitude, he has to flee abroad after ill-meditated violence ending in the murder of an Egyptian overseer, and radically reshape his task as Hebrew liberator.

Setting aside the actual location of the Burning Bush episode — there is more than one Mount Horeb — or even the botanical nature

of the Bush itself (most probably *Zizyphus Spina Christi*, the Wild Jujube), what matters to us is the central relevance of this theophany, this divine manifestation, to the Mosaic concept of law.

First of all, there is the notion of the god Yahweh as a personal God, intimate and awe-inspiring, but continuously present and always watchful. Such a notion can hardly have failed to seem revolutionary in a world where the gods, despite incarnation in familiar shapes such as those of a hawk or a jackal, must always have appeared extraordinarily remote from everyday experience.

God's omnipresence is closely linked with the concepts of his invisibility and his namelessness. Moses hears but does not see him, and there is here, as elsewhere in the story, the suggestion of an all too human perplexity at having to negotiate with a Creator who, when asked his name, riddlingly answers: 'I Am That I Am.' Both these concepts imply a universality which, in terms of what the Jews and other Middle Eastern peoples were then familiar with, seems almost arrogantly new-fangled.

The ensuing contest between an obdurate Pharaoh and Moses supported by his brother Aaron forms one of the Bible's greatest dramatic episodes. God's power, confirming the promises made to Abraham in Genesis (12:2), now shows itself in action, as plague follows plague in a lurid and terrible series. Yet only after the Red

Sea crossing and the final destruction of the pursuing Egyptian army is Moses called upon to act as lawgiver to the moody, turbulent tribes with whose leadership he has been entrusted.

In taking the Ten Commandments – the 'Decalogue' – from God on Mount Sinai, Moses was bringing to the Jews the kernel of a much greater body of laws designed to cover every area of civil, military and religious life. The Exodus narrative indeed breaks off at this point, as if conscious of the moment's importance, to include a kind of summary of the law itself, which will provide the basis of the Covenant entered into by God and the people. After the incident of the Golden Calf, in which the Israelites, impatient at Moses's delay on the mountain, turn for leadership to the plausible, smooth-tongued Aaron, who gives them a golden idol, this Covenant is renewed and Exodus closes with a detailed outline of solemn ritual observances, forming an introduction to the immense legal corpus known as Leviticus, 'the Priestly Book', which follows.

Leviticus is clearly not the work of Moses himself, but the result of accumulated centuries of hieratic legal tradition. Nor was Moses the earliest lawgiver among the peoples of the ancient Middle East: somewhere around the seventeenth century BC, Hammurabi, King of Babylon, had promulgated a detailed code of laws, whose original record, inscribed on a black basalt slab, has survived until the present day. There may well be a suggestion of Hammurabi's distantly-felt influence in the story of the Ten Commandments, in which law carved upon stone reflects a symbolic guarantee of permanence. Egypt, too, had its body of law, with which Moses and many of the Israelites were surely familiar, and the connection of this with the priesthood as its guardians and transliterators points ultimately to the theocratic character which early Jewish society was to assume.

The fundamental difference between Mosaic law and that of other Middle Eastern cultures lies in the absoluteness of its statements. It envisages the closest possible bond between God and the people. The essentially conditional character of, say, Hammurabi's ordinances, which postulate situations in which, *if* such-and-such happens, *then* such-and-such may happen, simply does not enter into a legal system which is presented from the start as an expression of the divine will. Invisible as Yahweh may be to the Israelites, he sees and hears all that they do, and is ready to supervise every aspect of their lives. He is identified not only as a personal god, concerned as much with the individual as with the community, but also as a god with a personality, a fatherly presence, sometimes chiding, often angry, but always, as the final legal authority, responsive to devout appeal.

The law ... embodies
a summons to unquestioning
obedience and loyalty

Moses breaking the tablets of the law by Rembrandt.

Above all, the Mosaic doctrine propagates the concept, already implied in the confrontation with God in the Burning Bush, of shared responsibility underlying a detailed pattern of social existence for the Israelites. God inspires the making of the law, providing, in the Decalogue, a blueprint for Israel's survival, either as nomads in the wilderness or as settled farmers in conquered Canaan. The law itself embodies a summons to unquestioning obedience and loyalty. As the theologian Martin Buber points out, the First Commandment — 'Thou shalt have no other gods before me' — does not necessarily carry an assumption that other gods do not exist, only that Israel's god is Yahweh alone. Once again we can detect a discreet nod in the direction of neighbouring cultures, and though Moses administers very harsh justice to the worshippers of the Golden Calf (they are made to drink the pulverized gold of the

shattered image mixed with water) a pure monotheism is only later clearly evolved.

Absolute and unconditional as the law was, this did not prevent a certain extempore quality, directly inherited from the legal administration by judges at city gates, a custom widespread throughout the ancient world, from lingering on in Jewish society. We find this kind of 'gate-law' appearing in the bizarre tale of the Judgment of Solomon (I Kings 3:16—28) where harlots squabbling over a baby carry both the case and the child directly to the King, whose instant judgment, involving the slicing of the baby in two, is admiringly quoted as an instance of regal wisdom in putting psychological pressure on the true mother.

It is these later books of the Old Testament which reveal both the faults and virtues of the Mosaic concept of law as a moral force directly related to the spiritual responsibility of the Jews for whom it was designed. Reflecting though it did the influence of arguably more sophisticated cultures, and incredibly detailed as it appears to have become (the details of the famous dietary laws alone, in the fourteenth chapter of Deuteronomy, are staggering in their particularity), it could scarcely have made allowance for Israel's later contact with the complex civilizations surrounding her. Hence the frequently censorious tone of the biblical accounts of the various kings of the two kingdoms into which the nation was ultimately to divide; hence too, perhaps, the understandable exasperation of Jesus, well schooled in the Mosaic law, with those for whom the law itself had become a fetish, taking pride of place over the duty to God which it was intended to guarantee.

Nevertheless, whether we see Moses merely as Yahweh's mouthpiece or as a more independent and forceful figure, we must acknowledge that history offers few comparable examples of a single human mind successfully binding together a demoralized nation and prescribing its course over successive centuries. Yet it should be emphasized that Moses used no ordinary dictatorial ploys in making his point with the Israelites or in compelling them to accept the system of law he claimed as divinely instigated: in the last analysis, he was always alone, a prey to complaints and reprimands from family, friends and fellow tribesmen, the solitary negotiator between a fretful, querulous people and the all-seeing, invisible God. If he was not the first of the individual intellects that have shaped our culture, then his influence as a lawgiver was deeply felt by the founders both of Christianity and of Islam, and, perhaps inevitably, must have touched Marx and Freud, into whose Jewish cultural backgrounds it was ingrained. How ironical, therefore, that he should have died before being able to enter that Promised Land for which his system of law had been meant.   J.K.

The Christian approach encourages man to be virtuous and right within himself. From this it is expected to follow that his relationships with other people will also be right. Confucius put all the emphasis on the relationship itself. This relationship would be proper if each party carried out its assigned role. If the relationship was correct it did not matter if each party was a scoundrel or not.

551-479 BC

Right: The *Analects* of Confucius; a paper fragment dating from the T'ang period.
Below: Confucius; from a fourth-century manuscript.

Confucius had no biographer, neither did he leave an account of his own life in his own hand. Even his thoughts had to wait to be written down by disciples many years after his death, so their closeness to his original words can only be surmised. But before considering what little we know of the man Confucius, we must consider the times in which he lived.

In 771 BC Hao, the capital of the Chou empire, which extended over the North China Plain, was sacked by rebel states aided and abetted by borderland barbarians. The royal household fled and set up a new capital at Loyang. They failed to regain their former power and glory, though nominally they still headed the empire, which consisted of another nine states (Ch'in, Chin, Yen, Ch'i, Lu, Sung, Wu, Ch'u and Yüeh) completely surrounding Chou at the centre. The peripheral states were able to extend their borders outwards, and so both increase their size and take in new ideas from non-Chinese cultures. Thus Chou gradually faded into insignificance while the other states struggled amongst themselves for supremacy.

Despite incessant warfare, strict rules of conduct were always observed on the battlefield and in negotiations. Summit conferences were held, treaties signed, alliances formed and political marriages arranged. In fact the whole period was one of feverish activity on the political front.

This then is the context in which we find Confucius, a period of political instability, excitement and danger. The name Confucius is the romanized form of K'ung Fu-tzǔ, which means Master K'ung. He was born in the year 551 BC in the state of Lu, which was to the east of Chou. Lu, like Chou, adhered to the old traditions, was not noted for its militancy and counted among its population many old-established aristocratic families. Though not born to a position of hereditary power, Confucius received a sound education, therefore we can assume that he stemmed from the lesser aristocracy who would still have deemed it necessary to be educated despite their lack of power or wealth. He seems to have lost both his parents at an early age, but presumably the Chinese extended-family system operated to a certain degree even then, and some kindly relative took care of him. When the time came for him to choose a career he decided he would like to be political adviser to his head of state. But this was not to be. It is quite probable that as a young man he secured some minor post in government, and that later on he held a sinecure, though this would seem to have been awarded him not on his own merit, but through the good offices of one of his pupils, born on a higher rung of the hierarchical ladder. This new appointment evidently upset him, for he resigned the post in Lu and spent the next ten years wandering from state to state in the hope of

finding a job as a practical politician elsewhere. Eventually he returned to his native land in 479 BC, to die a disappointed man and a failure.

Confucius himself wrote nothing. Books allegedly by him were rather edited by him. He sought to improve mankind by showing to them the old paragons of the early Chou period. In order to do this he collected together several kinds of literature, both written and oral, which he thought stemmed from that time. The *Shu Ching* (*Book of Records*) contains decrees put out by the various rulers of the empire from earliest times up to 629 BC. No one is entirely sure where Confucius got his material from, and the authenticity of the version in our possession now is highly dubious. We have no idea what the text he taught from was like, mainly because in the second century BC Ch'in Shih Huang-ti (the first emperor of the Ch'in Dynasty) embarked upon a rather efficient book-burning campaign of what he considered to be reactionary literature, Confucius included. What has come down to us is a later reconstruction of the *Book of Records* made up from salvaged fragments and from memory. The avid book-burner had also insisted on standardizing the written form of the Chinese language and stamping out the old forms of characters, so that in later years when ancient documents came to light it was not always easy to interpret them correctly.

The *Book of Odes* is a compilation of a different nature. Confucius chose 300 poems placing his own construction upon what are often no more than simple folk songs. The sentiments expressed by a young swain for his love he paralleled to those which a wise minister ought to feel for his ruler. But, bearing in mind that the *Book of Odes* also suffered at the hand of the book-burner, we cannot be sure what line Confucius really took.

Other works ascribed to Confucius, and not written by him, are the *Book of Ritual* (probably based on an oral tradition current during his lifetime but largely embroidered at a later date), and the *Spring and Autumn Annals* (which consist of bald records of events both trivial and important which took place in the state of Lu over the period 722–481 BC). Even the famous *Analects* of Confucius were not written by him either, though they give us the most insight into his life and teaching. Some disciple of his, or disciple's disciple, collected short Confucian aphorisms beginning with the phrase 'The Master spake . . .' The latter part of the *Analects* consists of short conversations between master and pupils framed by a piece of narrative.

From the outset it is important to be aware of the Chinese attitude to spiritual life and religion. Although they believed in a variety of hobgoblins and spirits, these were small fry compared with the Indian pantheon. The nearest they ever got to a godhead was *Shang-ti* (the First Ancestor) who was revered rather than worshipped, or *T'ien* (Heaven). Neither of these in any way approached the Almighty of the Judaeo-Christian tradition. The emperor was regarded as the Son of Heaven in receipt of Heaven's mandate to rule over the empire. A kind of humanism rather than theism has permeated thought from earliest times. This Chinese humanism must not be confused with Renaissance humanism, with its emphasis on the individual; in the Chinese case man is always thought of in relation to society, with the emphasis on society and the individual's responsibility to it. 'Do not do to others what you would not wish to have done to yourself' is an important Confucian maxim which parallels nicely the Christian 'Love thy neighbour as thyself'.

We have seen that the time in which Confucius lived was one of political turmoil, where power and possessions were all important. Confucius could not help but feel this was wrong, since it caused suffering to so many among the lower aristocracy and ordinary people, himself included. He saw that the only way to change the pattern was to influence the man at the top. And so he chose the career of practical politician. He may not have been able to influence heads of state as he had hoped, but he certainly caught the minds of other educated men, so that eventually his thoughts permeated the whole of the Chinese nation from top to bottom.

At first sight Confucianism seems rather flat-footed when compared with the high-flown theories of other systems. There is not the intellectual appeal of Platonism, there are no exciting discourses, long reasoned arguments or pithy sayings. The Master had a total disregard for the spirit world, concentrating solely on man and his relationship to other men, and the obligations this involves. An ardent student of antiquity, he advocated a return to the conduct of the Golden Age he thought existed in the early years of Chou as a remedy for the anarchy of his own time. He thought that each man should play a role appropriate to himself and no other: 'Let the ruler act as a ruler and the subject as a subject, let the father act as a father and the son as a son.' There is nothing, you might say, particularly novel or exciting so far. Confucius would agree with you, as he did not consider himself an innovator. Where he did open up new ground, quite unconsciously, was in considering government to be a question of ethics. Power was hereditary in China (except of course when usurped by conquest), and Confucius did not question this at all. He did, however, stipulate that the man in power should set a good example to his people by living a life tempered by certain virtues. In so doing the whole of his people would then be contented. This he maintained was what good government was all about, and what a ruler should be striving for.

The ideal Confucian man was the *chün-tzu*, which has been variously interpreted as 'ruler's son', 'noble', 'aristocrat', 'cultivated man', 'superior man', though it is best thought of as 'gentleman' in the sense of superior man. The *chün-tzu* was required to cultivate the following virtues:

chih	(integrity)	*shu*	(reciprocity)
i	(righteousness)	*jên*	(benevolence)
chung	(loyalty to others)		

The mere possession of such virtues was not sufficient. To these had to be added the visible attributes of *wên* (refinement) and *li* (ritual). No rough diamonds were allowed: 'Integrity without the control of etiquette is rudeness.'

The basis of good government was founded on these five virtues together with the two outward signs of their possession. If a ruler possessed them and the 'five relationships' were upheld in the

state, he could not fail to be a success, nor his people fail to be content. The 'five relationships' are those which ought to exist between: ruler and subject; father and son; husband and wife; elder brother and younger brother; and friend and friend. It cannot escape our notice that each of these, with the possible exception of the first, is close and personal, rather than large-scale and impersonal, yet if every person were to observe them a huge network would stretch throughout the state. This was in fact the way it worked out. Foreign visitors throughout history have remarked upon the familial organization of the Chinese state.

Disciples of Confucius such as Mencius (372–289 BC) and, much later, members of the Neo-Confucian movement (ninth–tenth century AD) worked over the Confucian classics, putting new constructions on the texts, adding footnotes, uncovering and deciphering largely apocryphal documents and generally building up a major school of philosophy which verged on a religious order. Strict observance of the now enlarged rules was demanded of the Confucian scholar almost to the exclusion of independent thought. This, however, had little to do with the basic work of K'ung Fu-tzŭ, small-time teacher from the state of Lu.

Before Confucius the state was ruled by warrior-administrators who seized and maintained their position by force. They ruled over the other three social classes — peasants, artisans and merchants. Confucius taught that good government was a question of ethics rather than force. Afterwards we find the same three social classes ruled over by scholar-administrators. 'The pen is mightier than the sword' could well have been a Confucian maxim.   P.G.

The ordinary man sits in his limited cave and sees only the shadow of reality. The philosopher turns round and looking out of the cave sees the truth itself. Plato insisted that the truth existed as true forms or absolute ideas below the surface appearance of things. He set philosophy on an eternal course of searching for the underlying truth.

c.428-348 BC

Plato, sometimes styled the father of all rationalist philosophers, was born in 428 BC, probably in Athens, though there is some doubt about the precise location. His parentage was distinguished enough; his father Ariston was supposedly descended by royal line from the god Poseidon, while his mother Perictione was related to the great lawmaker Solon. The family circumstances were apparently neither sumptuous nor spartan, while Plato's own will bespeaks the life of moderation so approved by the ancient Greeks: he was neither too rich nor too poor.

Plato never married. The dominant character in his life, as in his education, was Socrates, whom he described not as his master but as his 'older friend'. But when Socrates was executed on a charge of subverting the young, in 399 BC, Plato lost more than a friend. He abandoned the hopes he had entertained that the existing political arrangements might be conducted on a rational footing. The death of Socrates, signifying a scandalous rupture between philosophy and politics, was the pivot on which Plato's mature thinking turned.

His introduction to politics came early. He was sixteen years old when the oligarchy began in 411, twenty-three when Athens finally collapsed to the Thirty Tyrants. Attempts were made to draw him into the oligarchic party, but these he resisted, prudently preferring to await signs of the direction of events. These were not long in coming. Some generally draconian measures ended in an attempt to implicate Socrates in the 'framing' of an innocent citizen. This was the beginning of Plato's disillusionment. The restored democracy completed it by putting Socrates to death, a tragedy immortalized in three of Plato's dialogues, *Apology*, *Crito* and *Phaedo*.

After Socrates's death Plato spent the next few years travelling in Greece, Italy, and possibly Egypt. The personal highlight of this odyssey was the friendship made with Dion, son of the ruler of Sicily, whose admiration for Plato became comparable with that of Plato for Socrates. But it was more than personal regard. Dion came to believe Plato's political doctrines, which by this time had achieved a firm shape. The *Gorgias* was published, while the *Republic*, setting out the principle that 'until philosophers became kings, or kings philosophers, there would be no justice in the world' (S. 473), was being composed. He eventually returned permanently to Athens, where he spent a tranquil old age, writing and teaching in the Academy he had founded there.

Plato's work, comprising some dozen dialogues, plus some correspondence, has acquired classic status, and it is not hard to see why: it meets the test of providing something for everyone who has a more than cursory concern with the major civilized human achievements. The Platonic dialogues accord a systematic treatment to theories of knowledge, of aesthetics, education, of men's relations with their gods, of morals and politics. Some of Plato's work is an embellishment of Socratic teaching, some, particularly in the later dialogues, is his own; how much is Plato, how much is Socrates, has long been a puzzle to scholars.

But to acquire the status of a classic, a body of writing must be more than extensively miscellaneous, and if we ask wherein lies the thematic unity of Plato's work, the reply could be given, it lies in a pervasive doctrine about human thinking. A recurring motif in the dialogues is that in order to be rewarding, i.e. to produce either knowledge or dependable opinion, men's thought must be active, mobile and must take the fundamental form of a conversation, even with oneself. Philosophy is 'a dialogue of the soul with itself' (*Theaetetus* 187). Books, formal speeches, even fine discourses

Above: Plato and Socrates from a thirteenth-century English treatise on astronomy.
Left: A bust of Plato found at Herculaneum.

like those of Pericles, suffer the intrinsic defect of being unable to answer and converse. The proper value of books and all written characters is either to give recreation or to act as a memorandum.

The life and breath of thinking, then, lies in active exchange, and Plato has characteristically left his own work in the form of dialogues. Some of these, it is true, contain long Socratic monologues, but vocal exchange is the elementary shape.

Philosophy itself, however, is more than informal talk. It involves a definite interrogatory procedure designed to drive the proposer of an argument along a chain of questions, each inviting a yes or no answer, into a logical impasse. This is the famous dialectical or Socratic method, which Plato learned from Socrates. In the account of his trial in the *Apology* (S. 27), Socrates announced the method when he asks leave to 'put my argument in my accustomed manner', and proceeds to cross-examine his prosecutor as rigorously as he had reportedly cross-examined Cephalus, Glaucon, Adeimantus and Thrasymachus in the *Republic*.

On this earlier occasion, he had collected various definitions of justice, offered out of ordinary speech by non-philosophers. Each definition is worked over by the method, and its internal contradictions exposed. The formula 'Paying back what you owe' is shown to produce injustice when applied to the case of a knife borrowed from a man who has since become clearly homicidal. 'Justice is in the interest of the stronger' is demonstrated to make justice indistinguishable in principle from injustice.

What, in Plato's understanding, lies at the end of philosophy considered as a way of argument — i.e. what are the ultimate objects with which the philosopher is left? Plato's answer lies in the theory of forms, an explanatory device first outlined in the *Symposium*, developed in the *Phaedo*, and expounded fully in the *Republic*. This doctrine can be, and has been, seen as a search for timeless truths, for definitions, as an answer to the question of how it is possible to make intelligible a world where all seemed to be changing. A simpler approach is to see it as a theory of language, offering a method of distinguishing between proper and common nouns. Proper nouns generate no problems as to their meaning; John is so named by pointing, by designation, by authoritative procedure. It is pointless to ask what the name signifies; it is neither rational nor irrational. Where a name is shared by a whole class of things, however, the question arises, by what reason do they enjoy membership of the class designated by the common name? What is the alleged shared qualification of, for example, all the triangles, birds, or tables? In Platonist terminology, what is their essence or form, that without which they would not be what we recognize them to be?

Plato's Academy in Athens; a mosaic
from a villa near Pompeii.

All true science, Plato believed, consisted in laying bare these essences or forms, and their existence was not notional, nor reducible to conventional understandings of word-usage. They actually enjoy an existence, more real, more permanent than the world of half-truths, interests and received opinions in which men play out their daily lives. To perceive them, after the travail of argument, is an illumination. Plato invites us to imagine men living in an underground cave which is open towards the light. The forms, the ultimate entities of science, are intimated to the cave-dwellers by casting shadows upon the inner wall. The philosopher by contrast is the man dissatisfied with shadows, who dares to turn and face the light, there to see the forms in their unmixed distinctiveness.

The satisfaction accorded the philosopher by this unimpeded vision of truth, the fruit of hard dialectical labour, is great indeed. No human satisfaction can compare, for durability or intensity, with it. It is both the enjoyment and guarantee of the immortal life of the soul. In the *Republic* and the *Meno* Plato demonstrates that the apprehension of the forms is a recollection of eternal truths.

But what is the connection between this vision and what goes on at the bottom end of the cave? What is the use of philosophy? Here Plato is explicit. The forms are not to be found in the cave, which is the ordinary world of human projects. But neither are they merely useless objects of contemplation, the due and exclusive reward of the tireless dialectician. They also serve as models to be copied in shaping the world of space and time. The more an object, or a state of affairs in the world, can be made to approximate to its form, the more satisfactory and useful will it be to the cave-dwellers.

The philosopher, clearly, has a clerical duty as well as a contemplative right, and Plato delineates in detail the training of a philosopher which alone might bring a transcription into the mundane world of the most comprehensively important political form, that of the idea of justice. To perceive the form of justice is to see the proper division of the *polis* into the three principal classes of human talent, with each class allocated to its suitable area of occupation. The soul of a man can be analysed into three general areas of conduct: rational, spirited and appetitive. Intellectual achievement is the work of the rational faculty; courage that of the faculty of spirit; simply wanting things, and satisfying those wants, is appropriate to the faculty of desire. All men have all three faculties. What distinguishes one man's soul, or character from that of another, is the 'mixture' or proportions of the three elements. Those in whom the rational faculty is dominant are capable of being philosophers, those with a larger share of courage are cut out for military and executive duties, while those who are little more than a

bundle of desires are the producers of substantive needs of life. A just *polis*, like a just man, will have its faculties properly ordered; above all, it will be ruled by those pre-eminent for the faculty of reason, who will be able with the eye of reason to see how the struggles and fumblings of half-sighted men can be steered into truth-based achievement. The ultimate form, to which even the form of justice is subordinate, is the form of the good.

Here is an uncompromising statement that rulers cannot be merely ordinary. The 'common touch' is no part of policy-making, though it may well be, along with judicious use of half-truths and coercion, a part of the rhetorical equipment for getting policies accepted. And Plato contends that this is not only true of the 'ideal' or essential *polis*. It is true of any actual *polis* in so far as it manifests the principle of justice in the mutual relations of its citizens.

Two comments: first, Plato evinces the most intrepid disposition to a philosophical monism, i.e. a tendency to subsume all classes, forms or ideas, under one master principle, the idea or form of the good. Unlike Aristotle, who is content to allow multiple principles of classification to operate with some latitude, Plato gives a free rein to the philosophical impatience with an unresolved diversity.

Second, Plato's monism has a curious result for his political theory. The story of European thought is not short of Utopias, schemes for a drastic reorganization of public life, and Plato's *Republic* has been called a Utopia. But whereas other Utopias, e.g. Thomas More's *Utopia*, or Francis Bacon's *New Atlantis*, have offered a model for copying only, making no attempt to use it to explain the actual world, Plato's *Republic* claims to explain what is the essence of all political organization, i.e. it purports to be an explanatory model as well. The thesis is that to know the essence of something is also to know what is desirable. Plato, following the Socratic principle that virtue is knowledge, offers two models for the price of one.   R.O.

Alternative Approaches

Society arises from the rules of behaviour that determine how people behave towards each other and towards society itself. Moses, Confucius and Plato provide an extraordinary contrast in their approach to society. Through his approach Moses welded a group of tribes into a religion-race-nation that has survived intact for thousands of years in spite of the many hardships which it has suffered. Moreover the direct monotheistic style of Judaism set up by Moses provided both the background and style of Christianity and Islam. The Confucian approach has profoundly influenced the thinking and behaviour of the largest nation on earth: the eight hundred million Chinese. Plato is acknowledged by all as the father of Western philosophy and thinking. As Bertrand Russell wrote: 'The influence of Plato on philosophy is probably greater than that of any other man.'

Moses was an historical figure and a legend, and much that was attributed to him may have arisen from other sources. Confucius collected and edited the works of others, and his philosophy was only put into a coherent form by the neo-Confucians some time later. It is not easy to tell how much Plato derived from Pythagoras, Parmenides or Socrates. Nevertheless we can treat each of these thinkers as being responsible for the style of approach which they developed. With Moses the approach was that of religion. With Confucius the approach was one of ethics. With Plato the approach was philosophy. Moses made a god of God. Confucius made a god of society. Plato made a god of man's mind.

The supreme example of the lawgiver

Moses is the supreme example of the lawgiver. God gave him the Ten Commandments on Mount Sinai, and on these he and his followers gradually built the colossal legal structure that constitutes the Torah (or Law) of the Israelites. This is the Pentateuch, or first five books of the Bible. It includes the detailed priestly code of Leviticus and the covenant between God and the Jews. The law covers all aspects of behaviour, both religious and private, including the type of food that is to be eaten and the way it is to be cooked. It is true that much of this law is not very different from the Babylonian and Hittite laws that existed at the time of Moses. It is probably true that much of it, possibly including the Ten Commandments, was an encoding of the ethical standards of the time. What is important is the emphasis which Moses and his lawgiving successors placed on detailed law as the foundation of society.

If every act and aspect of behaviour in society is governed by a strict law then society takes form. The emphasis is not on the way people behave towards each other but how they behave *towards the law*. If everyone is observing the law then

**Identity is achieved
as much by action
as by belief**

everyone will be behaving correctly towards each other and towards society. Imagine the structure of a fishbone after the fish has been eaten. If at the end of each rib or spine we place a small lump of wax to represent an individual firmly adhering to the structure provided, then each lump of wax is automatically related to each other lump by virtue of the structure. This law-based method of constructing society has been most effective. The very detail of the law has preserved and reinforced the identity of the Jewish people and kept it intact in the face of dispersion and persecution. In a sense, identity is achieved as much by action as by belief. Because the law-ridden people must act in a certain way they retain their distinctness from the people around them. Moreover each little observance of the law reminds the people at each moment of their own identity. Identity through action is much more powerful than identity through belief.

The Hebrew religion is essentially untheological. The emphasis is much more on the detail of law than the complexity of belief. The belief in the existence of the single God (Yahweh) and his special Covenant with the Jewish people is enough. It is the observation of the detailed laws of this Covenant that matters, for this is carrying out God's will. The existence of detailed laws automatically implies a detailed structure in society. Since the laws are complicated there emerges a priesthood whose business it is to guard and interpret the law – and so preserve their own essential function in society. Their authority derives from the authority of the law. Stability and survival have been a feature of such law-intensive societies, which have included the Incas, the Aztecs and the Egyptians, although the latter never seemed to encode their laws in the way that is characteristic of the Jews.

Law is only as good as the authority on which it is based. Here Moses had *the* supreme advantage. His laws were personally handed to him by God himself. There can be no higher authority. As an organizing operation, Moses had first to insist on the belief in the one almighty God and then use him to establish the authority of the laws. The two processes fed one into the other. Nowadays with our ever-increasing sophistication in the behaviour of systems we are coming to accept that a system cannot be stable if it relies only on its own internal behaviour. For stability a system needs something outside of itself as a sort of reference system: the technical term is a meta-system. God is of course the supreme meta-system. So much so that when Plato advocated the development of laws by the wise men or guardians of his 'Republic' he suggested that they should pretend that the laws came from God. Clearly there is no arguing with the authority of God. It is the original God-given nature of the Hebrew laws and the very detail of them that has been so effective in building and preserving the identity of the Jewish people.

It is sufficient to obey the law, and if the law is detailed enough and sound enough and backed by enough authority then all will be well with society. The rules of behaviour are provided by the law and if the law is God-given then the rules of behaviour are provided by God – and one cannot hope to do better than that. Interpretation of the law is still left to man and can offer him scope for a human input. The more detailed the law, however, the less scope for interpretation even when the details seem arbitrary. Detailed laws of procedure are very much more durable than laws of belief because belief is always vulnerable to interpretation and heresies.

The approach to society offered by Confucius is strikingly different, even though at first sight it might seem the same. Confucius endeavoured to crystallize and reintroduce the principles of behaviour that had existed in the old, conservative and feudal past in China. This may seem to suggest an attention to hierarchy, rules and laws of behaviour, but the approach is an entirely different one. Instead of concentrating on a legal structure as did Moses, Confucius concentrates on what we may call the sociological structure: how people behaved towards one another. This is a very modern view. Law-based societies such as that of Moses set up a tight structure of law and insist that strict adherence to it will ensure the proper behaviour of people in that society. Individual-based societies such as that of Plato or Protestantism suggest that if people are good-thinking, God-fearing and generally proper people then they will also behave properly towards each other and towards society. The Confucian approach is different from both. Confucianism concentrates on the role of each individual in society and on the role-relationship. It is the carrying out of this role-relationship that matters. It is the *manners* of people that matter, not the excellence of their soul or their personal credit balance with God. A person can be a blackguard provided he fulfils his role scrupulously, provided his manners are perfect.

It is the <u>manners</u> of people that matter, not the excellence of their soul

Of course the roles looked at by Confucius do include a large element of spiritual value, so a person carrying out his role is expected to demonstrate the virtues of love (a general term covering 'humanity'), justice (the fulfilling of a person's proper place, duties and rights), reverence (and especially filial piety and ancestor respect), wisdom and sincerity. Nevertheless these are all behavioural roles, and if a person were able to play the part as required and then go home and remove the mask to reveal a cantankerous soul, this would be perfectly all right. The Mosaic ethic is to obey the law and hope that that obedience will improve your soul. The Platonic and Christian ethic is to put the soul right and all else will follow. The Confucian ethic is to get the interactions of society and the role playing exactly right and to be happy with that. Confucius was very popular with the feudal overlords in China because his insistence on everyone keeping his place and playing the role it involved made for stability in society and in the family.

When Christianity supported the feudal state in Europe the approach was somewhat different. People were not to *mind* their poverty and lowly position in society because the kingdom of God was to come in the next world and Christ had said that poverty, humility and suffering were no bar to salvation: on the contrary they were a positive asset. Confucius was not concerned with the next world or the improvement in the state of the soul but with the fulfilment of the established roles. This is not unlike the rigid caste system in Hindu India, where positions in society are ordained. Paradoxically, Marx, who set out to liberate the masses from the 'opiate' of religion which soothed their dissatisfaction with a lowly state, ended up by being responsible for even more feudal states in which the assigned place in society is very firmly fixed and role-playing of a high order of conformity is expected. While it is claimed that the new positions are based on merit or political power, the role-playing required can be even more exacting than that required by Confucius, since the soul too must now play its role overtly.

In the West we take so much for granted the existence of god-centred cultures

Confucianism supported the rigid social order of Chinese
feudalism which was divided into four estates: *shih*, the gentry;
nung, the peasant-farmers; *kung*, the artisans; and *shang*,
the merchants. This late Ch'ing illustration from
the *Shu Ching* shows the *kung* at work building the new city of Lo.

that Voltaire was able to declare that if God did not exist it would have been necessary to invent him. This is understandable if he is to play the part of the meta-system, which he so obviously does in Judaism and the religions and cultures that arose from it. It comes as a surprise to realize that Chinese culture has never been god-centred but has been purely secular. There is no god-given authority behind the laws. The society is not a legalistic one. Instead there is the Confucian emphasis on role-playing and manners. Government is not legalistic. Politicians, government officials, wisemen are all in their hierarchical positions as much as in the Mosaic culture. But they are not there to interpret, preserve and administer the law. They are there to fulfil and act out the role of 'ruler', which is as much a role as 'farmer'. General precepts are given to guide the fulfilment of that role but much is left to individual discretion within the boundaries of these precepts. A 'ruler' deals personally with a situation, not through application of the rigid rule of law. Unfortunately this requires highly cultured, compassionate and learned people, whereas strict application of the law makes less demands on human excellence. That is why the Confucian system is more vulnerable than the legalistic one, and that is why Confucius and his reluctant Communist inheritors in China today have to work so hard to define the proper roles both in behaviour and (today) in thinking.

The Confucian approach is organic because it depends on each interaction and relationship rather than the filling out of some grand scheme. It is also very modern because today most of the emphasis in psychology, philosophy, politics, ethics and sociology is on finding the sociological structures and defining both the roles and the relationships involved.

Confucius is the only example of an Eastern thinker included in this book, which is concerned with the thinkers involved in the emergence of Western civilization – except in so far as the thinking of men like Pavlov and Einstein is independent of culture. Confucius illustrates precisely the path which Western cultures and religions most definitely did *not* take. He is included in this section to show up the distinctiveness of the Mosaic and the Platonic approach to society, and to show how these were definite trends and not inevitable developments.

We come now to Plato and his approach to society. This is radically different from that of Moses and Confucius. Plato has influenced thinkers and philosophers directly, but his main importance is not this direct influence but the indirect effect his ideas have had on society, especially through their infiltration into Christianity. Indeed Plato's effect on society is quite different from his overt political work *The Republic*, which shows a rigid aristocracy of merit with no elements of democracy at all.

Plato's main contribution is his theory of forms. For Plato virtue is knowledge. Knowledge of what? Knowledge of the true and absolute *good*. This true and absolute good replaces God for Plato, but became God again when Christians took up Plato. Underneath the ordinary ephemeral appearance of things Plato insisted that there were absolute ideas which could be reached only by pure thought. 'Humanity' and 'beauty' are absolute ideas, but we can only become aware of them in particular instances which reflect some element of these pure ideas. We can look at a particular beautiful girl and in her see some reflection of both humanity and beauty, but the pure absolute ideas exist only through the use of the mind. The absolute 'good' is such a pure form and indicates 'that which is

Absolute ideas which could be reached only by pure thought

proper, in its proper place, and functioning properly'. That seems something of a circular definition, but it is a very usable one. Its use lies in the motivation it gives to philosophers to look below the immediate, surface appearance of things to discover the true and eternal truths. These true and eternal truths exist by analogy with mathematics, which was a subject that completely dominated the thinking of the Greek philosophers. One could look at all sorts of buildings and other structures before one discovered the eternal truth that the square of the longer side of a right-angled triangle equalled the sum of the squares on the other two sides. This is the sort of pattern, form or truth that Plato believed existed under the different surface appearances of things.

It is this insistence on the search for the absolute truth underneath the surface appearances that has set Western thinkers on an unending path of search that has been so successful in science and so very sterile in philosophy. The sterility in philosophy arises from the habit of looking more and more deeply into our language concepts and in doing so constructing further concepts that can also be looked into and eventually with much diligence coming exactly back to where we started. We have failed to appreciate that language, thinking and behaviour are part of a patterning world and not the concrete world of external existence. In this patterning world the surface appearances are the truth, and to look beyond them takes us further away from the truth rather than towards it. Of course the surface appearance never constitutes a single absolute truth in the Platonic sense, but only an arbitrary truth – one among many.

Judaism was a system of God-given laws with little speculation about God. The Platonic influence in Christianity was to set all the Christian thinkers searching furiously for the absolute truth underneath the concept of God. Hence Christianity became a very theological operation, with the traditional battles about the number of angels dancing on the head of a pin. The search for the absolute truth set people thinking and made gods of their thinking.

It is this emphasis on thinking things out that characterizes Plato's approach to society. Instead of adherence to the divine, and sometimes apparently arbitrary, laws of the Mosaic approach, instead of the manners and role-playing of the Confucian approach, there is a direct effort to think things out. People are going to act properly because they can perceive the truth and the good. Knowledge is virtue. If people can see the truth they will adjust their behaviour so as to reach that truth. In contrast to the Mosaic laws or the Confucian role the emphasis is no longer on the behaviour but on the purpose or destination of that behaviour. We can use a travelling analogy. The Mosaic law-based approach says: 'You must take the following roads and the following turnings.' No mention is made of destination but that naturally arises if you follow the route laid down. The Confucian approach says: 'It is proper to your role that you take a train from this station.' Again no destination is mentioned but since railway stations only serve a limited area and since the tracks of the train are set in certain directions only a small number of destinations are possible. The Platonic approach says: 'We are agreed that your proper destination is the town of London. I am content if you can see that. You choose the way you want to get there.'

To impose on every individual in society the great burden of thinking things out for himself with the skill of a philosopher is a little unrealistic – although this is exactly what Protestantism (very much influenced by Plato via St Augustine

31

and Luther) demands. Plato was practical. Philosophers were going to do the thinking for the rest of mankind. Sometimes the philosophers were going to turn up general and permanent truths; at other times their skilled thinking was going to deal with a situation as it arose and to sort it out in an ad hoc manner but according to basic principles. That is why Plato insisted that the statesmen at the head of communities must be *philosophers* as well as kings. Confucius put his rulers in place and asked them to perform the role of ruler. Plato insists that they can only play this role if they are thoroughly trained as philosophers. This is probably true in Plato's world, since in Confucius' world the ruled subjects are also playing their roles as such, but in Plato's world the ruler has to deal with a free-for-all.

Ever since Plato, Western society has been influenced by more or less profound thinkers who have built up concepts of humanity, justice, proper behaviour, theology, political science and related ideas. Today society operates very much on Platonic 'pure and absolute truths' such as 'equality', 'fairness', 'human compassion', 'brotherhood of man', 'justice' and other ideas that are used as the foundation of policies and the ammunition in arguments.

We owe a great deal to Plato, especially in our scientific advances. But in the field of human relations his approach has several very serious defects which have come close to wrecking society. The first defect is that if you have to search for the absolute truth then when you think you have found it, it must be both absolute and true. That means it must be both permanent and singular. It is not much use if someone else has found 'his' absolute truth which is quite different from yours. The system simply would not work. Since Plato's system never tells us how to decide when we have found this absolute truth anyone is entitled to feel that he has reached it. Since by definition this truth is absolute and true that person, or culture, not only has the right to regard everyone else as wrong but even the duty to bring their error to their attention – by force of arms or fire if necessary. In the Platonic tradition, one of the best ways of showing that you are right is by proving the other person wrong. In short the Platonic idiom has given rise to dogmatism, arrogance, intolerance and persecution because of the very nature of the idiom, not because Plato intended it that way.

Plato hoped that the true philosopher would agree with all other true philosophers in seeing the world in an agreed way, since truth was one. He neglected, as did all other Greek philosophers, the contingent nature of truth. Truth depends on a definition of the universe in which you are thinking. In the mathematical world, mathematical truths are true. But even that is a special universe. For instance on a plane surface the angles of a triangle always add up to two right angles. But on a spherical surface – a different universe – they add up to more than two right angles. Similarly a person may argue with perfect logic towards the absolute truth in his universe of values but arrive at a different absolute truth from someone else who is also arguing with perfect logic in his universe of values. By neglecting this difference of universe and putting the emphasis on the philosopher's clarity of search, Plato has created troubles which the Western world is a very long way from solving.

The Platonic idiom has given rise to dogmatism, arrogance, intolerance and persecution

Aristotle

Before Aristotle words were simply a means of communication. Words and concepts followed each other in the flow of language or thinking. Aristotle classified and categorized concepts in order to extract their full meaning and from this their relationship to each other. He went on to devise the syllogism which is a device for relating categories to each other and so extracting hidden logical truths.

384-322 BC

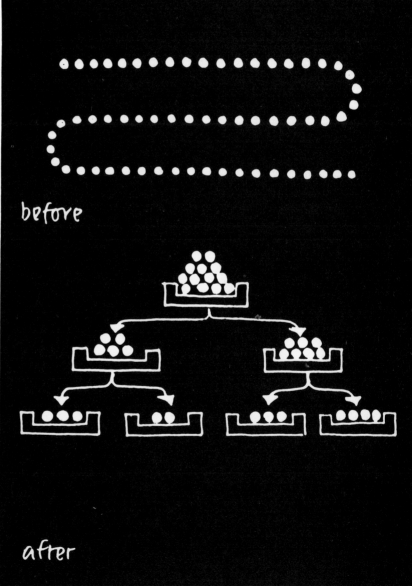

before

after

No philosopher has been more honoured or more reviled than Aristotle. Though he was a heathen Greek of the fourth century, fifteen hundred years afterwards his philosophy became a pillar of Christian doctrine. Before then he had become an acknowledged master in the Islamic world. And as late as the seventeenth century, English scholars were obliged by statute to recognize Aristotle's authority as 'paramount'. But on the other hand Luther called Aristotle a 'stinking philosopher'; Hobbes denounced him as the source of all the worst nonsense in metaphysics, ethics and politics; more recently Aristotle has been accused of distorting thought with the fallacies of 'naturalism' and 'essentialism'. And both sides of Aristotle's reputation get a tribute in Bertrand Russell's verdict that: 'every serious intellectual advance has had to begin with an attack on some Aristotelian doctrine.'

It is surprising to find at the centre of such adulation and hostility so ordinary a figure. No one thought that Aristotle looked impressive — a lisping dandy, with small eyes, thin legs, and not much hair on his head. Nor was he distinguished either as a recluse or a misogynist — not even as a reprobate. Though when asked why he preferred the company of pretty women, he replied that only a blind man could wonder, he lived steadily with his wife, and after her death, equally so with a concubine. His will is that of a man who efficiently arranged all his worldly affairs, from the freeing of his slaves to his own burial.

There is nothing remarkable either about Aristotle's education or career. He may have learned biology from his father who was a doctor at the court of Macedonia. At eighteen he did the usual thing for talented young men of his sort. He became a pupil in Plato's Academy, then he worked there for almost twenty years until Plato's death. There was no dramatic rupture between them, even though Aristotle went a different way. The only striking episode is the few years that Aristotle spent as tutor to Alexander of Macedonia, but his association with the conqueror of the ancient world was marked by neither the high hopes nor the despair in Plato's attempt to educate a philosopher-king for Syracuse. Though Aristotle was also charged with impiety, as Socrates had been, instead of a noble death scene we have Aristotle's remark on leaving Athens, that he wanted to save her from sinning twice against philosophy.

His conventional life seems to fit with the style of his writing — treatises full of divisions and subdivisions. Only Cicero's praise of the 'golden stream of Aristotle's eloquence' suggests that in the lost works we might have discovered a more colourful voice. Everything else indicates a mind of 'appalling tidiness'. In Aristotle's Lyceum, the courses of study and living arrangements were meticulously

regulated by rules. He was a formidable collector: hundreds of manuscripts and maps; geological and biological specimens; a complete list of the plays produced at Athens, including authors, producers, actors and winners of prizes; books detailing the problems of interpreting Homer, 158 Greek constitutions.

The same obsession with accumulating and sorting seems at first sight to be the chief distinction of his philosophy. But the classification is at least on so grand a scale that we are still indebted in every field to categories invented by Aristotle. He identified the subjects of logic, metaphysics, politics, ethics, rhetoric, psychology, physics, biology, meteorology. He gave us our distinctions between theoretical and practical, intellectual and moral, potential and actual; our classification of forms of government into constitutional and tyrannical, monarchy, aristocracy, oligarchy, democracy; the central terms of logic such as syllogism, universals, substance. Aristotle is the source also of the moral vocabulary of Europe, so incomparably rich in refined distinctions — between motive and intention, behaviour and character, between the generous and the magnanimous man, the courageous and the reckless man, the wit and the buffoon, the friend and the lover.

In spelling out all these distinctions, Aristotle anatomized what Plato only alluded to as the vision beyond language from which the philosopher-king drew his insight into reality. But the difference is not after all due to dreary pedantry, to a pedestrian insensitivity to nuances in words and ideas, not even to a commonsensical or utilitarian view of philosophy. Aristotle believed as passionately as Plato that if men are to reason at all, their thought must find an eternal, universal resting point. But there was besides another dimension to Aristotle's philosophical passion. He was bent on finding this fixity within human life, not beyond it, and without denying or belittling the reality of our everyday changing experience. He differs from Plato, as well as from our modern seekers after certainty, in refusing to see human life as a poor reflection of a non-human reality, whether of higher transcendental ideas or of lower biological and physical mechanisms.

Instead Aristotle wanted to explain why, though our ordinary experience seems like a kaleidoscope, it is not just a jumble of ever-changing images. He was not out to escape from change, but to find an orderly way of understanding and accommodating to it. The reality that interested Aristotle could not be grasped in a single ultimate vision. To discipline the wonder that inspires the philosopher's inquiry, to prevent an appreciation of the complexity of things from degenerating into a mindless burble, Aristotle relied on the precise use of language. That was why he took such trouble to sort out distinct subjects and to define the four 'causes', that is,

the different questions that had to be asked: What is this made of? What is its form or structure? How did it get to be this way? Why was it made? It was in order to answer these questions about the whole range of human experience that Aristotle collected his information and made his distinctions and categories. His logic is not an idle exercise in sticking labels; it is the ordering of thought by a man seeking to understand both its subject and objects.

The cosmos that emerges from Aristotle's philosophy is a hierarchy of species in which every kind of thing has its fixed place and is graded according to whether it is more or less self-moving. But it is a fixity of form or pattern, expressed in abstract universal principles that allow for a varying content. All living beings are seen as a set of fixed potentialities — what Aristotle called an 'essence' — that may or may not be actualized in time. Thus Aristotle offered a way of understanding what is common to an acorn and an oak, to Socrates and Alcibiades, without depreciating the differences between them or the alterations that take place in the course of their existence.

Human beings incorporate within themselves the ordering principle of the universe

Aristotle by Raphael; a detail from the fresco
entitled 'The School of Athens' in the apartments
of Pope Julius II in the Vatican.

In calling men rational animals, Aristotle meant that human beings incorporate within themselves the ordering principle of the universe. This is their reason, which enables them to apprehend the unchanging order as well as to see alternatives and to make choices, which renders them more completely self-moving than other beings and therefore the highest in the hierarchy. The good life for men consists in fulfilling all their capacities in the right order, that is, paying just enough attention to the lower bodily needs in order to develop the higher rational capacities. But unlike the acorn, they can and must choose how and whether to actualize their potentialities.

It is a commonplace that Aristotle's virtuous man pursues 'the mean'. But this is not at all, as it is often supposed, a matter of 'moderation'. It is doing the right thing in the right way at the right time. The courageous man does not face more danger than the coward and less than the reckless man. He risks danger when he should, whereas the coward runs away when he ought to stand fast, and the reckless man takes on dangers he ought to avoid.

What lies behind Aristotle's doctrine of 'the mean', and is a theme running through his philosophy, is the conception of different levels of abstraction in reasoning, a hierarchy that descends from necessarily true first principles, that are intuited, to conclusions deduced from them, to concrete decisions about how to interpret rules. In choosing 'the mean', the virtuous man correctly sees what practical decisions are required by the principles of right conduct in particular circumstances. And it is crucial according to Aristotle to distinguish between 'scientific reasoning' — the demonstration of necessarily true conclusions from first principles — and 'practical' or 'rhetorical' reasoning about things that could always be different from what they are.

This is the sort of reasoning that Aristotle considers appropriate to practical affairs, whether in daily life, politics, or the law courts. Unlike many later philosophers, he takes great pains to warn against wrongly preferring theoretical to practical knowledge, without however in any way denying or blurring the distinction. If we want to be healthy, he tells us, we had better ask the man who knows that chicken will cure us rather than the one who knows that 'light' meat is more digestible but cannot tell that it is to be found in chicken.

In the same way in politics, Aristotle said that the Athenians had the distinction of inventing laws and wheat, but whereas they made good use of their wheat, they did not know what to do with their laws. Though he considered the best form of government to be an association of equals who recognized the same laws, who ruled and were ruled in turn, because such men could most self-sufficiently run their own lives, he also says that what is practicable at any given time and place depends on whether the men there possess the required understanding and self-discipline.

All this analysis may bring to mind the monster whom Dr Johnson described as being so intent on dissecting a sunbeam that he could not enjoy a summer morning. By so meticulously separating in thought what comes together in experience, Aristotle seems to deny, or at any rate to encourage, ignoring the interdependence of the abstract and the concrete, the mystery of the one in the many with which poets and Christians have been preoccupied. His insistence on distinguishing and respecting both the certainty that men can have about abstract principles and the very different kind of conviction about the rightness of a particular action here and now is bound to irritate those who prefer a simple dichotomy between certainty and chaos.

The mixed reception of Aristotle that continues to our day comes of the extraordinary comprehensiveness and order in his philosophy combined with a repugnance to uniformity and simplicity. It is not a philosophy systematic in Kant's geometric sense of deducing all truths from one or a few universal propositions. Instead Aristotle shows that orderly thinking is compatible with and indeed requires recognizing a great variety of fine distinctions, not to divide and separate but in order to appreciate both the complexity and the connections of things, to make sense of human experience as a whole.   S.L.

Euclid

Euclid has been the envy of all thinkers. From a few basic axioms he built up
a great structure by the use of pure deduction. As each theorem arose it provided
the basis for still further theorems until it seemed that everything could be
explained by deduction from basic axioms. Euclid was, however, working
in a restricted universe of intersecting lines in two dimensional space.

c.300 B C

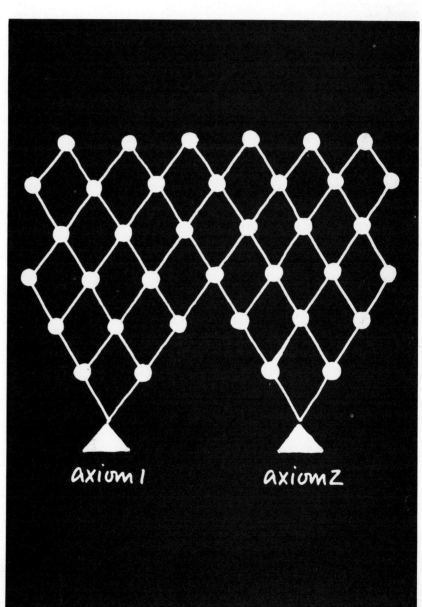

Some time around 1630 the English philosopher Thomas Hobbes came across the works of Euclid in a gentleman's library. It was a revelation, as the diarist John Aubrey tells us:

> Euclid's Elements lay open, and 'twas the 47 El. libri 1. He read the proposition and 'By G—,' sayd he, 'this is impossible!' So he reads the demonstration of it, which referred him back to such a proposition; which proposition he read. That referred him back to another, which he also read. Et sic deinceps, that at last he was demonstratively convinced of the trueth. This made him in love with geometry.

That such a meeting of minds could take place over a space of nearly two millennia, to such effect, is one of the most remarkable phenomena in the history of thought. What was true for Euclid, and true for Hobbes, remained more or less unchallenged until the late eighteenth century. And as one commentator wrote in 1848: 'There never has been, and till we see it we never shall believe that there can be, a system of geometry worthy of the name, which has any material departures (we do not speak of *corrections* or *extensions* or *developments*) from the plan laid down by Euclid.' Even now, although there are non-Euclidean geometries, Euclid's work has not been superseded. Within its own assumptions, it remains intact. Indeed, as we shall see, Euclid to some extent paved the way for his rivals of recent years.

He came from Greece, although we do not know either the date or the place of his birth. It is likely that he studied in Athens, learning philosophy and geometry from the pupils of Plato. But it was in Alexandria, during the time of Ptolemy the First (who reigned from 306 to 283 BC), that he did his major work, teaching geometry at the university and producing several books, of which the *Elements* is the most important. Proclus, an early commentator, recounts how Ptolemy asked whether there was any shorter approach to geometry than that of the *Elements*, to which Euclid gave the reply: 'There is no royal road to geometry.' Unfortunately, however, the same story is told of Alexander the Great and his tutor. The other traditions about Euclid are similarly dubious. It is said, for instance, that he was a man of uncommonly pleasant temperament, but there is no contemporary evidence about his character. Stobaeus tells the only story which is associated exclusively with Euclid: 'Someone who had begun to read geometry with Euclid, when he heard the first theorem, asked Euclid: "But what shall I get by learning these things?" Euclid called out to his slave: "Give him threepence, since he must make gain out of what he learns."'

In other words, Euclid was associated in the ancient world with the pursuit of pure science, of learning for its own sake. In this, he is unlike many of his predecessors. The word 'geometry' means land-measurement, or surveying. The Greeks considered, probably correctly, that it had originated as a practical pursuit in Egypt. The earliest Egyptian geometrical work we possess, that of Ahmes (1550 or 1700 BC), reflects an interest in geometry as a functional art, for use in association with architecture and in the measurement of volume and area. Greek geometry, on the other hand, was rarely functional. Certain figures could be used in order to calculate the distance of a ship at sea, and there was the association of geometry with astronomy. But the word 'geometry', by Euclid's time, had long since lost its primary meaning.

Indeed, as developed by Pythagoras, theoretical geometry seems to have had a largely religious significance. The Pythagoreans were

means also the letters of the alphabet). It remained *the* textbook
until the first part of this century, and many students used to call the
subject 'Euclid' rather than geometry. And yet the work is not
notably original. Of its thirteen books, numbers 1–4 and 6 are
concerned with Pythagorean or plane geometry, number 5 with
Eudoxus' theory of proportion, books 7–9 deal with the elementary
theory of numbers, and the last four with solid figures, showing the
influence of Theaetetus. Euclid's claim to fame is as a synthesizer
rather than as an originator of new theories.

Aubrey's description of Hobbes falling in love with geometry
provides a neat example of the Euclidean method at work. What
Hobbes read was in fact Pythagoras's theorem:

> In right-angled triangles the square on the side subtending the
> right angle is equal to the sum of the squares on the sides contain-
> ing the right angle.

Hobbes was not the first person to be excited by it. Pythagoras, so
Proclus tells us, had sacrificed an ox after making the discovery. It
gave a theoretical understanding of something that had long been
known empirically (the ancient Egyptians had known about the
$3:4:5$ triangle, but had not necessarily understood that it was
right-angled), and may also have shattered several of Pythagoras's
previous beliefs. It told him, for instance, that the diagonal of a
square whose side is one unit is $\sqrt{2}$, and he knew that $\sqrt{2}$ is an
irrational number — which may have upset his view that rational
numbers ruled the world.

However, the proof of the theorem that Hobbes read was not
devised by Pythagoras but by Euclid (a proof which Schopenhauer, unimpressed, referred to as 'a mousetrap proof'). In order to
understand the demonstration and be 'demonstratively convinced
of the trueth', Hobbes was referred back by Euclid to four previous
propositions. For instance 1.41:

> If a parallelogram have the same base with a triangle and be in
> the same parallels, the parallelogram is double of the triangles.

And in order to understand the demonstration of that, he was
referred back to two more propositions, for instance 1.34:

> In parallelogrammic areas the opposite sides and angles are
> equal to one another, and the diameter bisects the areas.

But before he could be convinced of *this*, Hobbes would have to
refer further back, to three more propositions and one 'common
notion'. 'Et sic deinceps' (and so on and so forth) until he came to
the beginning of the book. Then it was that, seeing how beautifully
the whole system hung together, he fell in love with geometry.

members of a closely knit secret society, with strict rules and
sanctions governing the conduct of the initiated. The properties of
numbers and the observation of proportion, the qualities of
geometrical figures, had a significance which would nowadays
be called magical.

Geometry was an occult science, then, and probably mixed up
with political intrigue. Nevertheless, it was a Pythagorean who first
began to teach the subject in order to earn a living, and among the
next generations of philosophers geometry developed its theoretical rather than magic character. Plato insisted that his students first
learn geometry before entering his Academy. The famous problems
that the Greek geometers set themselves to solve (squaring the
circle or doubling the cube) were to be solved theoretically rather
than by empirical measurement. A large body of theorems had been
amassed, and there were even some attempts at synthesis. But the
impression one gets is of a lively subject in need of a thorough
reorganization. This is what geometry found in Euclid.

Alexandria had been founded in 332 BC, and by the time that
Euclid went there, around the turn of the century, it was already a
thriving university town. Euclid founded a school, and wrote his
Elements to provide an ABC of geometry (the word 'elements'

Unctus est cuius ps nó est. ⸿Linea est
lógitudo fine latitudine cui⁹ quidé ex/
tremitates fr duo púcta. ⸿Linea recta
é ab vno púcto ad aliú breuissima exté/
fio i extremitates fuas vtrúq; eoz reci
piens. ⸿Supficies é q̃ lógitudiné z lati
tudiné tm h3:cui⁹ termi quidé fút linee.
⸿Supficies plana é ab vna linea ad a/
liã extélio i extremitates fuas recipiés
⸿Angulus planus é duarú linearú al/
ternus ptactus:quaz expãlio é fup fup/
ficié applicatioq3 nó directa. ⸿Quãdo aut angulum ptinét due
linee recte rectiline⁹ angulus noiaf. ⸿Qñ recta linea fup rectã
fleterit duoq3 anguli vtrobiq3 fuerit eqles:eoz vterq3 rect⁹erit
⸿Lineaq3 linee fupftãs ei cui fupftat ppendicularis vocaf. ⸿An
gulus vo qui recto maioz é obtufus dicif. ⸿Angul⁹vo minoz re
cto acut⁹appellaf. ⸿Termin⁹é qd vniuscuiuq3 finis é. ⸿Figura
é q̃ tmino vltermis ptinet. ⸿Circul⁹é figura plana vna qdem li
nea pteta: q̃ circúferentia noiaf:in cui⁹medio púct⁹é : a quo⁹oés
linee recte ad circúferétiã exeútes fibiinuicez fut equales. Et hic
quidé púct⁹cétrú circuli ds. ⸿Diameter circuli é linea recta que
fup ei⁹centz trãfiens extremitatesq3 fuas circúferétie applicans
circulú i duo media diuidit. ⸿Semicirculus é figura plana dia
metro circuli z medietate circúferentie pteta. ⸿Portio circu
li é figura plana recta linea z parte circúferétie pteta: femicircu
lo quidé aut maioz aut minoz. ⸿Rectilinee figure fút q̃ rectis li
neis cõtinent quarú quedã trilatere q̃ trib⁹rectis lineis: quedã
quadrilatere q̃ q̃tuor rectis lineis. q̃dã mltilatere que pluribus
q3 quatuor rectis lineis continenf. ⸿Figurarú trilaterarú:alia
est triangulus hñs tria latera equalia. Alia triangulus duo hñs
eq̃lia latera. Alia triangulus triú inequalium laterú. Daz iterú
alia est orthogoniú:vnú .f. rectum angulum habens. Alia é am
bligonium aliquem obtufum angulum habens. Alia est oxigoni
um:in qua tres anguli fut acuti. ⸿Figurarú auté quadrilateraz
Alia est q̃dratum quod est equilateru atq3 rectangulú. Alia est
retragon⁹long⁹:q̃ est figura rectangula : fed equilatera non est.
Alia est helmuaym: que est equilatera : fed rectangula non est.

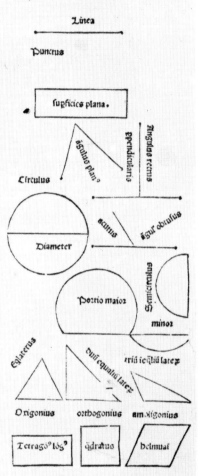

The opening page of the first
printed edition of Euclid's *Elements*
published in Venice in 1482.

**What Euclid had done . . . was
to create a completely
organic system**

What Euclid had done, in other words, was to create a completely organic system. Beginning with definitions, then postulates (apparent truths which he was nevertheless unable to prove), and then common notions (which were the basic logical laws by which he would work), he had built up, in a carefully chosen sequence, his series of propositions and proofs. The common method of proof, *reductio ad absurdum*, began by assuming the opposite of what was to be proved, and then proceeded by stages to show that the assumption was impossible. *Reductio ad absurdum* is a misnomer, since it is not enough to show that a conclusion is absurd. It must be actually impossible.

Euclid's Common Notions were not strongly contested. They include such rules as : 'Things which are equal to the same thing are also equal to each other' and : 'The whole is greater than the part.' The Definitions came in for more criticism, particularly the definition of a straight line ('a straight line is a line which lies evenly with the points on itself'). The Postulates, however, came in immediately for the closest scrutiny. There are five of them :

Let the following be postulated :
1 To draw a straight line from any point to any point.
2 To produce a finite straight line continuously in a straight line.
3 To describe a circle with any centre and distance.
4 That all right angles are equal to one another.
5 That, if a straight line falling on two straight lines make the interior angles on the same side less than two right angles, the two straight lines, if produced indefinitely, meet on that side on which are the angles less than two right angles.

What worried people most was the fifth, known as the Parallel Postulate. Euclid needed it in order to prove his propositions about parallels, but, absurd though it might seem, he could not prove it. If it could be proved, it would become a theorem. But those who tried to prove it found themselves involved in circular arguments. It has been held as a mark of Euclid's genius that he left it as it was, consciously exposed as an assumption. If it were true, everything else in Euclid's system would follow. The trouble was, it was impossible to prove.

When Alexandria gave way to Rome, geometry went into an eclipse. The Romans were only interested in geometry as a practical art, and did not advance it in any way. It was the Arabs who preserved Euclid's work (the *Elements* was one of the first books to be translated from Greek into Arabic), and when in the early twelfth century the English scholar Adelhard of Bath wanted to translate Euclid into Latin, he had to go to Spain disguised as a Mohammedan student in order to find the Arabic text. John Dee, the sixteenth-century scholar, located further Arabic texts, and by the eighteenth century a Greek text had been well established. The *Elements* was more than influential — it defined the subject.

But the nagging doubt over parallels remained. Savile in the seventeenth century pointed this out as a blemish. A hundred years later the Italian Saccheri, under the impression that he was justifying Euclid, raised the possibility that there might be geometries in which the Parallel Postulate did not hold. About a century later, by one of those odd coincidences in the history of ideas, three men were working out non-Euclidean geometries, completely independently of each other. Each of them, Gauss, Lobachevsky and Bolyai, began by questioning the postulate, which was finally in 1868 shown by Beltrami to be incapable of proof. The new geometries, in which space is curved and parallel lines do not exist, took some time to establish themselves. One of the last great defenders of Euclid was C. L. Dodgson, or Lewis Carroll. In *Euclid and his Modern Rivals*, a spirited and witty debunking work, Dodgson argued for the retention of the Euclidean system, as being the best proof against circular arguments and obscurantism.

Although we no longer learn 'Euclid' as a subject, the plane geometry which is taught in schools remains substantially the same as that propounded and systematized in Alexandria in 300 BC. There is really no equivalent of Euclid in the history of learning for the profoundness and longevity of his influence. He became his subject.   J.F.

Jesus

Jesus offered an alternative universe. Instead of the hierarchical universe of privilege and gain in which men struggled onto each others' shoulders in order to approach nearer to God, he offered the Kingdom of God in which all men were equal. In this universe there was place for the sinners as well as the saints, for the meek and humble as well as the righteous.

6 BC-AD 30

Jesus has had more influence on the world than any of the other thinkers described in this book. Yet, paradoxically, it is harder to reach the historical truth about him than about any of the others.

Almost all our information about Jesus is contained in the four Gospels bearing the names of his apostles Matthew and John, and Paul's companions, Mark and Luke — though they were certainly not the real authors of the works. Who these men were — the evangelists, from Greek *evangelion* (good news) — cannot now be determined. Nor do we know where the Gospels were written, or when; probably they reached their final form between thirty-five and sixty years after Jesus' death. But the main difficulty which these works present, from the historian's point of view, arises from their intention to edify, to spread belief in the divinity of Jesus — that is to say they were not designed primarily as historical evidence.

Thus researchers must throw away, for the time being, their beliefs or unbeliefs, and try to examine the Gospels with the same degree of objectivity as would be applied to any other informative pieces of ancient literature and distinguish between those passages which bear the stamp of the early Christian Church and those which, on the contrary, seem to go back to Jesus himself. In this way the mainlines of his career, thinking and teaching, can be to a substantial extent reconstructed.

Jesus was not born in AD 1 — a date based on a medieval miscalculation — but at some time during the last decade BC. His birth and career coincided with a very unhappy time for Palestine and Judaism. A thousand years earlier, the country had been great under David and Solomon. Then it had divided into two kingdoms which had fallen to the great imperial powers of Assyria and Babylonia respectively. Subsequently the Persians, and then the Greeks (Seleucids), had taken over the whole country. In the second century BC the Jewish nationalist movement of the Maccabees had won independence from the Greeks. But thereafter this dynasty had succumbed to the Romans, who had replaced them by the puppet monarch Herod the Great. Herod had died in 4 BC and by the time Jesus grew up, the core of Palestine had been directly annexed by the Romans as their province of Judaea, governed by a prefect who allowed the Jews a measure of self-government under a council (Sanhedrin) directed by their high priest. North and east of Judaea respectively were the territories of Galilee and Peraea which, in conjunction, formed the princedom of one of Herod the Great's sons, Herod Antipas, who ruled by the grace of Rome.

On the desert fringes of Judaea and Peraea, in about AD 28–9, there arose a mysterious Jewish preacher, John the Baptist (no connection with the later evangelist), who attracted widespread attention by proclaiming the imminence of the Kingdom (or rather Kingship) of God. This was not new; Jews had long believed that their miseries would one day end when the divine Kingship, which was potentially eternal, would in fact be realized upon earth, and the Lord would usher in perfection. They had also emphasized the need for repentance, and so did John, stressing that it must be a total change of heart. This achieved, he declared, the sins of men and women would be forgiven; and he set a seal on the process by conferring baptism — a new development of the periodical ritual ablutions, converted by the Baptist into a once-and-for-all event which radically and permanently transformed its recipients.

One of those who received John's baptism was Jesus — unquestionably an historical happening, since the early Church would have dearly liked to omit it (seeing that Jesus was supposedly sinless), but was unable to do so because of its authenticity. Jesus had probably been born not at Bethlehem in Judaea — a fiction inserted to fulfil a prophecy — but in Galilee, a country of fairly recent conversion to Judaism which produced numerous devout sages, though its people were looked down on

43

by Jerusalem as bucolic and incorrect in matters of religion. His birthplace may have been Nazareth. His mother was Mary. But, although the doctrine of the virgin birth later prevailed, two of the evangelists also ambiguously credit him with descent from King David (which the awaited Messiah was expected to possess) through Mary's husband Joseph, with the evident implication that he, not God, was Jesus' father.

Soon after Jesus had been baptized, John was arrested by Herod Antipas as potentially seditious. Thereupon Jesus returned to Galilee and began his mission. It contained the same ingredients as the Baptist's, but Jesus no longer preached, like the Baptist and other Jews before him, that the Kingdom of God was imminent, but that *it had already begun to arrive* — by his own agency, on the direct order of God. This sensational innovation was the key to Jesus' entire career: it totally dominated all his thoughts and actions, and every item of his ethical and social teaching — for example his many parables derived from and depended on this single-minded idea.

His alleged miracles — healings or exorcisms on the one hand, and conquests of nature (such as walking upon water) on the other — were 'signs' in the traditional Jewish sense of both prefiguring and in part actually constituting salvation. They were descriptive gestures or enacted parables, and, once again, they symbolized the Kingdom of God. His healings, in particular (some of which were surely authentic), were directly and explicitly related by him to the repentance and forgiveness of sins which were accompaniments of this dawning Kingdom. When Jesus proclaimed the forgiveness of sins, professedly on the grounds that he was ushering in God's Kingdom by God's authority, other Jews were shocked because he seemed to be usurping the divine prerogative and infringing upon their cherished monotheism.

But Jesus agreed with them that the full realization of the Kingdom had not taken place; like many other Jewish thinkers he believed that it would take place almost immediately. His entire programme of teachings and preachings was based on these two convictions: that the Kingdom would be brought into complete effect upon the earth almost at once, and that he himself, by God's will, was beginning to bring it into effect already. This placed everything in a new light. Repentance now meant not only a complete change of heart but a change of heart which specifically accepted Jesus' message. Later on the evangelists, and especially Luke, laid special stress on Jesus' compassion. No doubt he was a deeply compassionate man: but the prime motive behind his apparently compassionate gestures was, once more, his total concentration on the Kingdom of God.

In the same way, he extended his mission to the poor because they were 'poor in spirit', since, lacking material strengths of their own, they depended on God's help and were therefore most accessible to his invitation to enrol in the Kingdom. Sinners, too, received his welcome because their repentance would likewise secure them the same admission — all the more readily, because they were free from the complacency of the consciously virtuous. And forgive your enemy, he amazingly said, and turn the other cheek, because what can possibly be the point of petty worldly enmities in the face of this great opportunity for all to enrol in the Kingdom together? Suffer little children to come unto me, not for any sentimental reason, but because their simple, unspoilt directness perfectly exemplifies the approach needed to accept Jesus' message. And Jesus welcomed women around him, because it was absurd to suppose that the Kingdom was only open to men.

In this respect he differed from the Jewish teachers of the time, the scribes, who were not surrounded by women in this way. Nor, like him, did they go out of the synagogues and preach to a much wider public. He was a teacher and a brilliant one, but unorthodox. He was also, like John the Baptist before him, seen by many of his listeners as an heir to the ancient and now extinct succession of

'Jesus and the Woman taken in Adultery' by Titian.

prophets. And some hailed him as the Messiah or anointed one (Greek *Christos*), traditionally the personage belonging to the royal house of David who would eventually come to rescue oppressed Israel, and who, some had now come to believe, would need and receive the aid of superhuman hosts in performing this task. There was also a mysterious and variously applied designation 'Son of Man' or 'the Man', which had sometimes (in keeping with a Jewish tendency towards corporate, communal concepts) been used to denote all Israel, or the remnant of Israel that would be saved, though it may latterly have acquired a more specific reference to a future individual who would perform this liberation. Some also saw Jesus as Son of God; though all Israelites were, in a sense, this.

It seems probable that Jesus himself felt that none of these designations — except the suitably ambiguous Son of Man — were really appropriate for his mission, which he believed to be unique. In this respect he followed the Galilean sages before him, who likewise claimed an exceptional, personal, intimacy with God.

This could not fail to bring him into collision with the dominant group in the Jewish religious leadership, the Pharisees. In the face of this opposition his mission in Galilee, assisted by his twelve principle disciples (apostles), ended in failure — as he himself

openly admitted. As his support dwindled Herod Antipas saw a chance to get rid of this potentially subversive preacher and, it can be argued, it was he who compelled Jesus to leave Galilee.

At all events that is what Jesus did; and he proceeded by gradual stages to Jerusalem. He was going deliberately to the centre of the Jewish establishment, which he knew would not accept him; and he must have foreseen his death. Jesus, like other Jews, believed many of his actions had to fulfil the predictions and prefigurations of the Old Testament and deliberately directed them to this end: thus his entry into Jerusalem was carefully arranged, in keeping with a prophetic text, to show that his kingship was not of this world. Next, however, he deliberately challenged the most politically powerful Jewish group, the Sadducees, whose interests were represented by the high priests, by driving the traders out of the Temple. Before long, with the connivance of one of his twelve apostles, Judas Iscariot, who was probably disappointed by Jesus' refusal of an earthly role, the Sadducees arrested him. He was charged with threatening to destroy the Temple and with claiming to be the Messiah and Son of God — to which he gave no clear answer, since neither an affirmative nor a negative reply would have offered an adequate explanation to such an unsympathetic

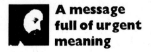

A message full of urgent meaning

An ivory plaque from a fourth-century, reliquary decorated with scenes of the arrest and trial of Jesus.

audience. He was then handed over to the prefect Pontius Pilate, who reluctantly gave orders for his crucifixion. Three days later, Jesus' followers believed they saw him resurrected upon the earth; and thus began the long process by which the failure of his lifetime was converted into triumph after death — almost the only revolution in the world's history that has lasted.

Of what did the revolution consist? In the first place, it comprised a religion which transformed Judaism by fastening it to a single figure and person, and a person moreover who (unlike the deities of Greek mystery religions) had actually appeared and lived upon earth. This *real* existence of Jesus among mankind, and his dramatic compassionate personality presented by the Gospels, were among the principal factors which enabled Christianity, throughout the centuries ahead, to attract enormously larger numbers of adherents than Judaism.

Thus the course of history and of human thought and perception was totally changed. And the revolution, quite apart from all those who have undergone its unconscious influence, still affects and directs millions of believers today. What many of them find perennially exciting about Jesus is this: in pursuit of his overriding idea, he was totally uncompromising in his refusal to bow to those, including those in authority, who rejected it and tried to silence him. His standard was an absolute one, and nothing short of it seemed to him of the slightest value. In this later twentieth century, an epoch of relative and shifting, sliding standards, that remains a message full of urgent meaning.   M.G.

Special Universes

To this day Euclid's systematized treatment of geometry remains the ideal example of thinking towards which all thinkers feel they ought to aim. He explored the nature of phenomena by stepwise deduction and established proofs that were beyond dispute. Aristotle set the pattern for and dominated logical thinking in the West for over two thousand years. Jesus founded what is probably the most powerful and certainly the most universal religion the world has known. The thinking of each of them was so effective because it created its own universe and then worked explicitly within that universe. It is this prior definition of a universe that allowed each of them to be so powerfully effective.

Most thinkers never define their universe but take it for granted that their thinking lies in the general universe of 'man' or 'nature'. A universe is a particular environment or set of circumstances within which certain truths are indeed true. Outside these circumstances the truths may not be true. Imagine a person to be holding a chunk of iron and a piece of wood in his hands. He releases both of them and they fall to the ground. Now imagine the same person to be in a spacecraft orbiting the earth. Again he releases the chunk of iron and the piece of wood. This time they float weightlessly. The universe of action has changed. Next we put the man under water in a diving suit and again ask him to release the wood and the iron. This time the iron sinks to the bottom but the wood floats upwards. In each of these instances the different behaviour of the wood and the iron would not have surprised the man because he would have realized that the 'universe' was different on each occasion. Imagine now that the man was strapped into a chair and so disorientated that he no longer knew whether he was upside down or right way up. He releases the wood and iron and finds, to his surprise, that they both fall upwards. Because he is aware of the usual behaviour of the wood and the iron and because he is unaware of any special universe change he deduces that he is in fact upside down. The main point is that the different behaviour of the wood and the iron is correct in each instance but the universe has altered. This is quite different from a situation in which the man, in semi-darkness, fails to notice that a nylon thread has been attached to the chunk of iron so that on release the wood falls but the iron remains suspended. In this last case the man is simply mistaken. Philosophers have tended to assume that we are all in the same universe and that man must seek to look beyond his mistakes. Thus the ancient Greek philosophers often failed to realize that the truths they were setting forward applied only to a rather specialized universe.

The universe of Euclid was the very circumscribed one of intersecting lines on

Pythagoras; from a fifteenth-century English manuscript. Euclid's achievement was to systematize the work of others, in particular, Pythagoras.

a flat two-dimensional surface. To some extent this universe is expressed in his starting axioms, and especially the famous 'parallel line' postulate. This postulate, which implies that parallel lines can never meet, seems true enough (but unprovable) in his two-dimensional flat surface but is not true for instance on a spherical surface. Euclid's geometry was a plane-surface geometry and many centuries after his death mathematicians such as Lobachevsky, Bolyai and Riemann showed that there were quite different geometries in which Euclid's truths did not hold at all. Euclid did not recognize that he was working in a specialized universe because he was not aware of the possibility of any other.

Euclid's systematic method has been the envy of almost all thinkers. Starting with his basic, hopefully self-evident, principles, by a sustained series of deductions he proved the whole range of plane geometry theorems. A theorem once proved could take part in the proof of a subsequent theorem until the whole imposing edifice was constructed. It matters not that much of the work was not Euclid's own, but that he put together and systematized the subject. His is the systematic effort and the deductive procedure. Most philosophers have searched for self-evident axioms about man and his world upon which to build, by logical deduction, a system as sound as Euclid's. What they forget is that the behaviour of Euclid's lines and angles is very much determined by, and limited to, the special circumstances of the universe in which he worked. In fact it is not too difficult to define a tight mathematical universe and to deduce behaviour in that universe from a set of axioms which themselves, as required by Gödel's theorem, are incapable of proof in that universe. The only trouble is that these constructed universes are very artificial and bear little resemblance to the actual universe of man or nature.

All that Euclid deduced was already implicit in his postulates, but could only be revealed by combining them in different ways. The discovery of what is implicit in a set of starting assumptions has been the main operation of philosophy and it is very worthwhile. Nevertheless it is quite different from discovering something new about the nature of what is observed. It cannot go beyond the given assumptions, postulates, axioms or premisses.

The universe of Aristotle was that of perception and language. It was the universe of man's interaction with the world in terms of his senses, his attention, his language ability to encode his perceptions as words and concepts. This is the world of 'logic' in its original sense of 'word' or 'measure'. We now know that the neurological behaviour of our brain, and probably of any self-educating system, makes it chop up the continuous world around us into small segments that can become the subject of attention.

Aristotle was the master classifier and categorizer. He looked very carefully at this process of 'chopping-up' and decided that he could formalize the segments chosen. For example he separated 'matter' from 'form'. Form is the particular shape or appearance and matter is what carries this: so in looking at a red apple we see the qualities of apple and redness, which are both forms, carried by the underlying matter. Clearly the distinction between noun and adjective is not important, since it depends on our habits of attention – for example a designer might say: 'Let's have some red in an apple form or appleness red.' In his classifying fervour Aristotle set out the following categories of statements that could be made about a substance: quality, quantity, relation, place, time, position, state, action and affection. Even the process of causality was subdivided into material cause, formal cause, efficient cause and final cause.

All this classifying and categorizing, which is said to have been influenced by Aristotle's background as a biologist, served as a basis for discriminating and distinguishing. Biologists are often, humorously, divided into 'lumpers' and 'splitters'. The splitters look for differences and subdivide a major species into any number of smaller species on the basis of such distinguishing features as a slight change in colour or shape. The lumpers do the opposite and by looking at the underlying similarities lump together what appear to be different species as one overall species with certain defined characteristics. Aristotle was a splitter, because he recognized that the only way to get clarity into philosophy was to know exactly what one was talking about. To some extent he was also a lumper, because he created large category concepts many of which are still in use today. He recognized that in the universe of the mind, language and the formation of concepts as attention areas was an effective form of thinking.

Aristotle set out to do for logic what Euclid had done for geometry. He did not actually state his axioms but they are implicit. The basic axiom is that of contradiction: something cannot be and not be at the same time. Without this axiom, which is only true in a certain universe, the whole of his logical system collapses. As a basic way of connecting up all the different categories and classifications he so busily devised he used the proposition which connects a subject to a predicate by the use of 'is' or identity. This type of relationship is already implied in our language structure and again is only valid in the universe of language. Finally he puts together two propositions in order to deduce a third proposition. The truth of the third proposition is, of course, implicit in the first two, but the 'syllogism' serves to make this truth obvious. For over two thousand years the syllogism remained the only form of argument recognized by logicians. An example syllogism might run: the basis of logic is to derive new truths from existing truths. The syllogism is a device for deriving new truths from existing truths. So the syllogism is a valid tool of logic. Unfortunately the syllogism often derived no new truth but merely made explicit what had already been taken for granted in the first place.

Just as a triangle can be regarded as being made up of three angles and three sides, so Aristotle tried to dissect out the different concepts that went into our ordinary perception. He then hoped to imitate Euclid by showing how such basic concepts could be combined in differing ways to give a better understanding of the world. It is only comparatively recently that philosophers have accepted that philosophers of the past were working in the universe of language, not of the world itself.

A change of universe

Jesus is perhaps the supreme example of the effects of a change of universe. In place of the universe of the present world Jesus preached the new universe of the Kingdom of God. Things that made sense in the current universe did not necessarily make sense in the new universe. Selfishness, power, ambition, an eye for an eye, adherence to the letter of the law, might all be effective ways of behaving in the world of man. Success and riches were desirable in the world of man. But in this new universe called the Kingdom of God things were very different: the poor and the humble had a place, riches were more of a hindrance than a help, turning the other cheek was encouraged. Instead of the development

**There was to be
only one law:
'Thou shalt love'**

of self there was to be self-denial in this new universe. Instead of the universe of strictly coded laws with which the Jews were familiar there was to be only one law: 'Thou shalt love.' This would be enough once people had absorbed the idiom of the new universe. It was a matter of perceiving this idiom through example and love rather than a matter of learning some laws. Love was important because the new universe was a patriarchal one in which God was in the role of Father who loved equally all his children. The children were to love each other as brothers, since there was no point, and no longer any need, to squabble for survival.

'The time is fulfilled and the Kingdom of God has drawn near.' This is an explicit statement of the new universe. The Pharisees had a great deal of difficulty understanding Jesus because they thought that he was quarrelling with their established truths in the existing universe. What he preached could not make sense until they were prepared to make the leap into the new universe. 'What shall it profit a man if he gains the whole world and lose his own soul?' Clearly the new universe was not a place for armies and glories but for the soul of man. Ambition and self-interest were to give way to a new ambition: the denial of self in the love of God and one's neighbours. This is very similar to the expressed intention of Eastern religions, which is to free man from his grasping self. The traditional paradox is that the harder man struggles to free himself from self the more he reinforces that self with satisfaction at his achievements. Nevertheless the direction of effort is clear enough.

The immediate mission of Jesus can be said to have been a failure, inasmuch as only one hundred and twenty disciples gathered together to spread his work after his death. But the purpose of the mission was not short-term success. The incredible spread of Christianity is all the more amazing when one considers how people were being asked to give up their immediate, tangible, sense-gratifying universe for a new universe which could not be apprehended by the senses. Many of the followers of Christ no doubt believed that the Kingdom of God was going to be in the next life as a compensation for the poverty and misery of this one. This seemed to be the view of the Church. For others the Kingdom of God was here and now and in the soul of every man who chose to enter it. Instead of simply obeying God's law in the universe of man, people were asked to enter the universe of the Kingdom of God. The change of universe brought about by the teachings of Jesus is without doubt the most powerful that has ever occurred in the history of man.

Augustine

Augustine introduced the concept of predestination. He thought that all men were predestined to damnation. No amount of effort on their part could alter this destiny. Only a gratuitous outpouring of grace by God could save a man's soul. This grace was not earned or deserved. But a man could open his soul to grace and rise with it to fulfil God's will and so achieve salvation.

354-430

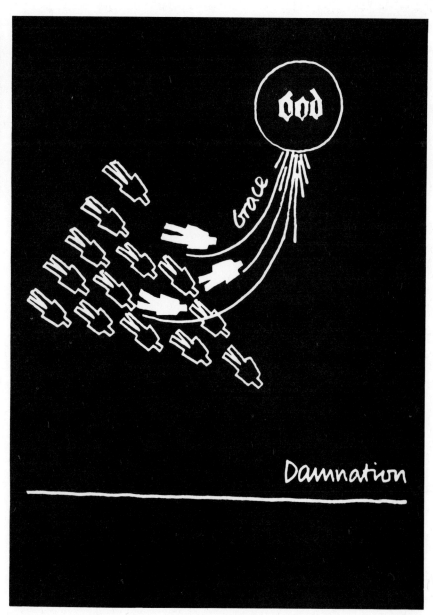

His thought was hammered out on the anvil of unceasing controversy

As a man and as a thinker Augustine compels response. Whether we see him as the pastoral Bishop, dying in besieged Hippo; or whether our impression is of the Christian controversialist relentlessly opposing false religion, heresy and schism; if we know anything of him we know that indifference is impossible. The outline of his life can be quickly told. Born in Thagaste, a small Numidian township, in the middle of the fourth century AD, rebellious against the simple piety of his Christian mother, a lover by his sixteenth year and a father by his eighteenth, his intellectual ability was early reflected by his gaining the position of professor of rhetoric at Carthage before he was twenty. Looking back on his life, he himself saw it as a spiritual pilgrimage, directed always to the pursuit of truth. He 'began now to arise, that I might return to Thee.' He sought the truth – in Manichaeanism, in scepticism – while continuing the pursuit of his own material ambitions, until at last, guided by the preaching of Ambrose of Milan, and the answers of Plotinus to the perplexing questions of spiritual reality and the origin and nature of evil, he found himself on his knees in a Milanese garden, the tears of repentance in his eyes, and before him a text of Paul: '... not in carousing and drunkenness, not in sexual promiscuity and sensuality, not in strife and jealousy, but put on the Lord Jesus Christ, and make no provision for the flesh ...' The intellectual sceptic had become a servant of God.

Significantly, Augustine's experience of conversion occurred at the level of morality and life-style rather than of intellectual belief. It was typical of the man for whom the closest bonds existed between the truth to which a man was committed and the conduct and life-style in which that commitment was made plain, and which in turn provided the context for commitment. It should not surprise us, therefore, to find the erstwhile rhetorician a Catholic presbyter within five years of his conversion. It was not Augustine's private desire, but he came to see it as of a piece with the pathway to God which he had already trodden. Inevitable, too, was the next step – his elevation to the episcopate in 396.

Thus Augustine found himself committed to the life of a Christian bishop and above all engaged in controversy – with Manichaeans, the followers of that mingling of oriental dualism with Greek and Christian thought forms that characterized the religious climate of the late Roman world; with Donatists, the fanatical schismatics of the North African Church, with their typically separatist claim to be the one pure Church; with pagans; and with the Pelagians. Augustine was no ivory-tower theologian. His thought was hammered out on the anvil of unceasing controversy.

As a result, it is perhaps misleading to speak as though his thought is systematic. There are few works of systematic

Left: St Augustine teaching
in the school of Rome;
a fresco painted by
Benozzo Gozzoli.
Opposite: St Augustine
by Botticelli.

theology amongst Augustine's writings. Perhaps the nearest he came to such an enterprise was the *Enchiridion* of 423, which brings much of his teaching together in a developed form suitable as a handbook for the Christian layman. Much better known, of course, are two earlier works, the *Confessions*, and the *City of God*. The *Confessions* are not polemical, but a reflection upon the course of his life, and they display already, and unmistakably, the characteristic theme of his thought. Man is part of God's creation, bearing about him both sin and mortality. The context of man's existence is the sphere of Providence, the unfathomable omnipotence to which man, despite the apparent autonomy of the human will, must ultimately bow. Augustine's life, therefore, is a spiritual pilgrimage, its destination known to God from all time, and Augustine's experiences are the outworking of that purpose of the sovereign God.

The theme is reiterated in the *City of God*, though here it appears in a different context. Augustine is replying to pagan critics of the Church who see in Alaric's sack of Rome in 410 the inevitable outcome of the abandonment of the old gods. But the *City of God* is much more than an apology. It is a Christian interpretation of history, and of the Christian's place within history, and in this context Augustine sets himself to answer not only pagans but also Christians who face the situation of a tottering Empire with pathetic bewilderment at their apparent desertion by God. For Augustine the outworking of the principle of the sovereignty of God in human history is that true participation in the meaning of life is possible only for those whose horizon includes an eternity where God is just as sovereign as in time. Fulfilment, therefore, does not belong to the present age, and no Christian should expect it as the result of God's government of the world. To be a Christian is to accept with

humility — a key word for Augustine — all that God sends, to recognize that suffering is God's means of refining and liberating his own. History, then, has meaning, and direction: direction by God to God's appointed end, the judgment and the eternal peace of God's Kingdom, and this direction is manifested in the eternal Church, the 'City of God', existing throughout time as the agent for God's purposes.

But over against this community is another city, the 'City of Earth'. 'Two cities have been formed by two loves: the earthly by the love of self, even to the contempt of God; the heavenly by the love of God, even to the contempt of self . . .' Their history can be traced throughout the history of man as the two cities struggle against each other on earth, and move towards their appointed ends of damnation and eternity. It is not chance or the upwelling of inherent principles that determine the course of this development, but the inscrutable will of the omnipotent God who is making up the number of his elect. What Augustine presents us with is the primitive Christian interpretation of history in terms of eschatology. Even the idea of two cities is borrowed — from the Donatist Ticonius. But what he has done is to create, for the first time, a philosophy of history. And the idea of the 'City of God', the eternal Church, was to prove equally influential in the medieval Catholic conception of Christendom, and the Protestant idea of the 'invisible Church' of which individual churches are the imperfect reflection.

If divine sovereignty dominated Augustinian thought on history, its correlative in the field of individual salvation was human dependence upon divine grace. At the personal level, this was fundamental to religion; indeed, it was borne out by Augustine's own experience. It was only when God had stepped in and changed his will by the operation of grace that Augustine had been able to make effective in his life a commitment to a truth he had for long perceived. Thus, for Augustine, grace meant being saved by God; its opposite was to save oneself. If grace was merely God's assistance of the human will, then a man might rescue himself from the results of his sin. If he could not rescue himself, then grace was not assistance but enabling. To say that God saves is to say that man cannot save himself. To be sure, the will is involved; but the work of grace is to transform the will from its natural inability to a God-given ability to turn to God. Thus Augustine's thought on personal salvation swung on an axis whose poles were divine sovereignty and human inability. The human will was bound to sin. Created free, it had bound itself in the Fall, and was now in bondage to its own evil character. Grace, therefore, meant God setting the will free to again do good in obeying God.

Like the vast majority of his predecessors and contemporaries, Augustine accepted that human nature was composite; man was a 'rational animal' made up of body and soul. The deep effect of the teachings of Plotinus left him with an unassailable conviction of the soul's spirituality. He strenuously rejected the idea that it is the soul which is the 'real man', imprisoned in the body, from which redemption will ultimately deliver it. Man is a union of the two, and the body is as much the man as the soul. Yet the two are united in the one man without intermixture, and the body is the properly appropriate counterpart of the soul. The result is that Augustine can speak positively of the body as good in itself, and take delight in physical beauty.

What Augustine meant by 'soul' is illustrated by the fact that he can use the terms 'soul' and 'mind' interchangeably. The soul is the inner man, the rational, spiritual, intellectual being, while the body is the outer man, material, tangible, visible. Where the Bible distinguishes body, soul and spirit, the soul is the spiritual principle as animating the body, while the spirit is the same principle as engaged in the activities of the mind. Accordingly, salvation, when complete, will extend to the body as well as soul. For soul as well as body requires salvation. The Fall destroyed the delicate relationship by which the body was subject to the soul; instead, the soul was now subjected to the carnal desires of the body through the bondage of the will, and because the first sin was essentially an act of the will − of the rational soul − the soul and body together are both fallen. And though the soul remains a spiritual entity, the rebellion of sin, in which all men were involved, both conveys an ineradicable burden of guilt upon all, and radically vitiates the original righteousness of human nature.

In the closing years of his life Augustine found himself confronted by a radically different interpretation of human nature in the teaching of Pelagius, which reduced grace to the level of divinely-offered inducements to perfection. God demanded perfection. The human will could achieve it. Therefore perfection was the duty of all who followed God. To Pelagius the idea of a radical inability to do good on the part of man was no more than a weak excuse for sin. For Augustine the danger in this approach was that it put man in the place of God, and overthrew the humility which was the keynote of man's relationship to God in the Augustinian order of things. Augustine appealed beyond Pelagius to Paul, and the rest of his life was given to the elaboration of the implications of the Apostle's gospel of salvation. The 'text' of Augustine's argument was Romans 9.16: 'So then it does not depend on the man who wills or the man who runs, but on God who has mercy.'

Inevitably, however, Augustine had to face the question why, if salvation were essentially freedom to good bestowed by grace, it is not bestowed universally. Like Paul, Augustine is forced at this point to fall back on the inscrutable purposes of God. Grace is evidenced in that God, out of the 'lump' of sinful humanity, has chosen to give grace to some, and such grace is undeserved or it would not be grace. Of the rest, Augustine would prefer to remain silent. The decree of predestination, the ultimate manifestation of God's glory and unconditioned grace, is not open to human speculation. Nevertheless, he was inevitably pushed further, especially by the pressure of continuing controversy. Even the rejection of those not elect is 'merited' on the grounds of their involvement in the universal sin of man.

Theologically, Augustine's views belong to the category known as infralapsarianism: God's 'decree' of election is a choosing of sinners to salvation, not a predestination of neutral souls to heaven or hell. Augustine recognized the danger of Pelagianism. It dethroned God, and made man the arbiter of his own salvation. But what man who knows himself could have any confidence in a salvation gained on those terms? Augustine rightly saw that the effect of Pelagianism was eventually to undercut that consciousness of ultimate dependence which is inherent in all true religion.

After Augustine, the Western Christian tradition could not be the same again. Thomas Aquinas would eventually construct the edifice of Catholic orthodoxy, but the conceptual framework was the work of Augustine. Neither does the heritage of Augustine belong to the Roman Catholic Church, any more than to the medieval Church. Luther was an Augustinian monk. Augustine's greatest expositors were John Calvin and Cornelius Jansen. Through the influence of the fifth-century Bishop of Hippo the theological lines of Western Christendom were laid once and for all.   D.S.

Aquinas

Before Aquinas it seemed that Christianity was bound to separate man's thinking into two distinct compartments. In one compartment there would be reason and philosophy and in the other there would be religion and belief. Aquinas reunited the compartments as natural theology in which reason and logic could live alongside belief and revelation. He achieved this by repackaging Aristotle.

c.1225-1274

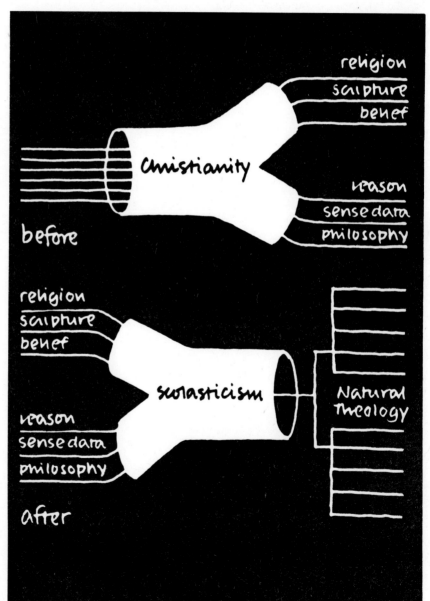

before

religion
scripture
belief

reason
sense data
philosophy

Christianity

religion
scripture
belief

reason
sense data
philosophy

scolasticism

Natural
Theology

after

A Dominican friar, canonized in the fourteenth century, whose teaching has been the official doctrine of the Roman Catholic Church, is hard to see as a rebel. On the surface, everything about St Thomas Aquinas, the rotund 'Angelic Doctor' with the broad placid face, suggests the same monumental solidity as his most famous work the *Summa Theologica*. But the assurance and order that we find there was the work of a man who opposed his family, his colleagues, and the most profoundly entrenched ideas of his Church.

St Thomas was born in 1225 into a powerful noble family near Naples, and died before he was fifty. When at the age of twenty he decided to enter the mendicant Dominican Order instead of becoming the Abbot of Monte Cassino, his family were so outraged that his brothers held him prisoner for a year, during which he prayed and studied and refused to relent. When he became Master of Theology at the University of Paris, St Thomas not only introduced new methods and proofs into his teaching, he fought the opposition of the secular Masters to letting members of the mendicant orders teach, and he had to defend himself against two mutually hostile parties, the Averroists who taught Aristotle in the Faculty of Arts, and the Augustinians on the Theological Faculty. Nor did the hostility to St Thomas end with his death. He was included in the condemnation of the 219 Averroist and Aristotelian articles by the Bishop of Paris in 1277; he was declared suspect by the General Chapter of the Franciscan Order in 1282; and in 1285 the whole of Thomism was denounced by the Archbishop of Canterbury.

Yet his writing looks about as tempestuous as a formal medieval tournament. The contests unroll in a series of Articles, each of which opens with the question to be disputed. The challengers advance their argument in a procession of Objections. Then the Doctor comes forward to refute error and defend truth. He announces his attack with: 'On the contrary' — here are the contradictory lines from Scripture; after which he declares: 'I answer that' — giving the proposition that refutes the false conclusion. And finally, he vanquishes the enemy with a flourish of Replies to the Objections. It is the quintessence of scholastic disputation. But behind the terse precision lay a turmoil of controversy about the most crucial questions for Christians.

St Thomas addressed himself to a crisis that beset the Church in the thirteenth century, of which the Reformation was only a continuation. A complete translation of Aristotle's physics had become available to Christian philosophers. And they found in it a formidably complete rational explanation of the order of the universe, incomparably superior to the fragmentary notions of the

older schoolmen. But the irresistible physics was wedded to ideas far from Christian.

For the Aristotelian universe has no beginning; it is governed by a God who is not a Creator; it includes no beatitude, immortal souls, or divine grace. Those clerics who became converted to Aristotle began to teach that there is but a single intelligence for the whole human race, denying God's providence, free will, and personal immortality. Though such Aristotelians argued that what their reason accepted did not affect their faith, it was at least plausible to suppose that Aristotle's physics was bound to endanger Christianity. The remedy found by St Thomas was inspired by his belief that reason and Revelation could not conflict because both came from God. If Aristotle's philosophy was true, then it must be compatible with, indeed supported by, Scripture. To demonstrate this was the task that St Thomas set himself.

St Thomas found in such a synthesis the answer to other questions as well, such as the controversy about universals that had been an issue for over a century. The dispute was over whether our abstract ideas — such as that of 'man' as opposed to our perception of 'this' man — exist independently and become known to us not through sense but through 'illumination', as Augustine had taught. Not just a theory of knowledge or logic was at issue. The differences over universals reflected a profound tension between two incompatible tendencies in Christianity — one toward a radical asceticism, a turning away from this world to the Heavenly City; the other, a disposition to humanism, to finding life on earth intrinsically worthy. The Augustinian party argued that asceticism was essential to accepting the Gospels, and that denying 'illumination' destroyed *a priori* proofs for God's existence, thus endangering faith. Their opponents insisted that knowledge must start from sense perception and that universals had no separate existence, but they had no coherent theology to support their contentions.

St Thomas attributed the whole tangle of disputes that plagued the Church of his time to the Platonic error, incorporated into Augustinian doctrine, of excluding matter from the reality of the world, thus denying the place of sense perception in thought and making it impossible to know the real existence of ordinary sensible things. St Thomas found the answer in Aristotle, but by producing a novel interpretation based on a new translation from the original Greek. What is central in the Thomist Aristotle is the doctrine that knowledge comes not by separation or escape from this world, but through the intellect's power to abstract unchanging truths from our changing sense perceptions. It followed that all our ideas have a sensory origin and that to reach God, men need not, indeed cannot, turn away from human life.

Of course, as a Christian, St Thomas acknowledged that there were truths inaccessible to reason. But he was equally certain that the human intellect could grasp some truths unaided by God's Revelation, and that the truths of reason could not conflict with Revelation. He went further to argue that faith was bound to take natural knowledge into account, even that the study of creation as naturally perceived might be useful for destroying errors in the interpretation of faith. It was therefore his task as a Christian philosopher to demonstrate the compatibility of the claims of reason with Scripture or to prove their falsity.

To fulfil this task, St Thomas produced a complete, finely articulated system of thought that covers the most remarkable variety of subjects, from proofs for God's existence and the nature of angels, to questions about when a foetus acquires a human identity, what constitutes virtue and vice in sexual love, and the justifications for civil disobedience. The systematic quality of Thomism comes of its being constructed on a small number of principles, all drawn from different aspects of the idea of being. There is a poetic quality about the formidable comprehensiveness and order that has inspired writers as diverse as Dante and James Joyce.

In the universe that St Thomas described, everything is linked in a

A world in which everything is essential to the economy of the whole

Right: 'The Apotheosis of St Thomas Aquinas' by Zurbaran.
Below: Aquinas disputing theology with Pope Urban IV;
a detail from 'The Disputà', a fresco by Raphael.

reality that has the form of a ladder leading to God. We are able to understand our relation to him and to the rest of creation because everything that exists shares to a greater or lesser degree in the being of which God is the unchanging source, though he is essentially different from and independent of his creation. St Thomas took the framework of the hierarchy from Aristotle; but he filled in the exact arrangements and degrees of operations within this framework by his conception of God. The knowledge came, he said, from reflecting on sense perceptions. He allowed as well for mystical knowledge, but he described it as an addition to, not a continuation of natural knowledge.

What made his synthesis a radical innovation in Christian thought and a harbinger of the modern outlook is that his emphasis falls not on the deficiencies of less perfect being, but on the contribution of the less to the more perfect. The result is a world in

which everything is essential to the economy of the whole. St Thomas saw in the union of body and soul a means by which the human soul achieves perfection.

But though this more amiable attitude to the Earthly City was inspired by firm Christian faith and may explain the endurance of Thomism in the modern world, it has also exposed St Thomas to enmity from Christians which came to a head in the Reformation. Luther was not alone in denouncing the 'ladder to God' as the invention of 'ungodly men' who 'presumed to ascend to Heaven' by their own wits. This denunciation denied that Christians could have systematic knowledge about God, or in other words, that there could be a valid natural theology such as St Thomas had invented.

What is at least distinctive about Thomism is the certainty that theology is the queen of the sciences, and has as good a claim to be considered knowledge as we attribute to Newton's physics, combined with an extraordinary interest in and prudence about earthly life in all its contingency and multiplicity. It is the attempt to account for the whole in all its complexity that produced the elaborate metaphysics and psychology, the special vocabulary and subtle distinctions, for which Scholasticism has been ridiculed.

It is why we find in St Thomas's political philosophy a belief in universal principles combined with a clear recognition that human knowledge is fallible. He suggests nothing like a theocracy, and he totally detached the need for rulers and laws from the Augustinian association with original sin. St Thomas understood political association not as a remedy for a defect, but as an essential feature of man's natural condition, a consequence of the plenitude of being in a rational creature who could see and choose among alternatives.

But if political association is part of the economy of the world, it must conform to a higher universal law. St Thomas's distinction between three different senses of law may serve as an apt summary of his outlook: the eternal law is God's ordering of the universe for all things in it; natural law is man's insight into or participation in this eternal law that gives the criteria for judging particular human decisions; human or positive law comprises the particular rules made at given times and places which must take into account differing concrete circumstances as well as accord with the principles of natural law.

In St Thomas Aquinas we see a mind capable of entertaining both faith and certainty without being tempted to extend it to everything, a quality rare even among those who find the universe more of a mystery. He was a unique sort of rebel, who was moved not by rejection but a serene acceptance of both God and man to oppose the going orthodoxy.   S.L.

Columbus

An example of how a strong idea could lead reason and action. Columbus did not discover America by accident but by a careful study of all the evidence and a determination to try things out. He set out to reach the Indies since he could not know America stood in the way. With the same equipment anyone could have set out on a similar task but no one else showed his determined thinking.

c.1451-1506

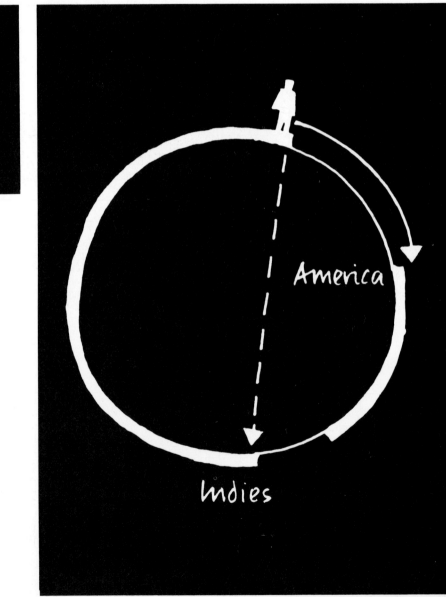

America

Indies

The course of history has perhaps been influenced as much by wrong thinking as by right. Columbus's own thought was ill-informed and misdirected, but it inspired actions as productive for the material condition of mankind and the increase of man's knowledge as almost any before or since. His achievement was the transnavigation of the Atlantic for the first time in recorded history and the discovery of an unknown and little-suspected continent. The immediate result was the most thoroughgoing revision of men's world picture that had ever occurred in Latin Christendom.

Columbus was born to a life of action, not of thought. The date was probably 1451 or late 1450. Genoa, his native city, was in the forefront of the maritime expansion of the late Middle Ages, but was intellectually the least distinguished of the great Italian towns. Moreover, Columbus' parentage was humble – his father was a weaver and marketer of woollen cloth – and as far as we know he never had the advantage of a formal education. That he should have taught himself enough Latin to absorb the geographical wisdom of his day and impress the fastidious scholars he later met at the Spanish and Portuguese courts is some indication of his mental calibre. But he was never truly learned; he read prodigiously but uncritically, wrote voluminously but obscurely. He absorbed knowledge at random, constructing improbable theories with flimsy evidence, rejecting or distorting whatever he read that failed to support his prejudices. His friend, the priest and historian Andrés de Bernáldez, summed him up as a man 'of great intellect, but little education'. The balance of his mind, moreover, was delicate and easily upset in adversity.

His practical training in seafaring began in his childhood though his experience of the sea can only have been limited, for Genoese records show him still ensconced in the family business at the age of twenty-one.

The direction his life was to take was confirmed by a shipwreck off Lisbon in 1476, which consigned him to a long period of residence in Portugal, a country which excelled even Genoa in exploration, and where the combined energies and intellects of the nation were dedicated to the search for an economical sea route to the Orient, the source of gold and spices. Columbus developed connections with the Genoese business community in Lisbon, visited the Atlantic archipelagoes and made an important step in his gradual social rise by marrying the daughter of a nobleman and explorer. It was a deliberate match. Columbus had already chosen exploration as a way of life.

It was probably in Lisbon that he began his voracious perusal of geographical books. From Ptolemy he learned that the earth was a perfect sphere – an inaccurate but serviceable observation – and that the known world extended in a continuous landmass from the western extremities of Europe to the easternmost confines of Asia. It appeared possible in theory, therefore, to cross from Europe to Asia by way of the Atlantic: only the distance seemed too great. From his reading of Marco Polo, however, Columbus deduced that Asia with its offshore islands extended beyond the limits suggested by Ptolemy and was therefore somewhat closer at hand. From a study, finally, of Pierre d'Ailly, the fifteenth-century reforming cardinal and cosmographer, Columbus took the most suggestive and least reliable of his data: Aristotle's observation that it was but a short way by sea from India to Spain, and the estimate of the length of a degree as $56\frac{2}{3}$ miles at the equator, made by the Arab geographer al-Farghani. Here Columbus's uncritical assimilation of information led him into a fantastic labyrinth of error; al-Farghani had been working in Arabic miles, but Columbus mistook them for Roman miles and thus computed a ridiculous under-estimate of the size of the globe; hence in turn he grossly underestimated the extent of ocean that might lie in his path. 'The Lord opened to me with His manifest hand,' he wrote, 'that it was possible to navigate from here to the Indies.' In fact, however, his plan for an ocean crossing was based not on divine inspiration but on a mathematical mistake. Henceforth, the idea became an ambition, and the ambition an obsession.

In order to realize his plan. Columbus needed a patron rich enough to finance the enterprise and powerful enough to guarantee its originator a share of any profits that might accrue. He spent the 1480s canvassing widely among the nobles and monarchs of western Europe, but at first he encountered only the almost universal hostility of prevailing scientific opinion. It must be stressed that the shape of the world was not at issue: there were possibly fewer educated men who believed in a flat earth in the fifteenth century than do so today. The unacceptable element in Columbus's plans was simply his belief in a navigably narrow Atlantic. In that respect only a handful of *savants*, mostly in Florence and Nuremberg, shared his world-picture. There were others in Portugal and Castile who were prepared to consider the possibility of an unknown 'antipodean' continent in the western ocean, but support on those grounds for Columbus's projected journey was considered too speculative by most cosmographers.

But Columbus persevered, directing most of his efforts to the court of Ferdinand and Isabella of Castile. Temperamentally incapable of contemplating failure, he was motivated in part, perhaps, by his strongly providential religious views, and was progressively heartened by the growth at court of a party of influential friends, won over by his tireless self-recommendation.

Most vital of all, Columbus had the admiration of Queen Isabella, who no doubt found his religious intensity sympathetic.

But this progress seemed negligible compared with the unfavourable chorus of learned opinions and the constricting exigencies of the royal finances at a time of war with the Moors of Granada.

At last, after a decade's unremitting effort a change in his fate occurred: the triumphant conclusion of the war freed resources for new adventures and on 3 August 1492 the great idea at last became seaborne. As it turned out, the route Columbus selected, via the Canary Islands, ensured his success, for it enabled him to exploit the prevailing winds, but the uncertainties of the journey taxed his qualities of leadership to the utmost.

On the four voyages he made to the New World between the first memorable landfall at San Salvador on 12 October 1492, and his last return to Spain in December 1502, Columbus discovered, explored and charted the southern Bahamas, the south coast of Cuba, Jamaica, Hispaniola, Puerto Rico and the Lesser Antilles, Trinidad, the mouth of the Orinoco and the coast immediately to its north, and the whole Central American coast from Honduras to the foot of the Isthmus of Panama. He became the first man to record the variation of the Pole Star. He brought a new continent and a new race of men within the cognizance of his fellow Europeans. But one has to consider how far he recognized the new lands for what they were, in order to gauge the importance of his thought as well as his actions. His original reaction was to confirm his prior opinion that it was Asia that lay on the far Atlantic shore. But when he found the American mainland in 1497 he was compelled to revise that opinion, and entered in his logbook some of the most significant words in the history of exploration: 'I believe that this is a very large continent, which hitherto has remained unknown.'

Most geographers who had absorbed the news of Columbus's discoveries identified the new lands as non-Asiatic and continental in nature. Though the existence of an 'Antipodean' continent had been vaguely suspected before, it was Columbus who found the evidence of it. And the rapid acceptance of the idea of a continent separate from the Eurasian landmass, which can be dated from Columbus's voyages, constituted the most significant single advance ever made in man's geographical knowledge.

The lustre of Columbus's achievement was dimmed by the reversals of his last years. Brilliantly successful as a navigator, he proved a dismal failure as an administrator of the territories he had brought to light, and was rapidly superannuated and disgraced. Only most reluctantly did the Castilian monarchs allow him to make his fourth voyage to the New World in 1502: the northward extension of the American continent was as yet unknown, and Columbus hoped to find a strait through it that led to the Asia he had sought unsuccessfully for so long. Struck by a hurricane, taxed beyond endurance by adverse winds, weakened by malaria, attacked by hostile Indians on the Panama coast, marooned at last on Jamaica, threatened with starvation, disappointed of his hopes and repudiated by many of his men, Columbus became literally

CRISTŌ: COLOMBO

deranged, driven into a mental refuge compounded of wishful thinking, mysticism and fantasy. He returned, for the rest of his life, to an uncompromising insistence, smack against the facts and the evidence of his own discoveries, that the newly found lands were merely an offshoot of Asia.

Columbus returned to Spain and permanent disfavour after the débâcle, a disillusioned, embittered, prematurely old and physically enfeebled man. He devoted his time to writing, mystical contemplation and the ordering of his financial affairs. After ratifying a will that sustained his habit of wishful thinking to the end — he left far more bequests than he could afford — he died on 20 May 1506.

It is not by the aberrations of his last years that Columbus's thinking must be judged, but by the process of formation of his one great idea. The strengths and defects of his thought were such as one might expect from an ingenious but uncultured mind. In some ways, he was a representative thinker of his times: his servility before the authority of geographical texts, combined with his paradoxical delight when from his own experience he was able to correct them, marks him out at once as one of the last torch-bearers of the Middle Ages, and one of the first beacons of the scientific revolution, whose glow was kindled from within by their preference for experiment over authority. In a sense, to test a theory by striking thousands of miles into an unknown and universally feared environment was a great triumph of the empirical method. One must remember, however, that Columbus was motivated not only by scientific curiosity but also by a mixture of religious fervour, personal ambition and the hope of material reward. Though curious from the historical and psychological points of view, Columbus's thought only takes on great importance by way of the actions it generated. He was an example of the power of will rather than thought. Clarity of mind, which Columbus lacked, may be necessary to comprehend the limits of the possible. But sometimes an effort of will, like Columbus's own, can challenge practical constraints and, by attempting the apparently impossible, promote human progress.   F.F.-A.

Above left: A map on oxhide believed to have
been used by Columbus.
Above: A portrait of Columbus by an unknown artist.
Right: The discovery of the Antilles; a woodcut
illustration from Columbus's report on his
first voyage published in 1493.

Thinking Backwards

Destinations had been established by dogma and by authority

It is characteristic of the thinking of Augustine, Aquinas and Columbus that they knew exactly where they were going. Like climbers on Mount Everest they knew that the summit was there and they could see it quite clearly. Their task was to get there. This involved exploring, finding and following a route. In the case of Columbus getting there was the important thing, but in the case of Augustine and Aquinas it was the route they established that was important.

This process of thinking backwards was typical of the Middle Ages. Destinations had been established by dogma and by authority. What was left to the energies of man's mind was the sort of exploration that would amplify, elaborate and support the conclusions that were known in advance. All this was in marked contrast to the thinking of the Greek philosophers, who were more concerned with exploration than with tidiness. The Greek philosophers set out to explore a subject not knowing where they were going and what they were going to find. The thinkers of the Middle Ages knew very well where they were going to arrive. This is the usual distinction made between the two types of thinking, and it is usually made in favour of the Greeks. What is usually forgotten is that outside of mathematics or geometry in particular, the Greek method was no more one of exploration than was that of the Middle Ages. The Greeks disliked experiment and believed that experiments with concepts in the mind were quite sufficient to tease out the nature of the universe. Mathematics by its nature was experimental in so far as one thing led on, inexorably, to the next.

It was the Greek mistake to imagine that all the universes of thinking were like those of mathematics. This led them to disdain experiment and observation in favour of deduction. Outside of mathematics this meant that their thinking was largely circular, since the exploration began with certain verbal concepts and ended up with the implications of those concepts, which were particular to their own civilization, and especially to the nature of the small city state. It is only because our own civilization has taken over those concepts almost entirely that we see them as 'true' and 'worthwhile'. To an outsider from another planet they may still seem worthwhile within the particular 'universe' that we have chosen, but by no means the only possible set of concepts.

In short the sharp distinction that is made between the free philosophical exploration of the Greeks and the circumscribed thinking of the Middle Ages is not quite as definite as is supposed. Both sets of thinkers knew where they wanted to end up. It is true that the Greeks did not use their thinking to provide logical support for their pantheon of gods or for matters of faith. They used their thinking to support their concepts of secular good behaviour and the proper nature of man. Plato's famous search for the 'good' is about as circular an argument as one might find anywhere (but a highly practical one: truth is that thing we are looking for when we are looking for the truth). For the thinkers of the Middle Ages the Christian religion was so powerful, and satisfactory, a universe that secular ethics and religious beliefs had become one. It is hardly surprising therefore to find that they employed their thinking to support these notions.

A dangerous habit

We are right in supposing that thinking backwards is a dangerous habit, since it can be used to support any manner of prejudice or superstition. Indeed, the most outstanding feature of ordinary thinking as practised by even the most brilliant is the habit of coming quickly to a decision and then using thinking to back up this decision. In a study of the thinking of schoolchildren this effect is so obvious as to be almost a caricature. There is a rush to instant judgment and then support of that judgment with as much skill as the thinker can control. This approach is by no means confined to schoolchildren, and is especially to be found amongst the most brilliant academic minds. The tragedy is that the more brilliant the mind the more successful it is going to be at supporting the initial judgment – whatever that may be. This means that the more brilliant the mind the less chance it has of ever changing its ideas.

Again this habit of thinking backwards may seem an obvious defect of thinking, and so it must be at the individual level. But ultimately it is the emotions and happiness of man that determine the purpose of his thinking. These themselves cannot be set up by any amount of thinking within the system because a system cannot set up its own 'meta-system'; they come from outside, either as the dogma or revelation of the medieval thinkers or the 'consensus emotion' which modern society purports to achieve. So ultimately thinking backwards is respectable so long as we never acknowledge it to be so. It must be done surreptitiously, under the pretence that it is an awful thing to do. It also follows that thinking backwards is perfectly all right so long as we agree with the beliefs from which we are thinking backwards – and quite improper if we do not subscribe to these beliefs.

It should also be noted that even in science, where we claim to think in a purely exploratory fashion, we are also guilty of thinking backwards. That is not to say that we juggle facts and experiments to prove an idea – though this sometimes happens, as in the case of Lysenko in Russia – but that science is impossible without an hypothesis. It is said that Chinese science came to a halt because it never developed the concept of an hypothesis. We pretend that an hypothesis is a temporary, tentative idea in the mind of the scientist. In fact it is more often a burning conviction every bit as strong as the conviction of Columbus that he could sail to the Indies by going westward. In theory a scientist is supposed to do experiments to prove that his own hypothesis is wrong. In practice the scientist works with zeal to collect enough data to support an hypothesis which, by definition, is no more than a sort of personal revelation.

St Augustine set the conceptual framework of Christendom. He set the framework for the Catholic Church, and even more so for the Protestant Church, which in its split from the Church of Rome reverted to an even purer form of Augustinianism. Luther was an Augustinian monk, and both Calvin and Jansen

He set out to square the Bible with Plato

advocated the severe concern with predestination, sinfulness and moral responsibility that originated with St Augustine. It could be said that St Augustine is responsible for the main difference in moral concepts between the Western and the Eastern world. He set the tone: either by originating the concepts or by formalizing and emphasizing attitudes that were implicit in the Church. He also set the tone by firmly blocking other directions, especially that of Pelagius, which were beginning to offer alternatives.

In what respect was St Augustine thinking backwards? It has been said that he set out to square the Bible with Plato just as St Thomas Aquinas set out to square it with Aristotle. This is a neat way of putting things, and has a lot of truth in it. St Augustine was a convert to the Church relatively late in his intellectual life; he had done a lot of thinking first. But he was not an intellectual convert. His conversion seems to have been more emotional and a result of the influence of his mother, and the way of life he observed amongst Christians. Ambrose was also a strong influence here. In his conversion he came to accept the Christian beliefs, including the Scriptures. In the particular case of St Augustine it was a matter of thinking backwards to square this concept of the Christian God with the Platonic thinking by which he had been strongly influenced, especially by Plotinus.

In general it may be said that at this time there was a good deal of intellectual effort going on in the Church. The untheological nature of Judaism, with its simple acceptance of Yahweh, had for a time been the model in the Christian Church. But the influence of Greek thought, especially Plato and Aristotle, was too strong for the intellectuals in the Church, and soon they began to think as well. For them it became a matter of accepting the Christian beliefs and then thinking backwards to square these with the secular Greek thinking. In St Augustine's case the process was somewhat in reverse, since he came to the Greek thinking first – but this only made the effort to square things more intense.

It is easy to say that St Augustine was influenced by three things: his supposedly profligate early life, the years he spent as a Manichaean, and his knowledge of Platonic thought. It is easy to say this, and like many things that are easy to say it is very probably true. St Augustine held the Platonic idea of God as the absolute truth or form of the 'good' that infused all his creations. He declared that: 'All knowledge comes directly or indirectly from God.' This may be contrasted with the opposite approach of St Thomas Aquinas who said: 'Nothing is in the intellect that has not first come through the senses.' The dilemma was that in the Platonic idiom God was something that infused all things in a pantheistic sort of way, whereas the Scriptures demanded the Old Testament God as a creator who stood apart from what he had created. St Augustine eventually solved this dilemma by the creation of the concept of grace, which was an infusion from God into the spirit of man.

If God was in all his creations then they should be as perfect as he was himself. This would leave no place for the Church to lead people to God. Moreover the manifest failure of people to be perfect could be put down to excess love of self – but what did this really mean? Here St Augustine's Manichaean background exerted a very strong influence. The Manichaeans believed that good and evil were two separate material principles which were admixed in things and people in various proportions. Evil was not just the absence of good but something as definite and as powerful. After his conversion St Augustine opposed the

Opposite: The chosen ones; a miniature from a fifteenth-century manuscript of St Augustine's *City of God.*

Manichaean heresy just as he busied himself opposing the Donatist and Pelagian heresies, but it is easy to see that his ideas were strongly influenced by Manichaean notions. If men had an admixture of evil then this would allow them to be infused in measure by God's spirit (in the Platonic sense) and would also offer a firm place both to the Church and to God, who would lead them to salvation. This firmly established the place of God and the role of the Church, which is what Augustine's thinking backwards was trying to achieve. But it was obvious that this approach was much too Manichaean.

The concepts with which St Augustine solved this problem have remained the basic concepts of Christianity. The Fall in the Garden of Eden was supposed to have weakened man's *will* to do good. This was crystallized in the concept of original sin. Original sin was not actually evil but a weakening of the will to do good – a turning away from God. This led on under pressure from the Pelagians to the idea that man was essentially damned and sinful, which immediately established the role of the Church – to mediate for man with God in order to achieve his salvation.

The followers of Pelagius held that man could, through his own good works and self-improvement, haul himself up by his bootstraps to salvation. This would of course remove the need for both Church and God's help. St Augustine insisted that man was powerless by himself and that it was only divine grace, which was given gratuitously, which could turn man's will towards God. It was then man's responsibility to accept this grace and operate his will in the right direction.

Only divine grace ... could turn man's will towards God

In this way St Augustine established the conceptual framework: that man is essentially sinful and damned; that this is due to a weakening of the will following original sin; that man can only be saved by grace from God; that this grace is not earned but given gratuitously by God; that nevertheless man is morally responsible for his actions. With slightly differing degrees of emphasis (for instance on predestination), we can recognize these as the fundamental concepts of both Catholic and Protestant Churches. The concepts arose by thinking backwards from the idea of the Christian God and trying to square it with Platonic thought. There was also the need to combat contemporary heresies (such as the Manichaeans and Pelagians), and this drove the concepts to an extreme they might not otherwise have reached. In his practical role in the Church St Augustine knew he had to oppose the heresies; he then had to think backwards to see how his opposition could be squared with his basic concepts on Christianity. It is interesting to speculate what would have happened to Christianity if the positive self-help doctrine of Pelagius had been adopted instead of the predestined damnation doctrine of St Augustine. Quite possibly the Church would have withered away for lack of a purpose and function.

St Thomas Aquinas is immensely important as a thinker for two reasons. First he became the official philosopher of the Church and in so doing provided the ideological philosophy for perhaps the most widespread thinking system of all time. Leo XIII in an encyclical of 1879 directed that the teachings of St Thomas should be taken as the basis of theology. This pronouncement was superfluous, since the teachings had been the basis of theology for centuries. The second reason for the importance of St Thomas was that he brought Aristotle right back into the mainstream of Western thinking. He did more for Aristotle than Aristotle could possibly have done for himself. Since the Church had exclusive control of education through the universities and monastic orders, the Aristotelian type of logic became established as the basic Western mode of thought, and it has persisted until this day, especially in our universities and academic establishments.

St Thomas set out to square Christian beliefs with Aristotelian reasoning. His approach was exactly opposite to the Platonic one used by St Augustine. In the Platonic idiom one moves from contemplation of absolute truth to its manifestation in various particular forms: from God to his creations. In the Aristotelian idiom one moves from observation and analysis of the sense data provided by the particulars to infer the existence of God.

St Thomas acknowledged that there were two sources of knowledge: reason and Revelation. Reason uses the power of the intellect to abstract unchanging truths from our changing sense perceptions. Reason provides natural knowledge, and the way this natural knowledge eventually leads to its predetermined destination (Christian beliefs) is called natural theology. Revelation transcends reason and arrives directly at these truths. For St Thomas there could be no conflict between the two, for any conflict would simply point to the inadequacy of the line of natural reasoning. St Thomas strove to show that natural reasoning was not something confined to the world of philosophy but that it could be used to lead to the truths that were otherwise accepted on the basis of Revelation.

This approach was the basis of Scholasticism, which dominated thinking between the eleventh and fourteenth centuries in Europe. At no time was the destination of the reasoning unknown. At no time was there any possibility that the line of reasoning would lead to an alteration in the ultimate truths that were to be reached. In other words, the path up the mountain could not alter the position or shape of the peak. Nevertheless the path was well worth finding. The destination was always determined by dogmatic theology, the path by natural theology.

In his many works, and especially in the *Summa contra Gentiles* and the *Summa Theologica*, St Thomas built a massive and coherent structure of philosophy. That it only proved what it set out to prove does not make that philosophy any the less valuable. The map-maker who explores the interior of a country is as important as the person who only discovers its boundaries.

St Thomas's famous five proofs of the existence of God are typical of the approach of natural theology. The first proof argues that every cause must be caused by another cause, and if we follow the chain back we must come to an uncaused cause that is God. The second proof does the same for movement and arrives back at the source of movement, which again is God. The third proof argues that all existence is contingent on something else and that only one entity can have necessary existence, which belongs to it by right, and this we call God. The fourth proof holds that all things contain some element of perfection and that therefore this perfection must exist separately in itself as God (a Platonic approach). The fifth proof is from the apparent design and purpose in nature to a designer.

St Thomas sought to bring together the two universes of belief and reason and to hold them together in a structure. For the most part he succeeded. There was much opposition. In particular the Franciscan philosophers (Roger Bacon, Duns Scotus, William of Ockham) tried hard to separate reason from faith and to

The destination was always determined

declare them as separate universes. They claimed that the criteria of reason could not be used in matters of religious belief and that religious dogma should not interfere with reasoning about natural phenomena. On the one hand this approach opened up natural observation and science, which no longer had to reach conclusions predetermined by the Scriptures. On the other hand this led to doubt and scepticism in matters of religious belief, since the boundaries between the two spheres could not easily be drawn. Moreover once natural reason had been given an area of dominance, faith would seem to be a rearguard action defending only those areas which had not yet fallen to natural reason. Wisely, in terms of the survival of the Church, the authorities preferred the Dominican approach of St Thomas to the Franciscan one. They felt that whereas reason could be used to support a belief that otherwise justified itself, if it were left to reason to create its own beliefs the way would be open to chaos.

Columbus is the most striking example of the process of thinking backwards. We underestimate Columbus if we regard him as a headstrong sailor who insisted on sailing westward and was lucky enough to find the American continent. We underestimate him even more if we assume that he stumbled on America by accident and that anyone could have done it. It is easy enough to say that America would have been discovered sooner or later and that whoever had the luck would merit no more than acknowledgment of this. The fact is that Columbus had no special ships or apparatus that had not been available to other mariners before him. He discovered America because he deserved to. Columbus was convinced that he could reach the Indies by sailing westward. To him this was as much a fixed idea or revelation as were the Scriptures to St Augustine and St Thomas. He then worked backwards from his idea in a methodical fashion. He even taught himself enough Latin to study the texts of the geographers. He supported his fixed idea with three lines of argument: natural reason; the theories of the geographers; the anecdotes, reports, traditions of mariners. From Ptolemy he took the idea that the world was a sphere. From Marco Polo he took the idea that the Indies extended further eastwards than was supposed. From the Arabs he misinterpreted measurements sufficiently to believe that his scheme was viable. Three times he had to argue his case before a council. Three times his scheme was rejected on the perfectly correct grounds that the distance to the Indies was too long. Finally we know that his *incorrect* thinking paid off. An exactly parallel thing happened to Marconi when he first tried to get wireless waves to cross the Atlantic. All physicists knew that the waves would not follow the curvature of the earth but would stream off into space. Marconi knew this too, but he persisted, and managed to transmit wireless waves from England to America. The unknown and unsuspected factor with Marconi was the ionized Heaviside layer which bounced the wireless waves back to earth. The unknown and unsuspected factor with Columbus was a whole new continent – indeed a whole new half of the world.

His incorrect thinking paid off

Columbus nicely illustrates the paradox of reason. Should ideas lead reason or should reason lead ideas?

Machiavelli

The idealist moves ahead hoping that things will turn out as he wishes. He nods at good fortune and copes with difficulties but feels that the true course of events should be even. Machiavelli's realist responded to things as they were instead of wishing them to be as they should. His realist was an opportunist who extracted the maximum from good fortune and even tried to turn misfortune to advantage.

1469-1527

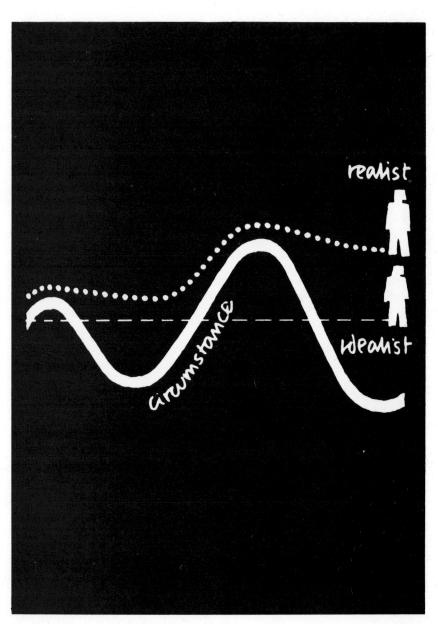

A new path...laying
bare the principles
of statecraft

Niccolò Machiavelli enjoyed a life notable for its diversity, both in vicissitudes of fortune and in range of interests. He was born in 1469 into the family of a Florentine attorney. His father barely scraped a living, so Niccolò did without a full-blown literary education. He managed to acquire Latin, but it is doubtful whether he knew any Greek beyond a few classical expressions. He did, however, have access to books, and indulged in a 'constant reading of ancient events'.

In 1498, after the downfall of the fiery Savonarola and the expulsion of the Medici from Florence, he became secretary to the ten magistrates who conducted the diplomatic and military affairs of the city. In this capacity he enjoyed a period of moderate prosperity and prominence under the patronage of Pier Soderini, who became Gonfalonier of Florence.

With the expulsion of Soderini and the return of the Medici in 1512, he lost both his job and his illusions, while his finances returned to their erstwhile meagreness. He withdrew to his small farm at San Casciano, in order to write, unable, as he put it, to do 'anything better'.

For the next fifteen years, until his death in 1527, he produced a remarkably rich and varied succession of publications. He is famed mainly for *The Prince* and the *Discourses on Livy*. But he also wrote some comedies, a *History of Florence*, a treatise on *The Art of War*, and many letters which, to put it mildly, are full of human, including venereal, interest. The literary motivation was probably complex. He undoubtedly enjoyed reading stories of 'great deeds' and 'eminent men', and writing up a contrast between ancient virtue and contemporary viciousness. But there is also reason to think that he wrote with an eye to a possible return to the public world. *The Prince* is prefaced by a fulsome dedication to Lorenzo de Medici, while the *Discourses on Livy* are also dedicated to the group who ruled Florence. He managed to secure some political assignments from Cardinal Giulio de Medici, who became Pope Clement VII in 1523. Before his career could arise from its ashes, however, he fell ill and died.

Machiavelli chose to write about what he calls 'the affairs of the world'. He also claims 'to tread a new path, which has not yet been followed by anyone' in laying bare the principles of statecraft. As a discursive writer then, he wears two hats, that of the general moralist, concerned with the totality of human affairs, and that of the political scientist, focusing narrowly upon the relationship of government and subject, and between government and government.

It may seem surprising to see the author of *The Prince*, the purveyor of a sour pessimism about human dependability, and

recommender of a ruthless cunning in dealing with it, described as a moralist. Yet the backcloth to Machiavelli's political advice is unmistakably a conception of how men ought to live together. They should be self-reliant, respecting the laws, faithful friends and good neighbours. They should, in short, display the virtues which, Machiavelli contended, characterized the inhabitants of the old Roman republic. From his readings of ancient writers he detected a state of public decency which the sixteenth-century world has lost. No longer are people enthusiastic for their laws, glad to form themselves into citizens' armies for the defence of the territory, embracing a religion grounded in patriotism. They have instead become self-seeking, preferring to leave defence to armies made up of mercenary soldiers. And in Christianity they have adopted a strange religion: not indigenous, but one of converts, which teaches the virtues of meekness rather than of vaunting independence.

His attitude to the Christian faith was ambivalent; while despising the New Testament teaching that the meek would inherit the earth, and deploring the corruption of the contemporary Papacy, he admired Jesus as the giver of a system of law (along with Solon, Lycurgus and Moses), and respected the founders of monastic orders, together with some Popes, such as Julius II, who had dared to ride an extraordinary run of luck in the conduct of diplomatic relationships. Machiavelli saw religion in two general lights: in that

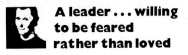

of a profound belief in the periodic necessity for a fresh start or renovation in human affairs, met by either a religious innovator or a lawgiver; and in that of the pre-eminence of patriotic virtue.

For Machiavelli the first step out of moral chaos is to produce a leader with the nerve and the moral equipment to grasp nettles, enforce laws, and be willing to be feared rather than loved. Fear is a more direct control over the actions of others than love; one may be loved, and even obeyed, but the effect is indirect and altogether uncertain. Such a feared but capable leader, Machiavelli hoped, Lorenzo would turn out to be, and *The Prince* specifies in detail the precepts of firm government. You must learn to avoid flatterers, and to recognize conspiracies when they are still forming, since it is as difficult to recognize political, or any other disease, early as it is to cure it late. You must, if you can, leave your subjects' property and women alone; most men are grazers rather than predators and will obey in return for security. But they will more readily forgive the killing of their fathers than the loss of their patrimony, and if you must kill, do it quickly and efficiently. If you employ a lieutenant to do your dirty work, don't hesitate to sacrifice him afterwards to popular demand for retribution. Avoid half-measures, be decisive. Cultivate the appearance of liberality, whilst remaining mean, since public liberality involves heavier taxation and will ultimately make you unpopular. Raise an army of citizen soldiers; they are cheaper, more reliable and better motivated than mercenaries. Use them as infantry in preference to shutting them up in fortresses, thereby gaining in flexibility. Acquire the reputation of piety, sobriety and probity. Keep faith with people as long as you are able; if reason of state demands that you break a treaty, make sure you appear to keep it, throwing the onus of bad faith on the other party.

'Reason of state': the phrase epitomizes the innovatory in Machiavelli. Medieval Christian Europe had not been lacking in advice books to rulers, nor in general treatises on principles of government. But the advice had hitherto been built into the general postulates of moral Christian conduct, drawing negligible attention to the specific assignments and problems of rulers. And the presumptions had been of an ideal society of citizens who were a mixture of moral beliefs and a practice which sometimes fell short. Machiavelli, by contrast, declared that the practice was the normal standard, that to expect human conduct to be other than greedy, treacherous, vainglorious, was to tread dangerously.

This is political advice of a novel kind. It states baldly that politics is as much a specialized profession as medicine or banking. Its standards are peculiar to itself, and are neither a part of, nor derived from, the general moral maxims which regulate informal and casual human relationships. Machiavelli frequently compares statecraft with medicine, an art which is diagnostic and prognostic. A doctor who relied upon abstract principles of health would be ill equipped to treat his patients. Likewise a prince whose only knowledge was of high-level principles would be set for disaster, unless carried along by sheer good fortune. Even the principle of 'reason of state' is a weapon to use after, not before, the action which only your judgment will tell you is necessary. And just as the Hippocratic oath makes the health of the patient the overriding professional obligation of the doctor, on occasion demanding that the patient be *not* told the truth, so the safety of the state, from enemies both internal and external, is the yardstick of political achievement. All this is what is meant by the autonomy of politics. You do not judge politicians by the standards of good family-men or friends.

How are they to exercise this specialized judgment? Having foresworn abstract principles of conduct, Machiavelli falls back upon the more modest use of precedents as the guidelines to decision. If you inspect the records of the past, and particularly of the Roman republic, you will find precedents for both successful and unsuccessful political action. The proper posture of the statesman, like that of the doctor, is towards past cases, his own or those of others, to try to fix an identity for the problem before him. It is difficult, and any response you make is subject to Fortune. But respond you must, and, like any professional person, you will be judged not by your intentions, still less by deeply-buried motives but by the results. To achieve an outcome favourable to your operation, you need to be extraordinarily self-disciplined, brave, far-sighted, caring little for the venial rewards of ordinary life, expecting only glory, probably posthumous, in return for an uncommonly dangerous career.

Machiavelli's moral views are in the end of a piece with his political recommendations. What distinguishes the ruler is the strict specification of his office, not his character. Part of the reason for the revilement of Machiavelli following his death lies in a dim recognition that he was challenging a large sector of Christian moral belief with a revived Stoicism.

He sees the human animal as a creature of circumstances, one of those circumstances being an inescapable challenge to choose and decide, a paradoxical conception, which fairly reflects both the excitement and the misery of being alive. A man is constantly faced with situations which are new and potentially hostile. Some of them are the direct outcome of his own or other people's intentions. More often they are the result, in part if not in whole, of the operations of Fortune.

Allusions to Fortune are common in classical letters, and the art forms of medieval Europe. She had signified various things

Cesare Borgia, the ruthless tyrant of the Romagna. Machiavelli admired Borgia's political realism and drew on Borgia's career in writing *The Prince*.

various times — the bringer of bounty, the ruler of the world, or, in the Christian version, the agent of God whose task it was to draw men's attention to the utter unpredictability of the mundane world, directing their eyes instead towards Heaven, where God rules with constant and reliable justice.

Machiavelli fits the ancient goddess neatly into his general moral beliefs. She is treacherous, nullifying rational endeavour and inflexibly planned projects. If she assists men at all, such assistance cannot be either forecast or relied upon.

Faced with this, what is a man to do? He may elect to drift wherever Fortune takes him. But this is not a commendable or safe course. Alternatively he might determine to stick to his guns and soldier on. This again is unsatisfactory; despite a worthy stubbornness, it suffers from the same defect as does adherence to abstract principles. It is unable to give actual circumstances their full weight, and thereby means relinquishing an open-eyed attempt to shape them to one's own ends.

The disposition recommended by Machiavelli is flexibility, a prescient grasping for the intimations of things to come. Think ahead, prepare in advance, and when the flood-tide arrives, keep your head above water, watching to see whom Fortune is favouring. Be ready to decide quickly whether to wait until the pace of events has slackened, when planning and foresight may bring predictable reward, or to counter-attack now. Machiavelli, despite constant tribute to the virtue of prudence, cannot conceal his admiration for the man of audacity who is willing to seize Fortune before she outruns him. The essence of audacious action is its speed in response to challenge, the token of a mind as energetic as it is courageous.

Such is virtue, in a world of contingent circumstance, where there are no sure rafts, no 'more certain word of God', only a few precious rules of thumb constructed from human experience, best treated as the fallible guides they are. Those who yearn for more are either in, or preparing for, eternity.   R.O.

Copernicus

Copernicus insisted on that most fundamental of truths: that the earth
was not the centre of the universe. He showed that instead of the sun
moving around the earth, it was the earth that moved around the sun.
The idea itself had been suggested before but it was Copernicus who
set off the revolution in thinking that was to follow.

1473-1543

Below: The Copernican heliocentric system of the universe from *De Revolutionibus Orbium Coelestium* published in Nuremberg in 1543.

Nicholas Koppernijk or Copernicus was born on 19 February 1473 in Torún, a city on the banks of the Vistula and some 180 kilometres north-west of Warsaw. His father, a well-to-do merchant and magistrate, died when Nicholas was only ten, and the family then came under the protection of an uncle, Lucas Waczenrode. Only four years after the adoption of his brother-in-law's family, Waczenrode was consecrated Bishop of Warmia — a position of high standing and no little temporal power. At his uncle's suggestion, it was agreed that Copernicus should enter the Church, and after a period of schooling in his home town he was sent to the university at Kraków (Cracow). Here, in a university city where his father had been born and where an elder married sister lived, Copernicus was swept up into a lively intellectual atmosphere. Here he was introduced to the new humanistic learning then spreading through Europe, and showed a predilection for mathematics and astronomy.

Copernicus stayed at Kraków for three years, but like many students at the time he left without taking a degree, and after his return home it was two years before he set off on further studies, this time to Italy. Copernicus' uncle had by now decided to offer his nephew a canonry in the cathedral at Frombork, on the shores of the Baltic, but the actual appointment had to await a suitable vacancy and it was in this interregnum that the young man was sent to study canon law at Bologna, then famous for its law school. The students elected the Rector and Council, and student life was pretty independent and somewhat riotous, with the result that Copernicus and his brother Andrew, who joined him there after two years, both ran through their allowances and had to appeal for more funds. Although elected to his canonry and installed, with his brother, in 1501, Copernicus was granted leave of absence to read medicine at Padua, then one of Europe's leading medical schools. From Padua he went to Ferrara where, in 1503, he was awarded a doctorate in canon law, thence back to Padua, and it was not until 1506 that Copernicus returned to Warmia.

For the rest of his working life Copernicus remained in Warmia, first as part of his uncle's entourage at the cathedral at Lidzbark, then either at Frombork or at Olsztyn, where his cathedral owned land. This is not to say that he did not travel on occasions to treat the sick — he was prized as a medical man — or move about Warmia on his administrative duties. As an administrator Copernicus was, in fact, exceptional; amongst other things, he organized a reform of currency during a period of economic difficulties following incursions by the warlike Order of the Teutonic Knights, whose lands surrounded most of Warmia. He was also a man of considerable determination; when the Teutonic Knights laid siege to Olsztyn he took a firm stand and saw that armed resistance was organized until reinforcements came and the city was relieved.

Copernicus was as bold in his thought as in his actions. Astronomy may have been no more than a hobby, but in his own time his scientific prowess was nevertheless well-known. His opinion was sought about calendar reform, and when his new ideas about the universe were publicly formulated in general terms, lectures on them were delivered in Rome. Yet Copernicus was cautious in promoting his theory, caution due not to any timidity in his character but to the fact that his hypothesis was so revolutionary. Naturally enough, he wanted to leave as few loopholes for his critics as possible, and so he kept trying to perfect his scheme. How long he might have prevaricated we do not know, for in the end he was persuaded to publish his complete theory by a Protestant mathematician, Georg Joachim, from Rhaetia (the Austrian Tyrol), and usually known as Rheticus. Rheticus had heard about Copernicus' belief that the sun, not the earth, lay at the centre of the universe, and in the spring of 1539 came to visit him. Considering the general animosity between Protestants and Roman Catholics at this time, no more than eighteen years after Luther's excommunication, it is surprising how well the two men

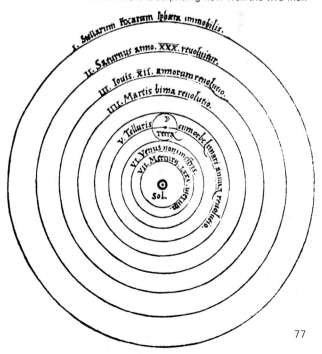

77

Copernicus's study in his uncle's
house in Frombork.

got on, for Rheticus stayed with Copernicus for more than two years. After a year's study, Copernicus allowed Rheticus to publish a summary of the theory, and in the end allowed himself to be persuaded by his younger colleague as well as his friends to publish the full text.

The actual publication of this momentous theory was fraught with difficulties. Rheticus undertook to have it printed and published in Nuremberg by the man who had done so well with his abridged version. With this end in view, Copernicus passed the manuscript to his friend Bishop Giese of Kulm who, having read it, handed it over to Rheticus, but Rheticus soon accepted the chair of mathematics at Leipzig and had to ask his old tutor Johannes Schoner and Andreas Osiander, a Lutheran priest, to see to the publication. Osiander was worried: the theory went contrary to a literal interpretation of the Scriptures, which spoke of a fixed earth, not one moving in orbit round the sun. He therefore took it upon himself to write an unsigned preface claiming that the theory was purely a mathematical device, and was no attempt to describe reality; in this way he hoped to disarm Protestant criticism. It seems that he altered the title of the book as well, for the book came out as *De Revolutionibus Orbium Coelestium (On the Revolution of the Celestial Orbs)*, thus perpetuating the age-old doctrine of the universe as a collection of celestial spheres nestling inside one another. Yet Rheticus scored out the words *Orbium Coelestium* in his copy of the book and it seems clear from this, and from the textual evidence of the book, that Copernicus wished to leave the title vague. Copernicus himself made no comment, but this was only because an advanced copy did not reach him until he was on his deathbed.

The essence of the Copernican theory was to demote the earth from its privileged position at the centre of the universe, and relegate it to the status of a mere planet orbiting the sun. Copernicus, it is true, had come across such an idea in his reading of ancient Greek authors, but his theory was no carbon copy of the earlier hypothesis. He had examined the current explanations of his time and found them wanting, not least because they did not make use of uniform motion in a circle to explain planetary motion. Certainly they paid lip-service to the idea, but even as early as the second century AD the Alexandrian astronomer Ptolemy had been forced to offset the centres of the planetary orbits from the centre of the earth: only in this way had he been able to fit theory to observation. This did not please Copernicus, who thought it an unfitting result for a perfect celestial system, and one that he could avoid by putting the earth in orbit. A moving earth, rotating daily on its axis, also seemed to offer other logical advantages, and

appeared better suited to earlier observations already available to him, as well as to his own. On all counts, then, he thought the heliocentric theory had everything to commend it.

De Revolutionibus was published in 1543 and raised a storm of criticisms. Some came from Protestant scholars, some from scientific men, but precious little from his own Catholic Church. The book was dedicated to and accepted by Pope Paul III, and its transfer to the Index of Prohibited Books only came later, as will become evident in a moment. The Protestant objections were scriptural, and the scientific ones arose primarily on two counts — the inherent improbability of a vast and apparently steady body like the earth moving at all, and the unchanging patterns of the stars. For if the earth did move as Copernicus claimed, annual changes in star positions should follow, and no such changes were, in fact, observed. Copernicus foresaw this criticism and countered it by claiming that the gap between Saturn, the outermost planet then known, and the stars was very large, but the existence of so vast an empty space appeared, at the time, to argue an uncharacteristic purposelessness in the Creator. However, the theory possessed undeniable advantages in mathematical elegance and was a break with a tradition that had come in for some severe censure by many Renaissance scholars; in time it came to be favoured by mathematically-minded astronomers.

Of those who promoted the new theory, the most important were Thomas Digges in England, Johannes Kepler in Germany and Galileo Galilei in Italy. England contained a number of pro-Copernicans, but the significance of Digges was that in 1576 he published a new edition of his late father's *Prognostication Everlasting*, and in this he not only argued in favour of the heliocentric theory but also printed a diagram identifying the sun as one of the myriads of stars which, he believed, extended outwards infinitely into space. Thus it was due to Digges that the Copernican theory gradually came to be associated with the concept of an infinite universe.

Modern research has also shown that it was from Digges that Giordano Bruno, an ex-Dominican friar with mystical and novel proposals for Church reform, learned of the Copernican theory, and this proved important too. Bruno was burned at the stake in 1600 for religious heresy, not heliocentric leanings, but as he had promoted Copernicanism along with his other ideas the new scientific outlook became tainted as far as some pious minds were concerned. Consequently when Galileo began to oppose accepted theories of the universe and to gravitate towards Copernicanism, he was for a time chary of making his views known. From 1609 onwards, when he had begun to use the telescope and gain

The door was open to a new and different assessment of the whole of creation

Nicholas Copernicus; a posthumous portrait.

observational evidence of the inadequacy of previous ideas and what he believed to be a positive proof of heliocentricism, he declared his opinion. It was now that Bruno's infection of Copernicanism, coupled with Galileo's own often tactless advocacy, brought the new theory into open conflict with the Roman Church, and led to Galileo's famous recantation.

Johannes Kepler was contemporaneous with Galileo, and his adoption of the heliocentric theory goes back to his student days when his tutor, although unable to teach it openly, brought it to his attention. Kepler's own concepts of the universe and of its divine harmony were based from the very beginning on the Copernican theory, and this led him, when he had the highly accurate observations of Tycho Brahe to work on, to discover that planetary orbits are elliptical, not circular — a discovery that was to be put to great use later by Newton.

Astronomically the Copernican theory was of fundamental importance, since sixteenth-century astronomy was almost exclusively concerned with the planetary system. A total rethinking of the whole planetary scheme could not but cause a revolution in outlook, more especially as the old laws of physics required fundamental revision if a heliocentric theory was to be accepted. For almost the next century after *De Revolutionibus* the validity of Copernican ideas was questioned, but finally the heliocentric hypothesis won the day, even if modified by the contributions of Digges and Kepler.

The theory Copernicus proposed had more than purely astronomical implications. The whole outlook of the sixteenth century was based on the conception of man as the centre point of divine creation, the focal point of the cosmos. He was the microcosm that echoed the macrocosm of the universe. With the displacement of the earth by the sun at the centre of all things, with the relegation of the earth to a lowlier status, the whole position of man was altered, degraded. His divine status was gone, and the door was open to a new and different assessment of the whole of creation.   C.A.R.

Luther

The Church had always insisted that it was man's travel agent for the journey to salvation. If man was to ascend to God, then the immense structure of the Church was necessary for the ascent. Luther maintained that man should carry his own ladder to salvation. Man could communicate directly and on a personal level with God without the intervention of the Church.

483-1546

before after

Martin Luther; a woodcut dated 1520.

EFFIGIES DOCTORIS MARTINI LVTHERI AVGVSTINIANI WITTENBERGĒSIS 1520

When he was a student at the university of Erfurt, his companions called Martin Luther 'The Philosopher'. It was a rather surprising choice of nickname for this large, brash Thuringian peasant. Perhaps there were overtones of irony in its choice, for in many ways Luther was a man of action rather than a contemplative. Indeed there is a certain irony in including him among the greatest thinkers, for his mind, though capable of great insights, was a far from clear one and quite often he contradicted himself when caught in an intellectual corner. Even so, there is no doubt that he earns his place among thinkers; the scheme of thought that he formulated, rather than originated, caused an intellectual, spiritual and political upheaval almost without parallel in the history of the world.

More than anything else, it was the expression of his ideas that sparked off the Reformation, splitting the Universal Church of Western Europe into two still-unreconciled camps, compassing, though long after his death, the destruction of the Church as a temporal power, opening up new ground for philosophical speculation on the nature of God and man in which questioning the authority of the Pope and the received theology of the Catholic Church need not necessarily be considered heresy, and finally, terribly, plunging Europe into a series of Wars of Religion that were to last for a hundred years.

In all this — and much of it happened after his death — Luther was a reluctant participant. The foundation of new Churches was no part of his philosophy. He was pushed by events. He happened to be the man with the power and courage to speak at the right moment. He had indeed a gift of words — simple, blunt, direct words needed to rouse the feelings of those who were intellectually or politically in sympathy with the anti-Papal views he was formulating. In another way Luther was lucky in the moment of his birth, which happened some thirty years after Gutenberg had set up the first printing press with movable type in Europe. Through the printed word Luther became the first great thinker to bring his arguments before what could be called the general public. For his disputations with theologians he used Latin, the universal language for intellectual argument, but at the same time he wrote his pamphlets in German, and these were printed and distributed widely to cleric and layman alike.

Martin Luther was born in Eisleben in Central Germany in 1483. His father was a free peasant who later became a copper miner. His was a pious home and, Luther was to write later, his upbringing was stern — no sparing of the rod at home or school. The young Martin showed early promise, with the result that at fourteen he was sent to Magdeburg to be prepared for a university. At

Magdeburg he sang in the cathedral choir, and, by tradition, also in the streets for food. In 1501 he moved on to the university of Erfurt, then regarded as the finest in Germany. His father was by now the manager of four smelting works and a town councillor, and could afford to pay for his son to read law. Four years later Martin graduated, the second out of seventeen successful candidates. As a student he had been the centre of a group that discussed philosophy and music. Surprisingly these young men were not much influenced by the humanism of the Italian scholars; they still adhered strictly to the views of the medieval Scholastic theologians, though Luther himself favoured the 'Modern' school, characterized by the fourteenth-century English Franciscan William of Ockham, which harked back to Augustine, rather than the 'Realism' of Aquinas and Duns Scotus.

Luther was set for a career in law, when suddenly on 17 July 1505 he changed his mind and entered the monastery of the Augustinian Eremites at Erfurt. Luther was very much a creature of impulse – we would call him manic now, his moments of depression being famous – and there is no reason to think he had been planning this move. His own story was that he was caught in a thunderstorm and prayed to St Anne, promising that if he were spared he would enter a religious life. For whatever reason, he was soon deeply immersed in the ritual of his Order. The Augustinians suited his cast of mind well: Luther needed a challenge, and no one was more punctilious in his observance than he. He fasted, scourged himself and threw himself into his theological studies. Just three years later he was sent to the university of Wittenberg to teach theology.

At this time there was still, as we can see from his surviving lecture notes, no sign that he was other than an orthodox Catholic theologian. Even his visit to Rome, which certainly sickened him when he saw the opulence of the court of Pope Leo X, did not alter his views. The change came during the winter of 1512/13, when Luther, now sub-prior of his Order, was living at the monastery at Wittenberg. Although he remained scrupulous, even over-scrupulous, in his devotions, monastic life was failing him. Slowly, for he was not a quick thinker, he was working himself towards the idea that the traditional view of salvation through good works was erroneous and that salvation must come through a personal bond between man and his Maker.

What led him to this conclusion – an extension of Augustine's ideas – was a long study of verses 16 and 17 of Chapter One of St Paul's Epistle to the Romans, a passage ending: 'The just shall live by faith.' Faith, in Luther's thinking, was the vital word. All men, he believed with Augustine, are sinners beyond redemption. It is God's infinite mercy that will judge them, saving some and condemning others. Luther believed completely in the idea of original sin, writing: 'Original sin is the lack of all rectitude and energy in our physical and mental faculties, both exterior and interior, the inclination to evil, disgust with the good . . . the love of error and darkness, avoidance and detestation of good works, zeal in wrongdoing.' Now it followed from this that if man's totally corrupt nature can only be saved by the mercy of God, then the Church has no special part to play. No superior power would rest with the clergy to grant remission of sins. The Church could only grant absolution for offences against its laws and not the laws of God. The Church could only command good works for its own purposes, not God's.

Not immediately, but within a few years of the first exposition of his doctrine of justification by faith alone, Luther had to go a stage further. And it was here that he broke with some of his contemporaries who agreed with him on his first step – Man's contract was direct with God and not through the Church – when he started to preach an extreme form of predestination: 'Through His will which is immutable, eternal and indefectible, God foresees, foretells and realizes all things. This principle is like a lightning flash, blasting and destroying human freedom absolutely.' If, then, there is no human freedom, then some must be destined to be saved, while the rest, come what may, are damned. Erasmus, who agreed wholeheartedly with Luther about the abuses present in the unreformed Church, could not agree with this. His more humanist views insisted on the paramountcy of free-will, man's power to shape his own destiny.

Luther believed that God imposes on man duties that he cannot possibly fulfil. Man must resign himself to eternal punishment, but at the moment of final despair God may save him. This promise of salvation is implicit in the New Testament: Jesus died to save us. If we have faith then we can be saved, however little we have done to justify this. These points form the centre of Luther's philosophy. It was some ten years before he had completed formulating them, but their first expression at Wittenberg, though popular with his immediate circle, otherwise caused little stir. A totally outside event turned Luther from an obscure academic into the nominal leader of a great religious movement.

For several hundred years successive Popes had claimed the right to remit sins on the basis of penances, which might consist of fasting or undertaking good works, but which might be compounded by the payment of a sum of money. This was a way of papal tax-gathering. Leo X in 1517 gave permission to the Archbishop of Mainz to allow the sale of indulgences (remissions of sins) in his diocese, the proceeds going officially to the

'I will have no reconciliation with the Pope for all eternity'

Bulla contra errores Martini Lutheri z fequacium.

Above: The title-page of the Bull excommunicating Luther issued by Pope Leo X in 1520.

Opposite: Vicious satirical attacks from both sides characterized the Lutheran rebellion against the Papacy.
Above: The Pope as antichrist.
Below: A Catholic counter-attack, *c.* 1535: the Devil plays Luther like a set of bagpipes.

rebuilding of St Peter's, but also to be used to help the Archbishop pay his debts. On 31 October of that year, Luther pinned ninety-five theses to the door of the Castle Church at Wittenberg, and the die, though no one knew it, was cast. All Luther was doing was to follow the normal practice of announcing that he was prepared to debate the question of indulgences and allied matters, and giving his views in brief. What was unusual was that when they came to be printed, this was done in German as well as the Latin used on the church door copies.

Totally by chance, the time was exactly ripe for Luther's characteristically strong statement of his case. Many people of all degrees were fed up with the indulgence salesmen, the luxury-loving clerics, the temporal power of the bishops. Luther had expressed what they wanted to hear. At first, the Pope was willing to assume that this was another minor heresy and was willing to let the matter die down, but the political situation, the death of the Emperor Maximilian and the election of his grandson Charles V in effect made the anticlerical movement Luther had started a political matter. Many of the rulers of the states that made up the Holy Roman Empire were restless at the power wielded by Charles, whose territories, in addition to the Empire, comprised Spain and the Netherlands. Public acclaim made Luther bolder, and he was soon denouncing the authority of the Pope.

Called by Charles V before the Imperial Diet, Luther refused to recant, and when the Pope issued a Bull (a formal edict) declaring Luther a heretic, he burnt the copy delivered to him. So Luther was excommunicated and, at the Diet of Worms, 1520, placed by Charles V under Ban of Empire. Luther would undoubtedly have been brought before the Inquisition had he not been protected by the Elector of Saxony, who hid him in his castle at Wartburg. There Luther remained for some time, pouring out a stream of sermons and pamphlets in his usual strong words. He could write: 'The die is cast! I despise the fury and favour of Rome. I will have no reconciliation with the Pope for all eternity.' As he countered the arguments of his opponents, among them Henry VIII of England, who wrote a denunciation of Luther's views, his ideas became more divorced from traditional thought. Soon he was advocating the marriage of clergy, and to prove his sincerity he himself in 1525 married Katharina von Bora, a former Cistercian nun who had left her convent after embracing his views. Later she bore him two children.

Luther's main contribution to Reformation thinking was nearly over; only one great controversy remained for him – the nature of the Sacrament. He could not accept the Catholic dogma of Transubstantiation, the changing of the bread and wine into the

flesh and blood of Christ at the moment of the Sacrament, nor yet was he willing to agree with the Swiss theologian Zwingli, that the Sacrament was purely symbolical. He proposed the compromise of Consubstantiation, whereby he declared that, though no transformation occurred, the presence of Christ could be assumed.

As Luther was approaching fifty his influence lessened. The Reformation was out of his hands. It had become to a great extent a political matter. He continued writing his pamphlets, translating both Testaments into German and composing his rousing hymns. The political side was in the hands of a group of Protestant princes, and the intellectual drive had been taken over by younger men like Melancthon, Calvin and Cranmer. Luther, at heart no revolutionary, felt a little bereft. As a young professor of theology he had dreamed of liberty and equality among all Christians, but he handed over the duty of securing this to the temporal rulers. Much of what had once belonged to Rome was now handed over to national Churches.

In 1546 he died, exhausted by a long illness, at Eisleben, his birthplace. On his deathbed one of his followers asked him if he remained steadfast to the doctrine he had taught. He replied, in a way that summed up the simplicity and directness of his thought, with the single word 'Yes'. It was his last.   D.H.

Breakaway

**The beginning of
new directions**

In spite of all the fuss that is made about it the Renaissance, and in particular the Italian Renaissance, produced few great thinkers. It is easy enough to hold the general opinion that the Renaissance was a period of great intellectual activity, but when it is examined closely there are few, if any, minds to equal the stature of the period that preceded or the period that followed it. Humanism is the term most often used to describe the philosophic outlook of the period, and thinkers like Erasmus and Thomas More are included under this term. The outlook of such thinkers is undoubtedly highly civilized and learned, and in its good sense has provided a foundation for much that follows, but it cannot be said to provide the sharp breakaway that is part of our mental image of the Renaissance.

It is possible that the Renaissance did not produce any great thinkers because thinking itself was exhausted. The old subjects had been worked out by masters such as St Thomas, and the new subjects had not yet acquired enough self-confidence. It is also possible that the thinkers of the day were too lost in admiration of the rediscovered Greek philosophers to do any more than comment on their texts. Nevertheless the period did provide a definite breakaway from the idiom of the Middle Ages. But the breakaway was the beginning of new directions in a more or less gentle manner, not the magnificent leap of a magnificent mind. It was only the fierce and sensible opposition of the Church that sometimes turned these small steps into chasms of division.

There are a number of mechanisms which lead up to a breakaway in thought and ideas. We often feel that there must come a time when accumulating experience and knowledge can no longer be forced into the mould of the old idea. The mould cracks and at once the available knowledge re-forms itself into a new idea that can accommodate it so much better. This process is, in fact, rarely the case. Human perception and thinking are so subtle that new information that should destroy the old idea is skilfully accommodated within it. Experience only becomes information when we look at it through the framework of an idea. If we look through the framework of the old idea then the experience will provide information that supports the old idea. It is more often the case that a new breakaway idea that is radically different from the old idea is only very slightly more effective in explaining the old experience. The classic example is that of Einstein, whose totally new concept of time and space explained only a tiny amount of experience beyond what was already explained by the old Newtonian idea. The bursting of the confines of the old idea by accumulated experience is a nice metaphor but not a reality.

Boredom, egomania and lack of education can be quite efficient mechanisms for the generation of breakaway ideas. Boredom arises when the old ideas seem so sound that little is left for the thinker to do, unless he is content to underline and elaborate the existing structure of ideas. This seems to have been the case with the Renaissance. The high competence of people like St Thomas had more or less established for all time the official thinking of the Church – and there was no other thinking to be done. It seems likely that this boredom gave rise both to the scientific impetus and also to such subjects as astrology and alchemy.

Egomania has been the mechanism of breakaway in many philosophers. The need to have some creative output of one's own has driven philosophers to oppose whatever was current doctrine. Having taken up this stance of opposition they then rely on their thinking skills to 'think backwards' and rationalize a sound base for this new position. Usually they have been successful, and this is why the history of philosophy is full of pendulum swings from nominalists to realists and back again. Sometimes the mechanism is disguised as a compulsion to search for the 'truth', and sometimes it is just that, but even in such cases it is difficult to decide which has come first.

**Lack of education ...
the most potent mechanism
for the production of
breakaway ideas**

Lack of education is possibly the most potent mechanism for the production of breakaway ideas. Someone who has not been thoroughly grounded in the existing perceptions can come to form his own perceptions and look at things in a new way without artificial effort. His new way of looking at things may be inefficient and crankish and much less satisfactory than the existing perception. But, occasionally, it may provide a brand new and innocent insight into something that should have been obvious long before. Machiavelli's lack of formal education may well have helped him in just this manner. Unfortunately, no matter how effective the process may be, no one is going to risk wasting a good mind by withholding education from it.

There is a theory of cancer which suggests that clumps of cancer cells may be forming all the time. Usually they are dealt with by the body through its auto-immune mechanisms. We only perceive the cancer when, for a variety of reasons, the cells are not suppressed but develop into a full-blown threat. There is a similar theory about the generation of breakaway ideas. It seems likely that throughout the reign of the current ideas, new ideas are bubbling up. But they never amount to anything and never even reach the public consciousness. No one will listen to the person with the new idea because he seems to be a crank – and very often is. Publishers are not interested in publishing his book because they cannot see a market for it. If sufficiently in doubt they will hand the book for examination to an expert who, by virtue of his expertise in the current idea, is bound to reject the new notion. If the idea does get further than this it usually becomes a welcome Aunt Sally for the pent-up intellectualism that can operate more easily in criticism than in generation. In the days when the Church was politically strong, the idea would have been denounced as heresy, and eminent thinkers like St Augustine would have thundered against it. There is nothing wrong with any of this. Most new ideas are crankish and offer no improvement on the existing idea. Most new ideas would be more disruptive than helpful. Unfortunately there is no mechanism for making an exception of the rare idea which may well be worth while. It arrives just like the others, and can never show its worth unless it happens to fall on exceptionally fertile ground.

It seems likely, therefore, that new ideas are happening all the time and what makes the difference is the climate of reception encountered by a particular idea at a particular time. This has little to do with the merit of the idea or the thinker who produced it. The idea may suit the political power of a ruler who has personal reasons for being dissatisfied with the existing state of affairs. Henry VIII's need for money and a new wife provided a suitable reception for ideas that challenged the authority of Rome. As we shall see, the success of Luther's breakaway idea had a similar political basis. This is not to say that the ideas were worthless and only succeeded because they suited someone's political machinations. On the contrary, the ideas may well have deserved to succeed but, undeservingly, would have aborted without the support offered by politically-motivated backers.

The breakaway idea that arises from a powerful mind of genius can be new in its entirety, but the breakaway idea that arises in other minds very often involves going back to previous ideas. Any current idea has a tremendous momentum that sweeps everyone past numbers of alternative roads. New directions can be generated by going back to these roads and taking them. This is what Copernicus did.

Machiavelli provided a marked breakaway in his thinking. Previous thinkers had been contemplative and speculative. They had thought about thoughts. They had felt, following the Greeks, that it was important to get the nature of thinking sorted out first before it could be applied to the world around. The coming of Christianity and the new universe of Christian beliefs put an even greater emphasis on metaphysical thinking. The Kingdom of God was not the material kingdom of this world but the kingdom of belief that man cultivated in his mind. So while men continued to be practical in their affairs their thinking was directed inwards and upwards in contemplation of the relationship between their souls and salvation. In contrast Machiavelli directed this thinking downwards and outwards: to man's opportunist nature and its political manoeuvrings.

Until Machiavelli, wise men were concerned with what things *should be*, with how the world *ought to* work. The books written for rulers were full of moral advice and the principles that should be followed. Some rulers may have managed to put these principles into action, others may have tried and failed. The majority probably paid lip-service to the principles and believed that they only applied to more saintly people or rulers with fewer immediate problems. A particular example is the meekness or other-cheekness of Christian ethics. This is very much directed towards the other world. In place of this other world Machiavelli placed his emphasis on immediate expediency, and power-plays replaced meekness.

Opportunism was his god

Machiavelli was concerned with down-to-earth practical action. Opportunism was his god. Moral considerations were totally replaced by expediency. He carried this amoral philosophy to the point where he appointed Cesare Borgia's chief assassin, Don Michelotto, to head the local Florentine militia which he had worked so hard to set up. He made it quite clear that rulers were not bound by conventional moral standards, and in place of them invented the new moral of expediency, which could be called 'reason of state' and applied in hindsight to any activity which seemed to offend moral susceptibilities.

Machiavelli was not concerned with what things ought to be or how people should behave but with what *is*. He was a realist and an operational realist. He himself had been involved in politics, diplomacy and intrigue, so his stance was not that of an academic theoretician. He attempted to codify what might otherwise be called rules-of-thumb or flying-by-the-seat-of-the-pants. He was thoroughly in favour of religion and a moral code – on the grounds that it made for political stability and made a people more governable.

Rulers, often with the political support of the Church, believed that they were there by divine right, by the legal right of inheritance or constitution, or through the moral acceptance of their subjects. Machiavelli saw it differently. He saw rulers retaining, or gaining, their position through the use of political skills often of the most jungle type. His yearning for a strong leader who might unite Italy and liberate it from ecclesiastical manipulations took this form of survival of the fittest.

It is fashionable to regard Machiavelli as an objective sociological observer and as the father of political science, and to maintain that he was amoral rather than immoral. It is claimed that his scientific detachment is what constitutes his breakaway from the thinking of his age; yet it is in no sense different from the detachment of those who observed and commented upon the spiritual behaviour of the mind. The breakaway lies more in his rejection of the Christian universe and his return to the universe of 'realpolitik'. His writings were roundly condemned by the Churchmen but had little effect on the conduct of the rulers, who probably felt that they had been acting as he recommended all along, and with a superior skill more suited to each occasion. Men of action have a natural arrogance which believes that reaction is better than thought and instinct more powerful than observation.

Copernicus made his profound breakaway by going not forwards but backwards. We acknowledge the profoundness of the breakaway because of the geometrical neatness of it. The reversal from regarding the earth as the centre of the universe with the sun going round it to regarding the sun as the centre with the earth going round it has an aesthetic appeal. What bigger change can there be than a total reversal – especially if it concerned a matter so central as our earth itself?

A total reversal

It seems almost certain that Copernicus first came across the heliocentric idea in his study of Greek philosophy. Aristarchus had put forward the idea, and in his time been roundly condemned by the Stoics for trying to upset the order of things. Copernicus also went back to Pythagoras for his belief that the universe could be better ordered than present explanations suggested. In fact when he did propose his heliocentric system he used perfect circles for orbits because these were nice and perfect. In its full form Copernicus' breakaway idea was not published until the year of his death, which made condemnation superfluous. In any case the Church reacted so mildly that the material was more or less approved. Interestingly, more opposition came from the Lutherans of the new revolutionary Church – it being a characteristic of revolutionaries that they are more intolerant of each other than of those against whom they are revolting (being essentially conservatives).

Copernicus did provide quite a lot of reasoned support for his reviving of the heliocentric theory, but little experimental data. As so often happens with

Jam poſtquam ſemel hujus rei periculum fecimus, audacia ſubvecti porro liberiores eſſe in hoc campo incipiemus. Nam conquiram tria vel quotcunque loca viſa MARTIS, Planeta ſemper eodem eccentrici loco verſante: & ex iis lege triangulorum inquiram totidem punctorum epicycli vel orbis annui diſtantias a puncto æqualitatis motus. Ac cum ex tribus punctis circulus deſcribatur, ex trinis igitur hujusmodi obſervationibus ſitum circuli, ejusque augium, quod prius ex præſuppoſito uſurpaveram, & eccentricitatem a puncto æqualitatis inquiram. Quod ſi quarta obſervatio accedet, ea erit loco probationis.

PRIMVM tempus eſto anno MDXCX D. v Martii veſperi H. VII M. x eo quod tunc ♂ latitudine pene caruit, ne quis impertinenti ſuſpicione ob hujus implicationem in percipienda demonſtratione impediatur. Reſpondent momenta hæc, quibus ♂ ad idem fixarum punctum redit: A. MDXCII D. XXI Jan. H. VI M. XLI: A. MDXCIII D. VIII Dec. H. VI. M. XII: A. MDXCV D. XXVI Octob. H. V M. XLIV. Eſtq; longitudo Martis primo tempore ex TYCHONIS reſtitutione i. 4. 38. 50: ſequentibus temporib. toties per í. 36 auctior. Hic enim eſt motus præceſſionis congruens tempori periodico unius reſtitutionis MARTIS Cumq; TYCHO apogæum ponat in 23 ½ ♌, æquatio ejus erit II. 14. 55: propterea lógitúdo coæquata anno MDXC í. 15. 53. 45.

Eodem vero tempore & commutatio ſeu differentia medii motus SOLIS a medio Martis colligitur ió. 18. 19. 56: coæquata ſeu differentia inter medium SOLIS & MARTIS coæquatum eccentricum ió. 7. 5. í.

PRIMVM hæc in forma COPERNICANA ut ſimpliciori ad ſenſum proponemus.

Sit a punctum æqualitatis circuitus terræ, qui putetur eſſe circulus ♂ ♈ ex a deſcriptus: & ſit Sol in partes β, ut a β linea apogæi

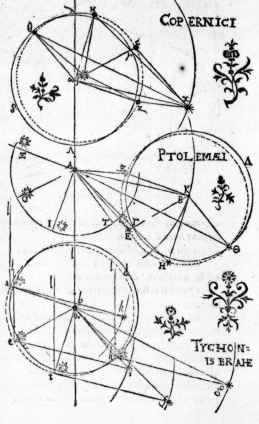

COPERNICI

PTOLEMÆI

TYCHONIS BRAHE

A diagram from Kepler's *Astronomia Nova* (1609) in which he used observations of Mars taken by Tycho Brahe to argue in favour of Copernican cosmology. The path of Mars according to Copernicus, Ptolemy and Brahe is shown.

breakaway ideas the whole thing might have collapsed (especially since his proposed circular orbits were so inadequate) had not the combination of Tycho Brahe and Kepler taken up the matter. Tycho Brahe provided the instruments and observations and Kepler knitted them into support for the heliocentric theory. Kepler went further, and following measurement of seven recorded oppositions of Mars came to the conclusion that the orbits were elliptical. Later the ideas got pulled into Church politics, as so many new ideas did, because dissidents made of them tools with which to attack the Church. Hence Galileo and his unfortunate experiences (with a less tragic ending than that of Socrates).

Copernicus revived an old idea in order to satisfy another old idea. He did not work things out very well. He was lucky to be followed by the combination of Brahe and Kepler. Nevertheless the first step in a breakaway is the one that deserves the credit.

Luther's breakaway from the Church was never intended to be one. He set out to be a reformer and purifier *within* the Church. That the Church set out to crush him indicates how very successful it must have been in crushing troublesome clerics, who were springing up all the time. Given Luther's character and temperament and the political dissatisfaction of the German princes with Rome, the whole thing escalated step by step to provide the definite breakaway that split the Church and provided national rather than supernational Churches. There is no doubt that Luther could not have succeeded without the specific military and political protection of the Elector of Saxony. The Bull of Excommunication which Emperor Charles v was required to serve on Luther, and Luther's subsequent condemnation at the Diet of Worms, would have been the end. The immediate military protection of the Elector saved him, and subsequent political support from other princes ensured that the movement could not be crushed directly from Rome. Indeed, the very word Protestant comes from the Appellation and Protestation signed by a number of German princes against the conclusions of the second Diet of Speyr, which had again come out against Luther.

But Luther had to have the qualities of intellect and character to sustain the breakaway as it proceeded from one escalation to another: burning Bulls of Condemnation, carrying on theological disputes, translating the Bible into German, studying and forming coherent points of disputes with the Church. By temperament and situation, Luther was remarkably similar to St Augustine. Both made apparently impulsive decisions: Luther to become an Augustinian monk and St Augustine to join the Church. Both were obsessed by a personal sense of sinfulness and the need for saving grace from God. Both were concerned with predestination and damnation. Both were driven by skilled dialectical opponents to ever more extreme positions of doctrine. It could be said that opposition crystallized in each a set of theological concepts. Luther started with a protestation against the sale of indulgences ostensibly to rebuild St Peter's in Rome but actually to pay the debts of the Archbishop of Mainz. The Church reacted immediately, and condemning him as a rebel and heretic required him to appear in Rome. In his disputation of 1519 he replied attacking the authority of the Church and upholding that of the Scriptures. The papal Bull of Condemnation of 1520 Luther burned. There followed the Bull of Excommunication and the condemnation at the Diet of Worms. The breakaway had

91

now become irretrievable. In fact in his statement at the Diet of Worms he held 'that it was not safe or right to act against conscience', and with those words established the idiom of Protestantism as the spiritual priesthood of all believers. In short, Luther, like many others, was dissatisfied with the Church's claim that it alone could act as the travel agent for salvation.

From a doctrinal point of view, Luther's notions were no more extreme than those of St Augustine in his time, but once camps were formed and polarized and political support lined up there was no going back. To solidify their beliefs people had to express them in action and persecutions, and the Wars of Religion followed. Luther's attack on the Zwinglian and Anabaptist sects and Henry VIII's attack on Luther illustrate how the righteousness of reformers blinds them to the fact of their breakaway and allows them the certainty that they have come back to the mainstream from which the current idea had strayed.

Since nature itself is so heavily dependent on the self-organization of chance events it is no surprise that breakaways in thinking also use the same mechanism. Whether as a focusing point for existing dissatisfaction or as the starting point for new investigations, a breakaway idea can only succeed if circumstances provide it with either protection or positive feedback. There seems to be no way other than survival by which we can assess whether an idea deserves to survive. But that initial survival depends very little on the quality of the idea.

Following Plato traditional philosophers had felt that truth resided in the mind of man and would shine forward to explain the surrounding world. Thinking had to come first and observation followed to confirm the thinking. Bacon insisted that truth only came from careful observation of nature. Truth flowed into man's mind and not out of it. Thus he came to be regarded as the father of the scientific method.

1561-1626

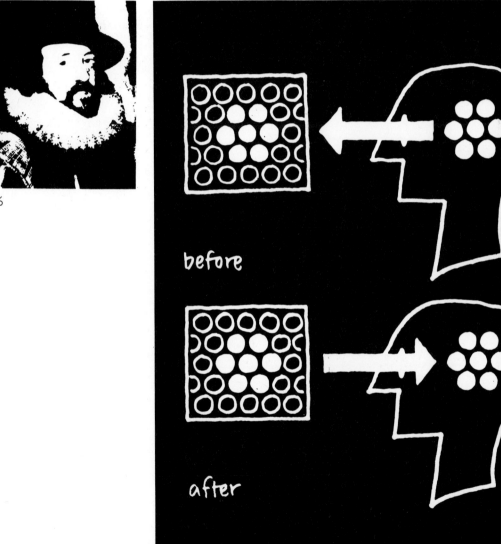

before

after

The father of scientific method

Francis Bacon has often been seen as the father of scientific method, indeed as the originator of a method which was soon to produce Newton as its first and greatest exponent. This is a half-truth. Bacon profoundly influenced that aspect of the scientific spirit which concerned itself with observation, classification, generalization and experiment. He was certainly one of the first to envisage scientific congresses and societies. On the other hand, he had little sense of the central importance of mathematics in science, unlike his near contemporary Descartes.

Francis Bacon was born in 1561. Bacon's father belonged to a Protestant family that had done well out of the dissolution of the monasteries, and he occupied the position of Lord Keeper of the Great Seal. Bacon's uncle on his mother's side was William Cecil, Lord Burghley, who was chief adviser to Elizabeth throughout her reign. Bacon trained for the law, and looked for his advancement to the favour of the government. His life was a continual calculation about advancement, a scramble up the ladders and down the snakes of position-holding; in many ways a cold and calculating man, his behaviour was such as to justify Pope's famous description of him as 'the wisest, brightest, meanest of mankind'. In 1593 he alienated the Queen's favour by a speech in the Commons, and subsequently became part of a group around the Queen's favourite the Earl of Essex. Essex treated him with the utmost kindness and solicited the Queen to advance him. When these endeavours proved fruitless, Essex himself gave Bacon an estate at Twickenham. In 1599 Essex raised a futile rebellion and was arrested and charged with treason. His friend Bacon was one of the two prosecutors, and he went about his task with a rancour which has been seen as exhibiting a poverty of moral feeling even in an age where there was such good reason to prefer political to personal ties. Bacon was later to write a defence of his actions in which he claimed to have put his duty as a citizen before his affections as a friend.

Bacon's career prospered much more under James I. He was knighted in 1603 and by 1618 he had reached the zenith of his power as Lord Chancellor of England, largely as a result of the influence of the King's favourite, George Villiers, Duke of Buckingham, whom Bacon had prudently taken care to cultivate. In 1621 he was made Viscount St Albans; soon afterwards he was accused of taking bribes and dismissed from his post. He was heavily fined, and ordered to be confined to the Tower, though he was soon released by James. He retired to his estate in Hertfordshire and gave all his time to the writing which had always taken a large share of his superabundant energy. The manner of his death in 1626 has always been seen as an emblem of the main interests of his life.

Opposite: Francis Bacon, Baron Verulam and Viscount St Albans; a portrait by an unknown artist.
Left: The Bacon family tree; at the bottom Francis's father, Nicholas, is shown with his two wives. Under the Tudors the fortunes of the Bacon family improved considerably and reached a peak in 1618 when Francis was appointed Lord Chancellor of England by James I.

Seeking to investigate the effect of cold in preserving animal flesh, he descended from his carriage and stuffed the entrails of a fowl with snow. He caught a chill and died a week later.

Bacon wrote a great deal of history, but his literary fame rests largely upon his small book of *Essays*, first published as a small collection of ten essays in 1597, and augmented in subsequent editions to a final total of fifty-eight. The essays constitute perhaps the most concentrated expression of practical wisdom in English literature, and many of the sentences, such as the remark about a wife and children being the hostages a man gives to fortune, have passed into common currency. Anyone looking for the attitudes of men towards political and moral matters at the beginning of the modern period cannot do better than to consult them.

In the wider current of scientific and philosophical thought,

however, Bacon's significance rests upon three features of his thought: His addiction to method, his belief in the technological exploitation of nature, and his elaboration of induction as a method of science. So far as method and technology are concerned, he was but one of many voices, though an influential one; but his method of induction was to become the basis of his enormous fame in later centuries.

Bacon is often linked with Descartes, each being seen as the founder of his country's modern philosophy. They were the two most influential proponents of the view that the knowledge inherited from the Middle Ages was riddled with error, and that men must begin again, starting from secure foundations and purging from the mind all the debris inherited from the past. But whereas Descartes sought to construct his foundation upon clear and

95

**He drew up the map
of what men had
to learn**

distinct principles, and is therefore called a rationalist, Bacon looked to the study of nature as the source of new and certain knowledge. For this reason he is usually called an empiricist. But this description is in one sense misleading, for Bacon was at one with Descartes in throwing over the tradition of knowledge, in seeking for certainty, and in believing he had found the beginnings of a rational method to get the task under way. In this important sense, both men may be described as 'rationalists' in one of the several meanings of that deeply ambiguous word. For a rationalist is one who seeks knowledge from reason rather than from experience, but he is also one who puts his faith in a rational method. Such a method discards both tradition and intuition in the building up of knowledge; indeed, at its most ambitious it seeks to discard also the natural difference of intelligence between men. Bacon is, then, one of the most influential exponents of what Michael Oakeshott has called 'the sovereignty of technique'.

What was the purpose of this technique? It was to glorify God by finding out about nature and using these findings for human ease and comfort, as God intended. Theologically, this doctrine derived from the book of Genesis, and in early modern times it came to be reinterpreted throughout Christian Europe and provided the moral justification for the expansion of technology that has marked the centuries since Bacon lived. The theology of the matter was important to Bacon because a concern with human ease and comfort might well seem to some Christians of the time a diversion from the primary task of caring for the soul. Bacon, however, was able to argue that it was not the interrogator of nature, but the speculator about divine things (like the scholastic philosophers of the Middle Ages) who exemplified an unseemly intellectual pride unbecoming to the human condition. He pointed out that it was the desire for moral knowledge, not for 'pure and uncorrupted natural knowledge' which occasioned the Fall, and he even goes on, rather charmingly, to suggest that God, in concealing the secrets of nature from the immediate view of men, is playing hide and seek with them. This line of argument can perhaps best be understood as Bacon's attempt to insulate the gathering of natural knowledge from the supervision of theologians.

In his unfinished Utopia *The New Atlantis*, Bacon describes a body of learned men called Saloman's House which was instituted 'for the finding of the true nature of all things (whereby God might have the more glory in the workmanship of them, and men the more fruit in the use of them).' This account has often been taken as the inspiration of the Royal Society, founded half a century later in 1660. It will be evident that Bacon's concern was thus essentially practical, and that what concerned him was technology rather than what we now call pure science. He himself would hardly have recognized the distinction. Further, in a typically practical way, he warned against too hasty an attempt to put knowledge to practical use, recognizing that some theoretical latitude was necessary to successful application. Bacon, then, is an important source of the beliefs we have about the universe in which we live: a universe from which omens and auguries, witches and hobgoblins, have been banished to make way for things described and explained in such a way that men may exploit and so live more prosperously.

Finally, what was the method by which man was to embark upon this adventure of practical knowledge? It is generally called induction, meaning the building up of universal rules from the observation of particular instances, but this is just a part of Baconian method. Bacon was by no means the mindless collector of data his modern critics have sometimes made him out to be. His view may perhaps be best encapsulated in terms of an insect fable to which he appealed. Spiders produce cobwebs out of their own bodies, just as the Scholastic philosophers were thought by Bacon to have spun out their elaborate speculations from their own thoughts rather than from any concern with the world in which they lived. Hardly more to be admired is the ant who scurries around collecting this and that without any plan — the very model of a mindless empiric. Bacon's favourite insect is the bee, who goes from flower to flower, or instance to instance, and then returns to the hive where the pollen is made into honey. Such is the procedure of the Baconian scientist, and it evidently requires a self-conscious and deliberate method if it is to succeed where earlier generations of men have failed. How are we to account for their failure? The human mind, Bacon tells us: 'is like a false mirror, which, receiving rays irregularly, distorts and discolours the nature of things by mingling its own nature with it.' The perceiving mind is, then, distorted by false notions, or 'Idols' as Bacon calls them. He distinguishes four types of Idol, and discusses each in turn. First there are the Idols of the Tribe, the distortions incident to the fact that man has five senses and each of them has a limited range. Secondly there are the Idols of the Cave, a reference to Plato's allegory of the cave in Book VII of *The Republic*. These idols are the distortions inevitably resulting from each individual's tastes, education, temperament and capacities. Here Bacon is recognizing that knowledge has a certain public character, and depends partly upon subjectivities cancelling out. Next come the Idols of the Market Place, which derive from the fact that men learn most of their ideas from each other and speak a language in which 'words are imposed according to the apprehension of the vulgar.' The solution to this difficulty is a language in which words have a fixed meaning, i.e. a

The title-page of Bacon's
Instauratio Magna published
in London in 1620.

fashion.' Bacon wants to tear down these theatres, and attend to the play of nature, and the first stage of his method is a purification of the mind conceived in terms of rejecting these four types of Idol.

Bacon's inductive method is a series of steps to be taken in the building up of certain information about nature. It involves the creation of a series of Tables of information about the particular phenomenon being studied — the example of heat is the one that Bacon himself uses most frequently. The first is called the Table of Essence and Presence, and requires the collection of known instances of the phenomenon. The second is a Table of Deviations, which 'presents to the understanding' those cases where one might expect the phenomenon to occur but it is in fact lacking. The moon's rays, for example, do not produce heat. These two Tables, although the language in which they are described sounds somewhat quaint, are similar to what John Stuart Mill introduced into the modern study of scientific method as the Joint Method of Agreement and Difference. Bacon's third Table is a study of the degrees to which the phenomenon is present in nature, and is called the Table of Degrees or the Table of Comparison. In Mill, it appears as the Method of Concomitant Variation. Here then is the material about nature which can be collected into axioms and constitutes what Bacon called the 'first vintage' of knowledge, a residue of the method which was expected to lead on to knowledge of increasing degrees of generality in the process of what Bacon called 'the human race seeking to recover its right over nature'.

This process of induction is to be stiffened by a further series of observations to which Bacon gave the name of 'prerogative instances'. There are twenty-seven of them, and they range from an attention to what would in modern terms be called crucial experiments, to a concern with striking features of phenomena, as in the case of the weight of quicksilver. This programme for the accumulation of natural knowledge will generate a series of natural histories from which may be distilled the laws of Metaphysics (which has a practical branch in a special sense of the word 'Magic') and Physics, whose practical branch is mechanics. We shall learn what nature does, and may be made to do.

Bacon's philosophy of science, from a twentieth-century point of view, is a script for a performance that never quite took place. The high road of science belonged to the mathematically inclined, those who proposed brilliant and imaginative hypotheses, rather than to the industrious natural historians of Bacon's imagination. But if he was not the philosopher of science, he was at least its prophet, the man whose vision excited generations after him, and who drew up, as Diderot later wrote, the map of what men had to learn.   K.M.

echnical vocabulary. Lacking this, men will be led away 'into numberless empty controversies and idle fantasies'. Finally, there are the Idols of the Theatre, by which Bacon means the ideas that philosophers have developed and which have remained in currency through respect for authority or simple neglect and indolence. This s perhaps an odd title for such a class of error, but Bacon tells us that: 'all the received systems are but so many stage plays, epresenting worlds of their own creation after an unreal and scenic

Descartes

Descartes' success in inventing analytical geometry convinced him that
even the most complicated situations can be broken down into simple parts
that are combined in a special way. By the power of thinking he sought
the simple parts that went to make up man's thinking and his destiny.
He hoped to do by analysis what Euclid had done by construction.

1596-1650

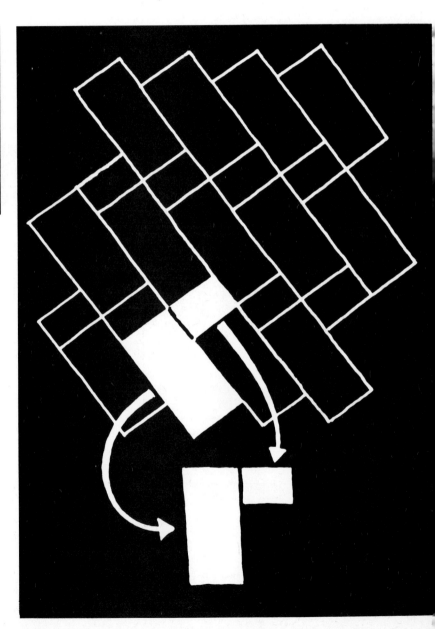

The relatively cosy, personal and purposive view of the universe which dominated much of ancient and medieval Western thought was quite literally torn asunder by the seventeenth-century revolution in scientific thought. René Descartes was one of the most important early contributors to this revolution, and probably the first thinker fully to appreciate the devastation it would wreak upon the existing European conception of the nature of knowledge itself. He had inherited enough to enable him to settle comfortably in liberal Holland, from where he carried on frequent and vigorous correspondence with the other important scholars of his day. Convinced that he had discovered the truth about the structure and meaning of the physical world, Descartes turned his attention to what he thought this implied for the generation of scientific knowledge and for the nature of minds capable of such knowledge. It was the exploration of the distinction between mind and matter and the consequences of this distinction which primarily occupied him until his death.

Unfortunately, Descartes' early speculations about nature were not published in any comprehensive form until after his death, even though he became well known during his lifetime because of his extensive correspondence. However, he did summarize his view of the world in his *Discourse On Method* (1637), and of the character of minds capable of successfully discovering the truth about the world in the *Meditations* (1641). Both have become philosophical classics, and have earned him the reputation of the 'father' of modern philosophy. In 1649 he accepted an invitation to teach his philosophical system to Queen Christina of Sweden. Part of his contract involved rising early in the cold climate to give the Queen morning lessons. After such a long time in comfortable seclusion he could not cope with such a regimen and died in 1650.

The scientific revolution involved a new conception of physical reality, one which was quite distanced from the near-identification of reality and appearance which had preceded it for so many years. There was renewed interest in the atomism of ancient Greece and more and more thinkers were beginning to argue that behind the complexity of ordinary experience was a quite extraordinary, unexperienced and simple reality. It consisted of countless impenetrable particles, in motion and interacting with each other in a variety of mechanical ways. The complexity of ordinary experience was interpreted as somehow resulting from the shapes of the particles, their interaction with each other and their interaction with the sense organs. Motion itself was also no longer what it appeared to be. It had previously been argued that some sorts of terrestrial and celestial motion were natural and/or purposively directed (i.e. heavy bodies fall downward because in some sense or other they

are meant to). Galileo effectively counterargued that many different types of motion seemed to have no directive purpose and could be successfully described and explained through assuming that they consisted of unobserved mathematical components. These combined in predictable ways to produce the unmathematical complexity of observed motion. Finally, completely new and, at the time, baffling physical concepts were being articulated for explanatory use. For example, the idea of some sort of 'force', analogous to magnetism, was gaining currency in explaining planetary orbits round the new centre of the world — the sun.

Descartes' earliest intellectual successes were in the field of mathematics. For example, he discovered that all the known mathematical techniques which had been employed in developing the new heliocentric views of motion could be expressed in geometrical and, therefore, spatial terms. He accepted the atomistic view that the world was just matter in motion and argued that both matter and motion were essentially mathematical in character and possessed no other properties than those which lent themselves to geometrical description and analysis.

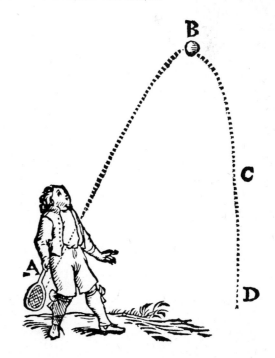

Descartes' geometrical system of the world involved three key assumptions. First, he claimed that the essence of matter was nothing other than geometrical or spatial extension. The measurable geometrical boundaries of matter constituted its reality. Second, he maintained that the essence of all motion is its mathematically describable features (i.e. the kind described by drawing a graph of a specific variation in velocity over a period of time) and that to that extent there is no favoured 'place', 'state' or purpose for or behind anything which is in motion. And third, all the motion which was in the world remained constant. That is to say, it might be mechanically communicated from one part of the world to another through direct contact but the overall system remained constant. It cannot be overemphasized how this simple result became vital for the development of physical thought. It stated that the variety of observed curved motions (and most observed motions are curved!) was the result of the mechanical interaction of matter in motion only describable and therefore explicable in

mathematical terms. In short, the overall picture was of a giant self-contained machine, transferring motion from one part to another oblivious to purpose, desire or any external direction.

Descartes ruthlessly attempted to specify the kind of world which must be assumed to exist if the role and success of mathematics in the new science was to be justified. It later became accepted that he had made his identification of nature with geometry too strong and that mathematics should be regarded as a tool in exploring nature but not her very substance. Yet Descartes was the first to ask a range of questions about the foundation and implications of the new science which would form the basis for practically all that which would follow. For example, what Newton did not take from him directly (e.g. Newton's first law of motion), he developed partly in an attempt to improve Descartes' mechanistic world view.

Clearly, Descartes did not acquire his supposed knowledge through observing reality as it really is. Nor did he acquire it through thinking about it in an arbitrary way. Yet he felt that his views concerning nature were quite literally beyond doubt. Doubt itself therefore became the foundation of his conception of the scientific method appropriate for the new world of geometrical reality. He would attempt to demonstrate that, beginning with the most systematic scepticism imaginable, his scientific results would inevitably still follow. He claimed that whatever else might be doubted, one thing could not be — doubt itself. And, he argued, where there was doubt, there must be a doubter. Or, as this view is almost universally now known: 'I think, therefore I am.' So beginning with this purported proof of his own existence, Descartes then argued in a variety of ways for the proof of other assumptions, including the existence of God and the reality of the view of the world he had earlier asserted. Consequently, Descartes' model of scientific method was the same as his model of geometrical method. Begin with self-evident and universal assumptions and then reason from them to particular conclusions about the world which, while not self-evident in themselves, still retain the certainty of the assumptions from which they follow. Descartes never really resolved the problem inherent in his method, of what happens when two people have conflicting general assumptions which they both regard as self-evident. However, the general standards which he set for himself in this respect would in turn establish argumentative criteria which would dominate scientific inquiry from then on.

Arising from Descartes' views on nature and scientific method was his other key contribution to modern thought — his formulation of what is known as the mind-body problem. If material reality is

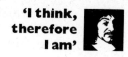
Opposite: Descartes
painted by Frans Hals.
Right: Descartes in his
study; an illustration from
Opera Philosophica, 1692.

nothing more than geometrical matter in geometrical motion, what sort of existence has the rich complexity of the rest of our experience and in what way is it related to this material reality? Descartes argued that all of the immediately non-measurable qualities of our experience were literally in the mind, and produced by the interaction of the mind with the material world. That is to say, our sensations of taste, colour, sound, etc, are all part of our private mental world and have, in themselves, no physical existence whatever. These qualities are just as real as material qualities. Their reality is simply of a different type. Descartes further argued that through our own volition we can mentally produce changes in the physical world. For example, I appear to be able to make my hand move at will. This appearance suggests that the mental world interacts with the physical world. Finally, he regards 'ideas' as the links between mind and matter, the mind — located near the centre of the brain — formulating and understanding them; the material world conforming to them provided they were initially conceived in accord with the proper method.

To conclude, Descartes recognized that the scientific revolution involved profound consequences for our conception of the inquir-

Descartes' illustration of the passage of a sensation by nervous impulse to the brain; from *Opera Philosophica*, 1692.

ing creator and recipient of knowledge. He accepted that the simple reality postulated by the new science was as strange to common sense as it was far from the rich complexity of perceptual experience. If reality is identified with what is physical and objective about the world and experience or appearance identified with what is mental and subjective, the study of the latter should involve different problems and methods and be directed toward different sets of attributes. In effect, therefore, for Descartes inquiring man is ultimately the prisoner of his own subjectivity. The real world is not the world of his experience. The world of his experience is only, at best, a confused approximation of the external world. Descartes developed his rules of reason in an attempt to show how the two worlds seemingly implied by the new science could be brought together and the epistemological bars of the prison be removed. However, his faith in reason as the bridge between mind and matter could not justify itself, and it collapsed into his faith that God (whose existence he had maintained that reason could demonstrate!) would surely not deceive us about these ideas we deemed beyond doubt.

Such a hard and fast split between mind and matter or the subjective inquirer and the physical object of his inquiry eventually crumbled, and with it the split between appearance and reality from which it seemed to follow. However, its destruction was to take centuries, and in some quarters of Western thought is still going on today. A brief example will illustrate the sort of problems involved. In recent years it has become clear that descriptions and explanations of both physical and mental aspects of our world depend for their practical meaning on the rules of our descriptive and explanatory language. For example, whether or not we regard the motion of the stars which we observe as real or simply as a byproduct of the motion of the earth will depend on which set of geocentric or heliocentric assumptions we accept to begin with. In other words, our characterization of reality of whatever kind is so dependent on what can be termed our particular modes of conceptual and linguistic behaviour that to drive a wedge between the knower and the known is to misunderstand the historical and cultural nature of different sorts of definitions of relations between the two. As Descartes himself would have accepted, we only meaningfully experience what we think we experience. What he would not have accepted was the impermanent character of the thoughts concerned.

So the debate continues. Even if Descartes' confidence in his solutions to the problems he posed turned out to be ill-founded, the significance of the problems themselves justifies his lofty reputation.   L.D.

Newton

Before Newton circular motion was circular motion. Newton showed that circular motion consisted of two components: motion in a straight line at a tangent to the circle and motion directed inwards towards the very centre of the circle. The latter was gravity. His concept of gravity and his mathematical treatment of it were to explain the mysteries of the orbits of the planets and the motion of the earth.

1642-1727

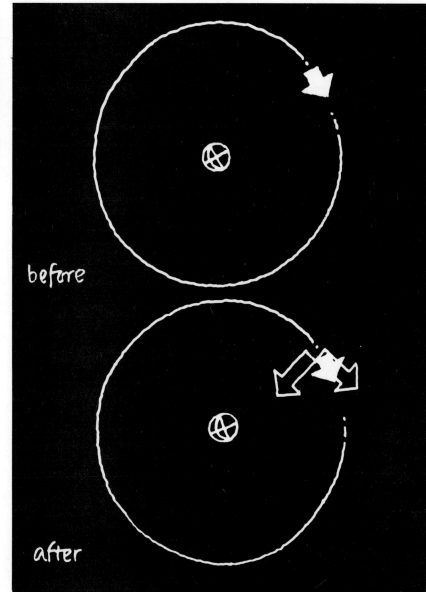

before

after

Isaac Newton was born on Christmas Day 1642 at the small manor house in the village of Woolsthorpe, near Grantham in Lincolnshire. A sickly premature infant, he had seemed unlikely to survive, yet in due course he was sturdy enough to go to local schools, where he stayed until his twice widowed mother brought him home to learn farming so that he could manage the small family estate. But Newton was no farmer — there are stories that he was more interested in making water wheels and sluices than in tending the sheep — and he showed no genius at school either, although over things that interested him he did display something of those extraordinary powers of concentration that were to be so characteristic later. Fortunately though, when the headmaster of his old grammar school was appointed rector of the adjacent parish, he recognized not only Newton's total unsuitability as a farmer but also something of his nascent academic ability, and persuaded his mother to send the boy to Cambridge, agreeing to coach Newton himself without fee. As a result Newton entered Trinity College in 1661. Here he lived quietly, as might be expected, since he was a subsizar and had to pay his way by doing various tasks, so that he can have had little spare money to throw around.

Academically Newton seemed no better and no worse than other undergraduates until, in 1663, he came under the influence of Isaac Barrow, the first holder of a new mathematical professorship. Barrow recognized Newton's latent genius and nurtured it to such effect that, six years later, he resigned his chair in favour of his pupil.

Newton's powers of independent thought first emerged in private, back at his home at Woolsthorpe. He had returned there in 1665, the year he took his degree, because the Great Plague had then found its way to Cambridge, and the university was closed. All who could dispersed to their own homes. At Woolsthorpe Newton carried out work in three fields — in optics, in gravitational theory, and in mathematics. The optical work was concerned with an investigation of the way in which lenses and prisms refract and disperse light, work that led Newton to realize that white light (sunlight) is compounded of all the colours of the spectrum. His research also led him to infer, mistakenly, that no lens telescope could ever be made which did not disperse light into its separate colours and so give images with coloured fringes. Yet if he was later to be proved wrong on this point, his mistake nevertheless led him, after he had returned to Cambridge, to design and build the first successful reflecting telescope, where instead of a lens to collect light and form an image, there is a concave mirror.

Newton's gravitational work was concerned with the motions of the planets round the sun and the orbiting of the moon about the earth. At this time various astronomers were considering the nature of the force that kept the planets in their orbits, and the idea of a specific gravitational force was being mooted. The trouble was that no one was capable of proving mathematically the kind of force it was, and so all they could do was to make conjectures. Newton found that he could obtain an answer by mathematical means, and he also saw a connection between the force needed to keep the moon and planets in their orbits and the force that makes terrestrial bodies fall to the ground. As frequently happens on such occasions, legends grow up around such an achievement, and Newton's favourite niece, Catherine Barton, never tired of telling how her uncle had been sitting under an apple tree in the garden at Woolsthorpe when an apple fell at his feet with a thud. This, she claimed, was what started him thinking of a link between the

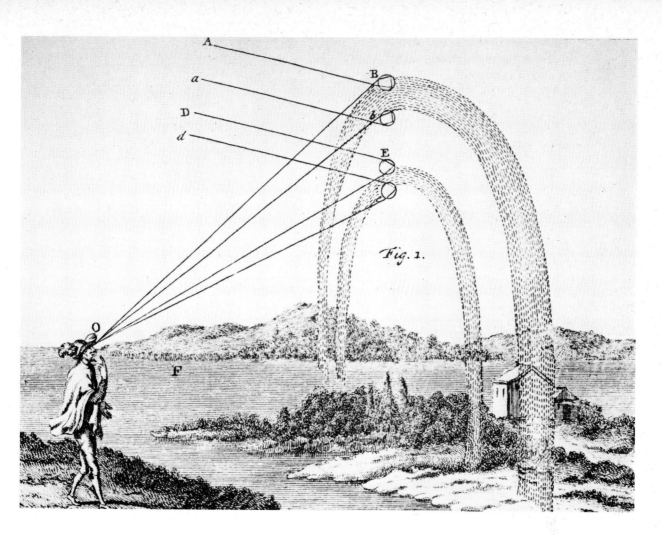

Fig. 1.

motion of the moon and falling bodies on earth; a link that could be forged by considering the moon's orbit as composed of two motions – one in a straight line and one perpendicular to it, directed towards the earth. The resulting path would be circular or elliptical, and whether or not Catherine Barton's story is true, it was certainly the separation of orbital motion into two components that enabled Newton to solve the problem. Along with Descartes, whose ideas Newton had recently studied at Cambridge, and Galileo, Newton took it that the first basic law of motion is that, once set moving, a body will continue to move at the same speed in the same direction unless some additional force acts on it. Newton, however, went further and specified that this motion could only be in a straight line. This meant that orbital motions had to be compounded of two separate movements, each in a straight line. Thus it was necessary to consider the moon's orbital motion, for instance, as a movement tangential to the orbit and a fall towards the centre of the earth. The orbits of the planets had to be treated in a similar way.

The moon's orbit, and those of the planets, are not a circle but ellipses, with the result that their speeds in their orbits are not constant; this severely complicates the mathematics. If one assumes a gravitational force that, for instance, depends for its strength on the distance between two bodies, then this strength will vary continuously during each orbit. Such a force was what scientific men were thinking about at that time, but its constantly changing effect is what baulked the mathematicians of the 1660s. It was this problem that Newton so brilliantly dealt with by a new type of mathematics that he called 'fluxions' (now known as the calculus). He did not develop this method completely at Woolsthorpe – that was to come later – but it was advanced enough for him to be able to use it to calculate the moon's orbit and obtain results which he found 'to answer pretty nearly' as far as the observations were concerned. Newton would have liked his results to be precisely correct, but at the time was not aware of all the new laws of elliptical planetary motion, nor could he obtain exact figures for the moon's changing distance. Moreover, he had to assume that Descartes was wrong in certain details of his theory of orbital motion, although he could not prove the error mathematically at this time. Newton had also to suppose that the power of gravitational attraction of both sun and moon lay at their centres, a fact that, again, he could not prove until later.

What Newton discovered while at Woolsthorpe was, in spite of its shortcomings, the basis of everything that he was later to achieve in astronomy and physics. But significant though it was, he said nothing about what he had done when he returned to

'The greatest intellectual stride that it has been granted to any man to make'

Left: Newton's reflecting telescope.
Right: A page from Newton's correspondence.

Cambridge in March 1667, even when he helped Barrow prepare his optical lectures. This reticence was probably due, partly, to Newton's dislike of controversy, for he would have realized that his theory of colours might well raise arguments – as in fact it was to do later – and partly to a natural secrecy that Newton cultivated. However, when Barrow resigned his chair in favour of Newton in November 1667, Newton's genius could not remain generally unknown for much longer, and after he had built his reflecting telescope it was a foregone conclusion that news of it would spread. In the event, the invention was examined by the Royal Society in London and a report of it sent to the continent. Newton was elected a member of the Society and, gratified with the response to his telescope, was persuaded to write up his theory of light and colours. But the theory was immediately attacked by Robert Hooke and others, so much to Newton's displeasure that he swore to do no more science. Fortunately, however, he was finally persuaded to develop his theory of light and, in due course, to continue his gravitational research and to write it up in the *Principia*, the most famous of all scientific books.

The writing of the *Principia* was to some extent fortuitous. In August 1684 Edmund Halley, who had been discussing gravitation and planetary orbits with Hooke and Sir Christopher Wren, visited Newton in Cambridge, and was astounded to find that he had solved the problem. The upshot was that Halley persuaded Newton to write up his results in full, and the Royal Society to agree to ultimate publication. In fact, Halley not only edited the manuscript and saw it through the press, but also paid for its production himself. And as if this were not enough, at one point Hooke raised such objections about the lack of acknowledgments to him, that it took all Halley's considerable tact to get Newton to complete the book.

The volume appeared in July 1687; its full title was *Philosophiae Naturalis Principia Mathematica* (The Mathematical Principles of Natural Philosophy), and although it could only be fully understood by a comparatively small number of experts, it was hailed as a work of genius. So it certainly was: in the compass of six hundred pages Newton was able to set out a closely-argued mathematical scheme of the universe; the laws of motion of bodies, long a contentious question, were clearly set out; the concept of universal gravitation was enunciated and then applied to astronomical questions. It was a magnificent *tour de force*, a veritable monument to the power of the human intellect, and after it Newton's position became virtually unassailable. He was elected as Member of Parliament for Cambridge University, but the mental exhaustion of writing the *Principia* gradually took its toll: in 1693 he suffered a

mental breakdown from which it took him a little time to recover.

After the *Principia* Newton's career was more administrative than scientific. In 1696 he was appointed Warden of the Mint during a period of national recoinage, and he did so well that in 1699 he was made Master, the most senior post but a far less onerous one. Yet in spite of his position it was not until after Hooke's death that Newton felt free enough from controversy to publish his *Opticks*. His reputation grew, and two years later, in 1706, when he had already received the first knighthood for scientific work and was elected President of the Royal Society, he had become a national figure. Yet even so he seemed never able to avoid conflicts. Arguments arose with the German mathematician Leibniz, who claimed to have invented the calculus earlier than Newton, and with the first Astronomer Royal, John Flamsteed, about the latter's reticence in publishing his observations. In some eyes Newton could do no wrong, and when he died in 1727 he was buried in Westminster Abbey with the pomp of what was virtually a state funeral.

Newton's contributions to natural science are almost impossible to overestimate. He solved finally the three-thousand-year-old problems associated with the motions of the planets and laid down the basic laws of behaviour of the physical universe. His theory of gravitation was confirmed time and again in the years following the *Principia* – in explaining cometary orbits, the behaviour of double stars, the movements of newly discovered planets – and became a fundamental principle in understanding the universe. His work on light and colours led to the development of the powerful analytical tool of spectroscopy, vital to chemist and astronomer alike, while the calculus ushered in whole new techniques of mathematics. Newton's achievements in science were nothing short of astonishing; the more so, perhaps, when it is realized that it was all achieved over a comparatively short period in his life, for he spent far more time on theological problems and on alchemy than he did on science. Yet there is no man since the Renaissance who has had more effect on our outlook, for it was Newton who finally changed man's concept of the cosmos from that of a creation with divine overtones to an impersonal machine of clockwork precision; from a spiritual universe to a mechanistic one. As Einstein later said, Newton achieved 'the greatest intellectual stride that it has been granted to any man to make'.   C.A.R.

3000×3500×5000=52500000
1008265007376.00.
14400
3,749014354
3749.
144

Knowledge and Method

Both Bacon and Descartes explicitly declared themselves thoroughly dissatisfied with the Scholastic approach to knowledge which had been taught them at school. The Scholastic approach was based on the work of St Thomas Aquinas, who had applied the classificatory approach and syllogistic method of Aristotle to human knowledge. In particular he set out to show how human knowledge supported Christian belief. Following the Scholastics it was possible to talk in a learned manner about the phenomena of the world and to offer descriptive explanations which made use of the terminology provided by them. It was not, however, possible to proceed beyond the descriptive phase and actually to turn that knowledge to practical use.

William of Ockham and the Franciscan philosophers had fought for the separation of matters of faith from matters of natural reason. They were quite happy to accept without the scrutiny of reason those matters which pertained directly to Christian belief. In return they wished to examine with reason the natural phenomena of the world in order to discover knowledge that was usable rather than merely descriptive. Although the Church had supported St Thomas and the Scholastics (which is why this approach was taught in school), the separation of the two spheres was beginning to be attractive, especially as there did not seem to be any further need for thinking in the field of theology. Both Bacon and Descartes set out to develop methods of obtaining natural knowledge. They took exactly opposite routes. Bacon eschewed the pure reasoning of the Scholastic philosophers and put the emphasis on direct observation of the material world. Descartes put the emphasis on pure reasoning, but the reasoning of the mathematical approach used by the Greek philosophers. Newton did not discourse directly on method but serves as a most successful example of both the mathematical and the experimental method.

Truths that could be put to practical use

Bacon was quite clear that he wanted to exploit nature. He wanted to discover truths that could be put to practical use. This in itself was something new. On the whole philosophers had been interested in pure knowledge for the sake of knowledge. This was reinforced by the purity of the mathematical approach. We know, for example, that Euclid instructed his servant to give some money to a pupil who had impertinently asked the practical value of geometry. It is probable that even for Descartes and Newton, as for many scientists, the pursuit of knowledge was an end in itself. If technologists want to make use of that knowledge that is their business. Bacon was an unashamed technologist.

We can look at some of the knowledge methods that have been in use at various times. They include: reference and authority, classification, induction, deduction, the mathematical approach, the experimental approach, model-building. Many of these overlap. Many are used in combination, for instance the mathematical and deductive. Descartes was very rude about the reference method, which set out to prove a point by offering quotations from a string of authorities, presumably on the grounds that if so many great minds had thought that way the matter must indeed be so. As Descartes, with his mathematical inclination, pointed out, the reference method has no value other than to demonstrate the wide reading of the writer. The method was prevalent at the time because, as in law, matters of subtle interpretation were referred to men of authority who had pronounced one way or another. It is fair to say that, taken in bulk, this method is still the dominant method of obtaining or transmitting knowledge in our culture today – so much so that this library function is virtually our definition of 'scholarly'. There is good reason for it because it provides work for minds not much capable of a higher generative function and because the essence of civilization is to preserve and build upon what has been accumulated.

The classification method was the one used by Aristotle and by the Scholastics. Everything was assigned its pigeonhole of classification, and the sum total of these classifications was held to constitute human knowledge. It was now possible to talk about any aspect of knowledge and to show how, in the classification tree, one thing was related to another. It is easy enough to sneer at the classification method on the grounds that putting a label on something creates no knowledge about it. Nevertheless the method does have a value because it carves out definite areas of attention by creating labelled concepts that can be attended to. Once attention can focus in an area it can acquire experience in that area and re-apply that experience by recognizing that area. The many-layered classifications in botany have had a real practical value. The benefits of medicine as a practical art have depended almost entirely on the classificatory approach. The scientific basis of medicine has been very slow to catch up with the operative needs of medicine because the human body is so very complex a system. Meanwhile patients cannot wait. They are treated on the classification basis. Diseases are recognized and labelled on the basis of a sort of classification of manifestations. Experience and observation attached to one classification is fed back as treatment. Now and then further understanding breaks down and re-sorts the classifications.

Chemistry is another field that has operated on the classification basis. It is observed that certain types of chemicals react in a certain way. It is observed that organic chemicals with certain radicals have certain characteristics. Classifications are attempted and succeed in guiding practical behaviour and even thinking about the structures involved. The legal system has always operated, effectively enough, on a classification basis. Theology is itself created by the classification process.

There is no doubt that classification has its dangers. The multiplication of classificatory jargon in a field like psychology gives a spurious impression of understanding and probably inhibits the development of unifying concepts that might cut across the classification boxes. For instance our habit of talking about 'memory' and 'recall' immediately exclude from consideration whole types of information-processing that might be going on in the brain.

A new tool of inquiry . . . induction

In place of the Aristotelian syllogism Bacon wanted to put a new tool of inquiry. This was to be induction. Aristotle himself had touched on induction but in Bacon's hands it was to be put forward as a more positive tool. His approach was to combine induction with a sort of classificatory approach. If a phenomenon was to be investigated then three lists would be drawn up. In the first list would be those things which exhibited the phenomenon. In the next list would be those which definitely did not exhibit the phenomenon. In the final list would be those things which exhibited the phenomenon in varying degrees. Bacon claimed that by analysis of such lists it would be possible to define in exact terms the behaviour of the phenomenon under examination. This method is the subject of ridicule both by experimenters and especially by mathematicians, who point out that no hypothesis could possibly emerge from such an examination of data. They also point out that the listing would have to be complete for it to be of any use.

Paradoxically, these objections to Bacon's approach were more valid in his day than they are now. In certain fields the direct approach by hypothesis and well-designed experiment has been much more fruitful than simple accumulation of data. But in more complex fields such experiments by isolation are not possible. Instead we collect a mass of observations. We also have available which Bacon did not, sophisticated statistical techniques for analysing the data. In many ways these processes of correlation are functionally similar to Bacon's three lists. Finally we have the supreme tool of the computer, which at once makes possible the immense computations that would otherwise be out of the question. The result of all this is that most of the scientific research being done today follows the Baconian mode: measure everything in sight, correlate the information, obtain a result.

The excellence of our statistical and computer equipment has, of course, led us to overdo the process. We almost believe that the excellence with which we handle the data makes it superfluous to pay any attention to the ideas involved in collecting them. Some useful ideas have emerged from this mass-data approach: the relationship between cigarette-smoking and lung cancer; the relationship between foetal malformation and thalidomide; the relationship between German measles in the mother and foetal damage. It is difficult to see how else such knowledge could have emerged. Nevertheless the method is being overdone, and the value of ideas and hypotheses is in considerable danger of being neglected.

Surprisingly, Descartes praised Bacon's approach though he wanted none of it for himself. Descartes' approach was exactly the opposite; it was the mathematical-deductive one favoured by the Greeks. In fact he virtually echoed Euclid word for word. He wanted a set of 'first principles that are given by intuition alone', and on these he would build an edifice of knowledge by the use of pure reasoning. He regarded knowledge as a sort of illumination which the mind could direct as a searchlight on the matter to be investigated. He set out four principles. First, never accept anything except clear and distinct ideas. Second, divide each problem into as many parts as are required to solve it. Third, order your thoughts so that you proceed always from the simple to the more complex. Fourth, check thoroughly at each point. These admirable principles were a hindsight description of how he thought he had developed the process of analytical geometry. This valuable mathematical invention, or at least systematization, of Descartes' showed how families of geometric curves could be represented by the relationship expressed in a simple equation. This early mathematical success so impressed him that he set out to develop a sort of universal mathematics 'that shall be applicable to all kinds of investigations'.

It is easy to see why the lure of the mathematical approach is so irresistible. Complex nature is seen suddenly to yield to a simple relationship that can be expressed mathematically. With a mathematical insight Newton explained the age-old problem of the motion of the planets. And the final explanation seemed so very simple. What a difference from the massive data collection suggested by Bacon. Descartes, like so many others, worshipped mathematics because of the certainty of its demonstrations and the obviousness of its reasoning. A mathematical proof instantly proved itself. This ease of testing, checking and proving certainly makes the approach attractive, for the emphasis is only on the generation of concepts. With most other approaches the idea stage takes very little time compared to the time needed to check or test the idea in the real world.

In his work, Newton showed a combination of the mathematical approach and the experimental. His work on the binomial theorem and on both the integral and differential calculus was pure mathematics. His word on the laws of motion was a mixture of applied reasoning and mathematics. First he set out the three laws of motion (derived in part from Galileo and Descartes) and then he deduced a full account of dynamics. Finally he applied this to an explanation of the heliocentric theory in so thorough a manner that his concepts survived intact right up to the time of Einstein and, in the area to which they specifically apply, they still hold.

Underlying the mathematical approach is the intuitive feeling that apparently complex phenomena are really made up of simpler phenomena interacting together. Thus Newton showed how curved motion was made up of two simpler components of straight motion in different directions. The more we know about matter the more likely it seems that differences are no more than differences in organization, and that means in mathematical relationships. The difference between radio waves and light waves is only a matter of wavelength. There seems little doubt that at the fundamental level true knowledge is mathematical, since it is organizational. Nevertheless the mathematical approach has severe limitations, because in many fields we are so far away from this fundamental level that other steps have to be taken first. It is often forgotten that mathematics presupposes a rather restricted universe. We have seen that Euclid's deductions worked only for plane surfaces. We know that mathematical concepts work well in space both for the motion of the planets and also to guide spaceships to the moon, because space is a very simple universe in which the effects can be isolated. Even the simplest biological universe is much more complicated, as are the universes of human behaviour. This complication is due to the different layers of organization (molecular, cellular, functional), and especially to the interactive nature of such universes. The sheer complexity of the situation makes it exceedingly unlikely that a pure mathematical approach will yield anything. In fact most of the work has to be directed to mapping out the universe itself. Until that is done there is not much to be gained by trying to work out the mathematics of the behaviour within that universe. Where the

An illustration from William Harvey's *De Motu Cordis* in which he proved the circulation of the blood.

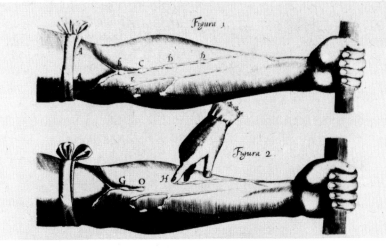

mathematical approach has been successful the universe itself has been relatively simple.

There is a subtle danger in the mathematical approach when it is applied to other fields. This danger is illustrated rather nicely by examples from the work of both Descartes and Newton. Descartes disagreed with William Harvey about the circulation of the blood. The philosopher supposed that the blood entered the heart, where it was heated up. He suggested that it was the consequent expansion of the heated blood which caused the circulation. It is easy to see how this idea could make sense in a mathematician's mind: heating causes expansion; the blood has to be heated somewhere, why not the heart; in conjunction with the valves, expansion of blood in the heart would cause a circulation. Pure thought can get so far. A little experimental work would have shown: that the volume of expansion caused by that degree of heat would be quite insufficient to cause circulation (especially since the heart is not a rigid vessel) and that the blood entering the heart is not at a lower temperature than the blood leaving the heart. The physical contraction of the heart and its ejection of the blood by pumping would have been obvious.

Surprisingly Newton fell into a parallel trap. His brilliant work on the separation of light into component colours by a prism led him to theorize that another prism was inserted to recombine the colours then the deflection would also be cancelled. In other words if a lens caused a coloured fringe through diverging the different wavelengths then this 'chromatic aberration' could not be cancelled out without cancelling the focusing effect of the lens itself. It is easy to see the line of reasoning: a prism causes dispersion of the colours; if we recombine the colours by use of another prism then we thereby cancel the effect of the first prism (or lens). It was this reasoning which lead him to invent the reflecting telescope which overcame the problem by using mirrors instead of lenses. In fact within a few years of Newton's death lenses that were free from the chromatic aberration were in use. Had he done some more experiments instead of reasoning it out, he might have realized his error.

The limitation of the mathematical approach becomes more obvious when we consider the theological and metaphysical thinking of both Descartes and

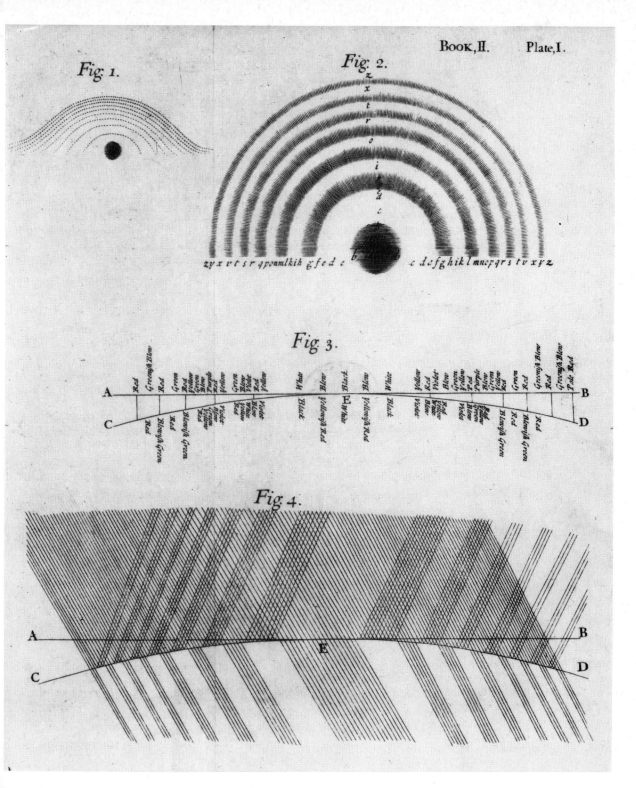

Newton's rings; a page
from *Optiks* published in 1704.

Newton. It is interesting to note that Newton spent a great deal of time on both metaphysics and alchemy without much success in either. We know much more about the metaphysics of Descartes, who tried hard to apply his mathematical approach to this subject but ended up by being even more unsatisfactory than the scholastic philosophers he so roundly condemned. He sought for his basic starting principle and reckoned that he had found it with his famous: 'I think, therefore I am.' In this he really referred to doubting, since one can doubt anything except the certainty that one is doubting. From this, his next step was the direct one to the ontological proof of God's existence that had been suggested by St Anselm and ridiculed by St Thomas: if the thinking mind can conceive of a perfect being then existence must be part of that perfection – so God must exist. Once God existed then he could create the external world. Since there was no reason to suppose that God would deliberately set out to mislead man, our perception of the external world could offer useful knowledge. At this point Descartes' systematic doubt came into play, for obviously errors and illusions were also based on the external world. Descartes' famous duality of mind and body was just as unsatisfactory, and was forced on him by prior suppositions about matter. The method that had proved so very successful in the development of analytical geometry seemed somewhat less successful in metaphysics.

Different approaches seem suited to different fields. The experimental method has proved most effective in the physical sciences, but in the study of human behaviour it has proved less useful, since it is not so easy to isolate the variables. The statistical analysis of observations may be more helpful. We may yet develop new types of mathematics to deal with complex organizations. A weakness in our method has always been the generation of hypotheses. The experimental method relies on hypotheses, and yet we have no definite way of generating them. An hypothesis is suggested by data but is usually so far ahead of the data (it has to be in order to be more than just a summary) that the human mind has to generate the major part of it as an idea. We run into the same problem in the soft sciences where cause and effect are established on the basis of correlations rather than repeatable experiments. We may imagine a causal relationship between two things simply because we cannot imagine any other mechanism to account for the correlation. In other words, in many situations proof is no more than lack of imagination.

Proof is no more than lack of imagination

Rousseau

ousseau tried to draw attention to the real feeling man that was somewhere nder the hard shell of social appearance which man had forced himself to wear. e drew attention to man's feelings and vulnerability, to the needs of s soul. He railed against the artifice of both art and science and all the disguises hich man wore in order to satisfy the expectations of society.

12-1778

Set up a pole, crowned with flowers, in the middle of the public square, have the people assemble — and you will have a festival. Better still, let the spectators partake in the spectacle, make them actors themselves, let each person see himself and love himself *in* the others, and they will be more closely united.

This concept of the 'festival', as a joyous and apparently spontaneous expression of the 'collective will', recurs throughout the work of Jean-Jacques Rousseau, proud bearer of the title 'Citizen of Geneva'. In *La Nouvelle Héloïse* (published in France, 1761), his best-selling epistolary novel, it takes the form of a rustic wine festival, during which the workers can forget about the inequalities which exist in their everyday lives. In Rousseau's political writings, it often takes the form of a public assembly, competition or games, in the course of which the participants will display their sense of fraternity, and of shared freedom: they will remain themselves whilst contributing to, and participating in, an expression of their *general* will.

Rousseau's notion of the 'festival' is clearly intended to convey some of his most fundamental ideas: that people should not be dependent on other individuals in a political state, but remain independent within a collective social situation; that the expression of this form of independence should not take the form of the 'will of everyone' (which implies a chaos of selfish considerations) or even the 'majority will' (which implies 'mere' head-counting and oppression for the minority), but rather an aggregate of wills, or the 'general will'; that social relationships should not be mediated through a repressive set of cultural and social 'rules' but should rather be unmediated (immediate), and based on honesty to oneself as well as to others, or, to put it Rousseau's way, 'transparency'; that modern society resembled nothing so much as a gigantic theatre, in which the cast of thousands were so intent on developing their *'amour propre'* (sense of self as defined by the opinions of others) that they had forgotten all about *'amour de soi'* (their sense of personal identity, or genuine-self-esteem).

Rousseau's theatrical event does not require a classical proscenium arch, a separation of audience and actor, or even a specific scenario — just a public square, an assembly of citizens, a keen sense of commitment to the idea of sharing, and a great deal of 'public spirit'. His version of the 'Social Contract' (of which the 'festival' is a central symbol) differs from that of John Locke and other apologists for 'possessive individualism' in the great emphasis that Rousseau places on the *community* aspects of the Contract, on the control that this community should exercise over its chosen government (a control which does not imply any sort of two-way contract), and on the political state as servant of t 'general will' or 'sovereign people' (rather than as a 'referee', whc function it is to prevent individuals from abusing the freedom th have been allowed — the classic liberal position).

But even street theatre needs some form of direction. When t Jacobins in the French Revolution ritually burned the symbols the feudal Old Regime, they then substituted a fresh set of symb (the triangle for equality, the scales for justice, the tree for libe the eye for vigilance, and the bundle of rods or fasces for unity a indivisibility). As many recent commentaries on Rousseau's pol cal and social ideas have pointed out, the concept of the 'gene will' may be intended to preserve 'that feeling of individual libe

which men would seem to have been born', and to pose the
estion of how much private liberty we must 'alienate' if we are to
ticipate in a just social and political order, but Rousseau's
nouncements on the 'collective will' in action can be interpreted
nore sinister ways than he could possibly have intended.

he punchy epigrammatic style of *Du contrat social* (published
52) does not help – much of the book was intended to redefine
d-eighteenth-century orthodoxies about the roots of political
igation: 'Whoever refuses to obey the general will shall be
strained to do so by the whole body, which means nothing
er than that he shall be forced to be free.' Rousseau means by
that if an individual or specific group stands resolutely outside
general will, or social pact, then the purposes for which the pact
set up can never hope to be achieved. But the association
ween the words 'force' and 'freedom' remains sinister in
lication.

n *Emile* (published 1762) – Rousseau's study of the psycho-
etic principle in education – the central relationship between
tutor and Emile may be intended explicitly to criticize more
litional theories of interaction between teacher and pupil, but
bizarre cat-and-mouse games with which Rousseau replaces
se theories again imply a great deal of direction and stage-
nagement: Emile is not taught formally how to read, but a
ation is created (by the tutor) in which he cannot join his friends
a party until he learns how to understand the invitation. In
usseau's political state, the legislator or lawgiver helps the
neral will' to express itself on what form of 'government'
ecutive) it considers most suitable: he is then supposed to
se himself out, his function as initiator completed. No wonder
usseau considered that 'it would require Gods to give men laws'.
roll-call of great lawgivers includes, Moses, Lycurgus and
vin, and these were 'exceptional cases'.

ess 'exceptional' lawgivers might well interpret *Du contrat
ial* in very different ways. The Jacobins in the French Re-
ution, who thought they were disciples of the Genevan prophet,
d the fasces and the eye as primary symbols of their regime,
sumably in an attempt to instil the feeling that 'Big Brother is
tching You'. To commentators who stress this aspect of
usseau's thought – associating it as much with the author
self as with the 'ism' created by his disciples – Rousseau's
sion of the 'festival', the country estate, or the city-state
omes a fairy-tale Asylum for the criminally Romantic. Even
usseau's popular opera, *Le Devin du village* has been associated
h a 'totalitarian impulse'. These commentators insist that
usseau's intentions were as sinister as the political leaders who

derived their inspiration from his works: that Rousseau's own
obsessional personality was seeking for a tutor, an employer, even a
lawgiver, to help him adjust to an unfriendly world. The 'justifi-
catory works' which Rousseau wrote at a later stage in his life, at a
time when most of his acquaintances considered him to be
clinically insane (suffering from an acute persecution mania), the
Confessions (1764–70), the *Dialogues* (1772–6), and the unfinished *Rêveries du promeneur solitaire* (1776–8), certainly
suggest that within ten years of writing his major works on
educational and socio-political theory, Rousseau's maladjusted
personality was prone to daydreaming about individuals who
might have been able to help him and even social situations in
which he would have been at peace. But this does not necessarily
mean that the writings of 1756–62 were also the products of a sick
mind.

It was Rousseau's life (or at least the version contained in the
Confessions) as much as his theoretical works, that appealed to the
early Romantics in France, England and Germany. They visited the
shores of Lake Geneva to relive their favourite moments from *La
Nouvelle Héloïse*, which they thought was an autobiographical
work. They were convinced that they owed the revival of interest in
nostalgia, folklore, exoticism, tourism and the concept of the
'misunderstood genius' at odds with society, to the example of
Rousseau. They insisted on interpreting his social theories in terms

Rousseau, the philosopher of the French Revolution.

**'Back to human nature'
rather than
'drop out of society'**

of primitivism, the 'noble savage' and 'back to nature', ignoring the fact that Rousseau's famous dictum really meant 'back to human nature' rather than 'drop out of society'. As Claude Lévi-Strauss has often pointed out, Rousseau was the first political thinker to see the significance of social anthropology in the study of the origins and development of society, language and socio-political relationships: but Rousseau's eighteenth-century critics even mistook the well-documented anthropology of the *Discours sur l'inégalité* for a mindless hankering after a state of 'noble savagery'.

The *Confessions* provided these early Romantics with a model odyssey – a journey through life by a man who had tried publicly to square his conscience, and to explain his feeling of alienation, by getting away from the prevailing notion of an autobiography as 'a profile view with only the better half shown': Rousseau reacted strongly against the two famous portraits of him (by La Tour and Ramsay), because they did not succeed in revealing what he considered to be the 'inner man', but rather emphasized society's view of him. The *Confessions* was, according to Rousseau, a unique exercise in self-analysis, bearing no resemblance to those 'clever novels constructed around some exterior acts' which masqueraded as genuine autobiographical statements. Most memoirs of the time were gossipy works of fiction which, at best, used the most spectacular events of the author's public life as an excuse to drop famous names. Rousseau, by contrast, sought to evoke the impact of the exterior environment on the 'inner man', and had a profound influence on Romantic 'novels of self-discovery' by Goethe, Stendhal and others.

The book tells of Rousseau's origins as the son of a Genevan clock-maker, and of his unhappy early experiences as an apprentice, which, he claimed, drove him to respond in antisocial ways – he stole from his employers, wasted his time in idle daydreaming, and, eventually, hit the road as a tramp. In 1729, he met Madame de Warens in Annecy: she initiated him in sexual and social mores, and he responded by thinking of her as his 'Mama'. After various adventures in Savoy, Paris and Venice (1740–5) – he was attracted by the glittering world of the Parisian literary salons. In Paris, he wrote fashionable entertainments, including light comedies and popular orchestral pieces – as well as contributing articles on music to Diderot's *Encyclopédie*.

In October 1749, Rousseau underwent something of a 'Damascus Road' experience, sitting under a tree near Vincennes, when he read in the *Mercure de France* that the Academy of Dijon was sponsoring an essay prize on the subject of the relationship between progress in the Arts and Sciences, and social morality. Rousseau apparently repudiated his earlier social aspirations on the spot, and entered the competition with the thesis that the Arts and Sciences had merely served to 'enslave men's minds', and had significantly contributed to the progressive corruption of society. The thesis was not particularly original but it won Rousseau the prize, and made him famous. Shortly after this, when a comedy dating from his earlier, more ambitious days (*Narcisse, ou l'Amant de lui-même*) was performed, Rousseau added a new preface, in which he remarked: 'Thank God this play has not succeeded. If it had, I would despair for humanity.'

Clearly, this 'conversion' laid Rousseau wide open to charges of intellectual inconsistency, and it was to counter these and other charges that he first embarked in his justifactory *Confessions*. The fifteen years between the publication of Rousseau's first *Discours* (when he was thirty-eight), and his flight from persecutions (both real and imaginary) into the *'pays des chimères'* were the most creative of Rousseau's life. Between 1756 and 1760, he worked on *La Nouvelle Héloïse*, *Emile*, the *Lettre à d'Alembert* and *Du contrat social* (an extract from a much more substantial treatise on political theory which he was never able to finish) all at the same time.

The aspects of Rousseau's mature thought which most appealed to European Romantics in the latter part of the eighteenth century are precisely those which have divided commentators on his work ever since that time: the intense subjectivism (even *Du contrat social* begins with the word *'Je'* and ends with *'moi'*); the creation of 'other worlds' (are they blueprints, or simply fairy-tales designed to make people think afresh about their role in society?); the apparent primitivism; the sense of election; the communion with nature; Rousseau the anti-artist, the critic of *'le monde'*, the creator of slogans, the proud Citizen, the persecuted genius who put his name to all his writings (instead of hiding behind a pseudonym) and as a result was on the run for the last fifteen years of his life. All these aspects of Rousseau's writings have been interpreted and reinterpreted in the light of changing political and social concerns.

Jean-Jacques Rousseau thought that he was a simple man, that his fundamental ideas could by no stretch of the imagination be called complex: he could never understand what all the fuss was about. Rousseauism has proved him wrong.   C.F.

119

The rationalists felt that truth emerged in the mind and was then seen to be reflected in the world around. The empiricists took the opposite view and felt that truth dwelt in the world around but could be observed and extracted by the mind. Kant suggested that the mind already held fixed ways of looking at things and that the observed world was fitted into these fixed ways.

1724-1804

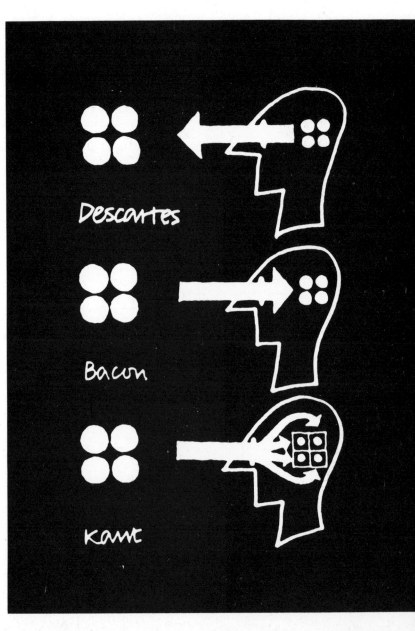

Descartes

Bacon

Kant

A German stamp issued in 1974 to commemorate Immanuel Kant.

Accompanying the seventeenth-century revolution in natural thought was an equally dramatic change in accepted views about the origin and structure of knowledge. This transition was marked by two different, supposedly incompatible tendencies. Some thinkers (e.g. Francis Bacon) argued that natural knowledge must be based on separate, infallible units of experience, methodically progressing from them to general truths about nature. The other sort of thinker (e.g. René Descartes) claimed that natural knowledge had to be based on infallible and self-evident general ideas about nature and the deduction from such truths of specific natural consequences which might not appear self-evident. These two apparently contradictory approaches to knowledge of the natural world possess three important similarities.

First, they both view the inquirer as a 'spectator' who through either his systematically processed experience or his systematically processed reason, attempts to describe and explain natural events (i.e. reality) from which he is totally separated. Second, these natural events simply are what they are in that their vital characteristics are in no way dependent on the desires, feelings or thoughts of the inquiring subject. And third, the truth about these characteristics will be manifest to the inquirer provided that he does not distort his systematic observational or systematic rational link with them. Such distortion would result from allowing his subjectivity to interfere with the link specified by whichever theory of knowledge he accepts.

Variations of these theories of knowledge have remained influential in Western culture. This is especially interesting in light of the fact that they were both devastatingly criticized as early as 1738 in David Hume's *A Treatise of Human Nature*. Hume argued that according to both theories, knowledge – if it was knowledge – of causal connections between natural events was both certain and necessary. This assumption was also the basis of the confidence and optimism of the Enlightenment and the general acceptance that Newton had discovered the basic truth about all important aspects of nature. Therefore, Hume simply asked whether or not the origin of the assumption or its actual use could be accounted for on purely experimental or rational grounds. He rejected the former because he argued that all we observe when we think we have detected a necessary causal link is a regular and recurring sequence of events. However, clearly, in light of our awareness of accidental experiential regularities (e.g. Big Ben strikes twelve noon and thousands of workers on Tyneside down tools) we must mean something more by such necessity. Similarly, he claimed, when we assert that a necessary causal connection exists between two events, we are clearly at the same time assuming that the future will resemble the past. But, Hume suggested, there can be nothing rationally necessary about this assumption given the many situations in which it does not hold. Does this mean we have to give up our conception of natural order in the world? If we did, we would surely go mad, for then we would be unable to have stable expectations about anything. So from where do we get this capacity to make the causal judgments on which our ordered world is predicated?

Immanuel Kant provided an answer to this. It was in a sense fitting that the problem of meaningfully justifying our utilization of assumptions concerning order and regularity in nature should have been confronted directly by a man whose own personal life was for fifty years a paradigm of order and regularity. He was born in Königsberg in East Prussia where he spent most of his life. At the local university he lectured on, among other things, philosophy. Kant was especially interested in the natural sciences, particularly Newtonian theory, and his early writing was mostly in this area. Most of his main works were published relatively late in life. The principal of these was the *Critique of Pure Reason* (1781), in which he articulated his theory of knowledge of the natural world. In the *Critique of Practical Reason* (1788) and the *Critique of Judgment* (1790), he focused on what he thought the differences to be between natural knowledge and moral and aesthetic knowledge. Although the full impact of his work was not recognized during his lifetime, it is now recognized by practically all schools of philosophy as constituting an important watershed in the history of Western thought.

Both versions of the 'spectator' theory of knowledge presupposed that the inquirer had to remain passive if accurate contact was to be made with reality either through experience or reason. Kant rejected this position for the same reason that Hume had. He could not give any adequate account of several aspects of judgment and experience which seemed to him to be crucial to our everyday perceptions as well as to more specialized scientific understanding of the world. In fact, he suggested that these activities should be regarded as somehow operative prior to all understandable experience if the possibility of its immediately meaningful character was successfully to be explained. For example, when we make evidently simple judgments like: 'All tables are brown' or: 'It is not the case that my car needs repairing' or: 'Bacteria cause specific types of infection' or: 'It is possible that I may die tomorrow', we are involved in two different sorts of conceptual activity. Unless we are merely engaged in defining words in specific ways, we are making particular informative judgments about various aspects of our experience. On the other

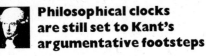

hand, these particular judgments are all examples of the more general judgmental forms: 'All x's are y's' or: 'It is not the case that x' or: 'X's cause y's' or: 'It is possible that x rather than y.' Of course, the specific values of the variables in question are all directly related to different aspects of our experience. Kant argued that we clearly could not have acquired the capacity to make such specific judgments from experience alone because meaning or understandability of experience at its most primitive and least abstract, still presupposed general judgmental capacities not related as such to the specific experiential content of any given judgment. Through the structure of our minds, he argued that we impose general structure on to raw experience which otherwise could only be a jumbled confusion. This Kant argued, despite the fact that because we are always involved in the activity of such imposition, we never actually experience it as such. Indeed, he asserted that our internal experience of ourselves is just as subject to the imposition of such judgmental forms as our experience of the physical world.

Kant included in this line of argument the concepts of space and time. What sense can it make to suggest that the spatial and temporal character of our meaningful experience is somehow initially derived from it? This cannot be the case, since all our meaningful experience is already spatial and temporal. In short, Kant agreed with those who emphasized the role of the mind in the acquisition of knowledge through stressing that its structure acts as a sort of filter through which we actively sort our raw experience into different categories. Each category corresponded to a specific example of the general forms of judgment already mentioned. For example, Kant identified plurality as a category of quantitative judgment, negation as a category of qualitative judgment, cause and effect as a category of relational judgment and possibility and impossibility as a category of modal judgment. Kant's point was that the specific content of informative statements as well as the assessment of their truth or falsity was grounded in experience, however, the capacity to make informative judgments in the first

place cannot also be so grounded. He argued that it depends upon and presupposes the existence and successful use of categories like these above. He further argued that he had discovered all the key categories of the four forms of judgment he had identified, and to this extent had discovered an exhaustive list of the basic concepts which any possible specific and testable assertion about nature would necessarily presuppose. Consequently, contrary to the spectator theory, the knower is active and projects patterns of order and regularity on to the relative chaos of unsynthesized experience.

Therefore, returning again to Hume, our conviction that there is causal order in the world is not acquired from experience. It is imposed by our minds onto that experience. The same situation applies to our quantitative, qualitative and modal judgments. If we cannot, Kant argued, conceivably imagine meaningful experience without them, they must be 'transcendental' to such experience. Similarly, space and time would also count as part of the necessary conditions for meaningful experience. So much for our ability to understand the possibility of the meaningful experience of our everyday world. What about the Newtonian world of atoms interacting with other atoms in absolute space and time in ways governed by their respective attractive and repulsive forces? During the eighteenth century, most thinking people viewed Newton's conception of nature as being just as certain as their own confident expectations about everyday life. However, given what we now know about Hume, even if we accept as Kant did the assumption that Newton's views are in some sense necessary, how can this necessity be accounted for? Kant attempted to answer this question through arguing that Newton's key assumptions actually followed from the more straightforward judgmental categories already mentioned.

A clear tension existed between Kant's theory of natural knowledge and his theory of value. According to what we can term Kant's naturalistic conception of self, the self consists of the same type of experience as any other aspect of the world and, to this extent, is equally subject to being filtered or actively synthesized by the forms of judgment. These forms cannot in themselves be regarded as constitutive of self, for all our meaningful experience of ourselves presupposes them in the way already illustrated. Consequently, this experience is subject to the causal form of judgment and this means that it is experienced deterministically. That is to say, what has happened to me in the past will determine what I do in the future. Even given this view, however, Kant equally believed in the reality of our value or moral experience and asked similar questions of this type of experience to those he posed for our experience of nature. One thing is clear. He suggests that without

assuming in some sense the existence of another non-experienced but somehow real self which had the capacity to choose right from wrong, good from bad and beauty from ugliness, we could make no sense whatever of our moral or aesthetic experience. Men should be treated as equals, not because it might give us momentary satisfaction to treat them that way, but precisely because they are men. But for this prescription to make sense we must be able to choose to treat men as equals. Kant was never really able successfully to resolve this tension in his philosophical work between free will and determinism.

The details of Kant's theory of natural knowledge have been severely and successfully criticized since his death. For example, Kant believed that he had shown that both Euclidean geometry and even Newtonian physics itself were preconditions for meaningful experience. However, non-Euclidean geometry in the nineteenth century and Einsteinian physics in the twentieth proved damning in this respect. The even more recent discovery and description of cultures using quite different modes of, say, causal judgment to those characteristic of the West has been just as damaging. However, Kant's clear perception of the active character of the relation between inquirer and object of inquiry still dominates epistemological discussion. The key difference is that now the necessary conditions for meaningful experience are seen as pluralistic and changing both historically and culturally. And, finally, contemporary analysis of the relation between the natural and social sciences raises exactly the same problems concerning the different character of the experience under analysis which Kant himself had raised concerning the differences between natural and moral judgment. In one way or another philosophical clocks are still set to Kant's argumentative footsteps.   L.D.

Malthus focused attention on something that became obvious once someone had stated it. He showed that if food production increased in an arithmetic fashion (straight line) and population increased in a geometric fashion (upward curving line) the widening gap between the two could only be filled by misery. He saw nothing in nature which would halt the geometric growth of population.

1766-1834

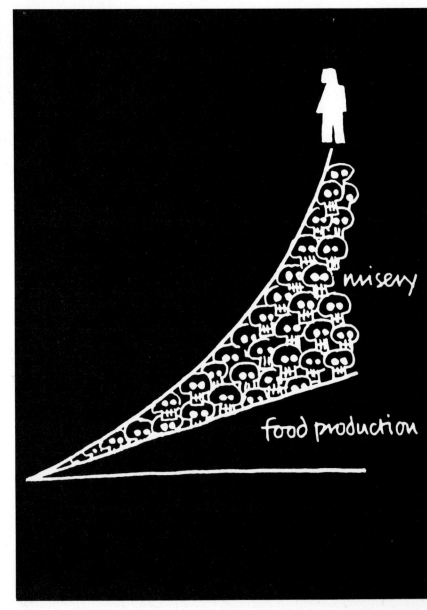

misery

food production

It is easy to get the impression that Thomas Malthus was a rather solemn character, rather doom-laden and concerned with the rapid growth in numbers of that somewhat unpleasant and sordid rabble known as the lower classes. Take what Karl Marx has to say of him in his essay 'Theories of Surplus Value':

> The hatred of the English working class against Malthus — the 'mountebank-parson' as Cobbett rudely calls him — is therefore entirely justified. The people were right here in sensing instinctively that they were confronted not with a *man of science* but with a *bought advocate*, a pleader on behalf of their enemies, shameless sycophant of the ruling classes.

And on the doom-laden side? Although he occasionally wrote that he hoped his fears were unfounded, he saw little scope for anything but oppression and misery for the majority of society and observed severe constraints beginning to act upon the physical viability of the world. Both of these are concerns shared by many writers and politicians today and, to that extent, the present appreciation of Malthus is no doubt influenced by the feeling that perhaps he was right after all.

What did this English clergyman and schoolmaster do to get himself into this situation?

He published a book in 1798 called *An Essay on the Principle of Population*, in which he presented a rather strong view on the prospects for humanity.

> I think that I may fairly make two postulata. First, that food is necessary to the existence of man. Secondly, that the passion between the sexes is necessary, and will remain nearly in its present state.
>
> These two laws ever since we have had any knowledge of mankind, appear to have been fixed laws of our nature; and as we have not hitherto seen any alteration to them, we have no right to conclude that they will ever cease to be what they are now, without an immediate act of power in that Being who first arranged the system of the universe; and for the advantage of his creatures, still executes, according to fixed laws, all its various operations.
>
> ... Assuming then, my postulates as granted, I say, that the power of population is indefinitely greater than the power in the earth to provide subsistence for men.
>
> Population, when unchecked, increases in a geometrical ratio. Subsistence increases only in an arithmetical ratio.

So, unless something is done to control population growth (be it controlled by deliberate policies or by natural causes), the number of mouths to be fed is going to keep on doubling; he put the doubling-time as twenty-five years. Thus agricultural production must also keep doubling — meaning that in 100 years' time, each farm in Britain would require eight times its then current yield, in 200 years 128 times, in 300 over 2000 times. Quite clearly, such an increase in the production of food was totally out of the question. Thus something had to be done to keep the number of mouths down.

The bare bones of the implications he drew, although somewhat complex in reality, can be expressed simply. Nature offered checks to growth either by 'positive' means (such as famine, disease, war and so on) or by 'preventive' means (such as late marriage reducing the consequences of the 'passion between the sexes'). In later editions of his book, he changed the list slightly, but the idea remained similar.

There is one other element to consider: what would happen if, by some means, people did succeed in becoming better fed and more prosperous? Answer: the situation would be even worse, because the population would grow even faster. Slowly (if not rapidly) the additional prosperity would be mopped up by the extra people, and so reduce them all to misery and poverty once again. Secondly, with the death toll reduced by the elimination of, for instance, disease and famines, yields on farms would have to increase, not two thousand fold within 300 years, but yet more times. The chances of achieving this are even less.

So, what can be done? One temporary solution would be to open up the lands across the seas — America, Australia and the like. However, not only would this be of temporary benefit, but the implied emigration 'must involve much war and extermination'. (Given what happened to the indigenous populations of these areas when colonialists arrived, he was quite near the mark on this point.)

This really leaves only one sensible option: accept the current situation, with its checks on population, as the only possible way of organizing society; any attempts to improve things will only be counterproductive.

And thus we have the root of Marx's label, a pleader on behalf of the enemies of the working class. Malthus found himself opposing any well-intentioned attempt at improving the lot of the poor. The Poor Laws, for instance, would only result in additional misery in the end, and to interfere in the effects of the Irish potato famine, his disciples argued with Parliament (and, indeed, within it) was not a wise course of action. The 1836 edition of Malthus's *Principles of Political Economy* contained the comment: *'The Essay on*

'The Essay on Population and
the Poor Laws Amendment Bill
will stand or fall together'

Population and the Poor Laws Amendment Bill, will stand or fall together. They have the same friends and the same enemies ... [They] form a great experiment ... upon the result of which, the due and harmonious adjustment of the relationship between the rich and the poor will hereafter mainly depend.' And anyway, Malthus did not regard the gap between the rich and the poor as being so undesirable. 'By securing to a portion of society the necessary leisure for the progress of the arts and sciences, it must be allowed that a check to increase of cultivation confers on society a most signal benefit.'

Malthus was born near Guildford. It is not too surprising to find that his father was a scholar, although admittedly not of great repute; he communicated with Rousseau, wrote several books himself, but was somewhat unostentatious and retiring. In this general respect, he was not unlike his son. Thomas (or, as he was then called, Bob) received his education mainly from private tutors, all well-known and respected at the time. Given this background, Malthus certainly had opportunities to build on whatever innate talents he may have received from his father.

A sense of humour is not something that one would expect from reading much of his writings. However, such a personal feature was noted by, amongst others, one of his tutors; Bob, it seems, was one of the few schoolboys of the time to find the humour in such works as the *Hecyra* of Terence or in Juvenal's satires. This humour, according to one biographer, 'was prevalent throughout his youth, and even survived a portion of his manhood'. While at Cambridge, he was capable of 'a very comic expression of features, and a most peculiar intonation of voice ...' This situation acquires extra pungence when one finds that his speech was 'hopelessly imperfect, from defect in the palate'. This, in turn, adds to Harriet Martineau's claim, in her *Autobiography*, that he was the only person she could understand without her ear trumpet. But, when the problems of population fell upon his shoulders, this sense of humour (and, apparently, of the ridiculous) left him.

Malthus spent some time at Jesus College, Cambridge. He was a hard worker and enjoyed the challenges provided by his feeling that the philosophy and science courses were somewhat too narrow. This he overcame by attending the lectures of the year ahead of him; thus during his third year he was able to study the things that had not been covered.

Despite all the gloom — and his faded sense of humour — it seems that Malthus was content as a person. Harriet Martineau says that she asked him how he had reacted to the criticism lavished upon him: 'I wonder if it ever kept you awake?' — 'Never after the first fortnight,' he replied. It is hard to discern the extent to which

Opposite: Thomas Robert Malthus; a portrait after Linnell.
Below: Malthus's warnings about the dangers of overpopulation
were borne out in the industrial revolution of nineteenth-
century England. The French artist Gustave Doré was appalled
by the squalor and poverty of London's slums in the 1850s.

Domestic virtue and happiness should be placed within the reach of all

A nineteenth-century comment on the population explosion.

Just what you want.

what you get.

Malthus felt upset and persuaded by his opponents because, while he had many friends and converts and, furthermore, enjoyed a good fight, one still feels at times that he saw something malicious in those who opposed him, that he had the truth, and, for reasons best known to themselves, they refused to be friendly and agreeable. And, whatever else might be said of him, he is frequently described as a friendly man.

And friends, Malthus did have, both political and personal. Harriet Martineau, a somewhat prolific writer, combined both. Malthus, she said, desired above all that 'domestic virtue and happiness should be placed within the reach of all . . . He found, in his day, that a portion of the people were underfed, leading to "fearful" infant mortality and the growth of recklessness among the destitute which caused infanticide, corruption of morals and, at best, marriage between pauper boys and girls, while multitudes of respectable men and women, who paid rates rather than consuming them, were unmarried at forty, or never married at all.' Was it really too much to ask people to behave sensibly and look after themselves?

Thus it seems that in the case of Malthus, if few others, his writings convey a relatively accurate view of his opinions and concerns, and (apart from youthful humour and the like) perhaps only omit to convey his enjoyment of the intellectual side – and the not amazing fact that he was very popular with his friends and converts.

Was Malthus right? The argument is still going on today. His view that increased affluence can only lead to an increased family size is now accepted as erroneous (although time lags between achieving affluence and the levelling-off of population size may be very important) and, while agricultural yields may not be a thousandfold the levels of his days, they have certainly increased beyond his wildest dreams of what was possible. And, while less to do with facts, his politics are something that few of his present disciples can swallow readily.

Bob Malthus left us with three things. Firstly, a point of view that helps to inspire many present-day writers concerned with population, food, mineral reserves, pollution, the future of the developing countries, and so on. Secondly, he illustrates the danger of believing in the irrefutable logic of an argument but forgetting to question its underlying assumptions – something not too rare in current forecasts of the world's situation. And finally, he illustrates how easy it is to acknowledge that things have changed in the past – and to forget how much they may change in the future.

A great thinker? Debatable perhaps – but certainly a very influential one   W.P.

Feats of Attention

A hippy commune somewhere in California would illustrate, in its most purified form, the philosophy of Rousseau. There would be the simple life. There would be communion with nature and a sensitivity to the beauty of nature. Organization would be effected through the 'general will'. Feelings would provide the only guide to behaviour and sufficient honesty of feeling would justify anything. This is Rousseau carried to an extreme that is hardly practical. But in less extreme a form we can recognize the sentiments as being very much part of current yearnings and values.

Our growing concern with ecology and the limited resources of 'spaceship Earth' is a direct inheritance from Malthus, who was the first to turn attention in this direction. His basic concern with a population increase that was sure to outstrip the available food supply is probably the major concern in the world today.

Anthropology, sociology and psychology are, today, very much concerned with the fixed perceptions through which people view the world around them. If, through culture or early upbringing, we are predisposed to view the world in a certain way, then that is the way we shall view it. The notion that we bring to the world a particular way of perceiving it can be traced back to Kant and his categories of perception.

So we see Rousseau, Kant and Malthus directing their attention to areas that have assumed an even greater importance in our life today. Rousseau and Malthus were not profound thinkers or even rigorous ones. Rousseau was inconsistent and most incomplete: his theories were never pulled together and for the most part were lace-like in their scantiness. Malthus worked out a logical structure on the basis of premises which he never questioned. Their feats were not feats of abstraction or logic but feats of attention. Kant was a more rigorous thinker, but old-fashioned in the sense that his approach almost harked back to the Scholastic one with its definitions and classifications and Aristotelian categories. Nevertheless he solved a most important problem by a feat of attention that allowed him to separate understanding from reason.

The most important characteristic of the mind

Attention is the most neglected, the least understood and yet the most important characteristic of mind. Attention had no place in the ancient philosophies because it was taken for granted. In later philosophies it became an operation of the 'will' and almost the definition of will: the choice of doing something or looking in a certain direction. But to describe it as will says nothing about it, and seems incorrect, since attention is not always a matter of will.

Attention is a powerful source of knowledge. In the two fields of astronomy and medicine most of the knowledge has come by means of attention. For instance it was Alexander Fleming's direction of attention to a contaminated culture plate that eventually opened up the most powerful group of drugs ever developed. Another powerful group of drugs, the diuretics, were developed from the attention paid to the excessive amount of urine which patients under mercurial treatment for syphilis seemed to be producing. To acknowledge the importance of observation is not the same as to acknowledge the place of attention, since attention precedes observation and prepares the area in which the observations will be made.

In our proper respect for the benefits of the Greek idiom of thinking, as exemplified by Pythagoras, Euclid, Plato and Aristotle, we must not overlook the stultifying effects of this idiom. It is fascinating to speculate what our thinking might have been like if it had not been firmly set in this track by these influences. Quite possibly it would not have got going at all, because the incentive to search for truth and the explanations underlying reality might never have been found in another idiom. On the other hand our attention might have been able to wander much more freely. It is perhaps an indication of the restriction of attention of this idiom that we had to wait for Galileo to demonstrate that objects of differing weight fell with the same acceleration. It seems incredible that no one had performed this simple experiment before. Clearly the matter had not been important enough to merit attention beyond the obvious application of reason which insisted that objects of differing weights must fall with differing accelerations.

The Greek idiom insisted that fundamental matters must be dealt with first. The nature of man, the nature of existence and the nature of knowledge underlay everything else, so attention had to be directed to these rather than to anything else. Besides they were suitable matters for the internal, language-based, contemplation and discussion that the Greek philosophers favoured. Their love of talking and discussion very much determined the nature of their thinking. There was also the conviction, carried on by almost all later philosophers, that once the building blocks of matter and knowledge had been established then it would be a simple matter to use them to explain other less central affairs. This centrifugal attitude was strongly reinforced by the mathematical inclinations of these philosophers. Their considerable mathematical skill and successes assured them that this was the right path. By its nature mathematics is centrifugal. Work things out by the light of pure reason and then apply the principles – as Descartes and Newton did. We can now admit that the mathematical approach has been extraordinarily sterile in terms of the knowledge of ordinary human affairs that it has contributed.

The coming of Christianity and the need to concentrate the best minds on building theological structures maintained the restricted attention area of Western thinking. God, man's soul and his salvation were added to the central list of matters fit for attention. The emphasis on the importance of the Kingdom of God resulted in a parallel de-emphasis on the matters of this world. Again there was the search for central structures and explanations, as in the *Summa Theologica* of St Thomas Aquinas, which strove to include all human knowledge within the theological framework. If God created all things then it is enough to

The restricted attention area of Western thinking

David Hume (1711–66)
painted by Ramsay

understand him and his method of operation in order to understand all things.

Nor should the effect of continuity be neglected. Pupils were taught the current philosophy at school and later at university. The current philosophy meant the established rather than the contemporary philosophy. The philosophy and logic that was taught to Kant would not have been very different from that which had been taught for centuries. Philosophy would consist, as it still does, of reference to what had gone before. The thinking of previous thinkers is the very fuel of philosophy, which has not yet had the self-consciousness to separate its history from its operation. A philosopher would establish his reputation by criticizing another philosopher. Lesser philosophers would establish theirs by commenting upon and elaborating on their betters. Occasionally a philosopher, like David Hume, would be honest enough to declare that he had come upon an insoluble problem. This would be a gift to subsequent philosophers, who would spend their lives solving this problem just as Kant set out to solve the problem posed by Hume. In the practical area of employment, university appointments and the like, the continuity of philosophy was ensured because if someone directed his attention to a new area he would simply not belong in the faculty of philosophy.

Rousseau's feat of attention arose from the fact that he strayed from the field of literature into the field of philosophy. The areas which he treated with so much skill, the passions of the heart and the beauties of nature, had long been the province of literature. Rousseau made a god of feeling. In philosophy this was remarkable; in literature it was commonplace, since feeling had always been one of the twin gods – Fortune being the other. Rousseau's vision of the noble savage was not based on his experience, or even his expected experience. It was his metaphor for a state in which feelings determined man's conduct rather than the artificial social structures which he was required to satisfy. It is neither here nor there that anthropology may show some 'savages' to be less than noble or even more hemmed in by social structures.

Philosophy had paid no attention at all to the sort of feelings which Rousseau elevated into an ethic. The Greeks had disdained to concern themselves with feelings because they had seemed Dionysiac and gross and because they tended to lead away from the certainty of mathematics to the cloudland of mysticism. The Christian era was based briefly on love, but very soon on administration. St Paul, who virtually created international Christianity single-handed, had a low regard for feelings and proposed a stern discipline for overcoming them. The Church, quite rightly, regarded the self-interest of feelings as the basis of that selfishness which automatically excluded man from the Kingdom of God. In a sense the whole structure of the Church was a meta-system to help man overcome his immediate self-interest (gratification of feelings) for a higher goal. Feelings were equated with the seven deadly sins unless they were a God-directed passion. Thinkers like St Augustine and Luther had such a consciousness of temptation and sinfulness that the reformed Church had even less time for feelings.

To be fair, Rousseau was not trying to rehabilitate the grosser feelings that had been so condemned by the Church. He tried to draw attention to the more gentle feelings such as love of nature, mild jollification and the anguish of his paranoia. As a person described by Hume as 'having no skin', Rousseau found that feelings played a large part in his life. In his *Confessions* he adopted the modern idiom of supposing that an honest description of raw feelings must be of interest to everyone else – and he was right. That Rousseau should have had feelings was hardly remarkable. That he should have made a philosophy of them – consistent in its incoherence with the incoherence of feelings – was a feat of attention. It is true that his adoption by the French Revolution as an idol who had railed against the artificiality of the 'establishment' helped his reputation. It is true that Byron's identification with the misunderstood genius of sensitivity established Rousseau as the patron saint of the Romantic movement. Nevertheless his success in directing attention to an area that had been neglected for far too long must be acknowledged. Feelings may have a dangerous subjectivity and expediency, like Machiavelli's power-plays, but they cannot be put in their proper place either by condemnation or by being ignored.

Kant's feat of attention was of a somewhat different nature. Rousseau directed attention to an area that was known but ignored. Malthus directed attention to a completely new area. Kant, however, was working in the oldest and most tediously worked over field of them all: the nature of human knowledge.

The polarization of philosophers into rationalists and empiricists was based, as is so often the case, on the inability of the parties to realize that they were looking at two different things that happened to be called by the same name: knowledge. The rationalists, like Descartes, believed that pure thought carries out its reasoning and then used the result to explain the world around. This is the obvious approach of a mathematician and the Platonic idiom. Empiricists believed that our knowledge is derived from accumulated experience which we process by abstraction and generalization in order to arrive at universal truths. The British empiricists, like Locke, followed this approach. Kant's feat of attention was to insert between the polarized parties of 'pure thought' and 'experience' a whole new area. This was the area of 'understanding', which was quite distinct from that of reason. Kant held that pure experience was impossible. The mind could only look at raw sense data through in-built organizing frameworks which he called categories. An obvious category was that of 'cause and effect'. Because we had to look through this framework we would see the phenomenon of cause and effect instead of two things that happened one after the other. Kant felt that these categories were innate properties of the mind. He also felt that because of these categories cognition was limited, since we could only see experience that had been organized in these fixed ways.

It is quite easy to see that the whole problem of experience and Kant's attempt to solve the problem only arise from the philosopher's habit of analysing everything into small units and then supposing that wholes are built up by relating units to each other in such ways as 'cause and effect'. If we take the opposite approach and suppose that at first a child has overall blurry perceptions which later get fined down into different areas of attention the problem never arises. Even so, Kant's contribution is considerable, since he directed attention to the contribution of the mind in the process of perception itself.

The contribution of the mind in the process of perception itself

The feat of attention of Malthus was powerful. It is true that the success of vaccination may have made overpopulation a more real danger, but the world must still have seemed large enough to cope with any possible increase. After Malthus it became impossible to ignore this area of attention. So much so that it is said that Darwin's ideas were directly stimulated by the work of Malthus.

Clausewitz

Clausewitz was concerned with practical operations rather than metaphysical analyses. He was concerned specifically with the practical operation of war. For him war and politics were not distinct: war was only politics carried on by different means. His interest in strategy, tactics and operations makes him the father of management science. He was interested in action not in essence.

780-1831

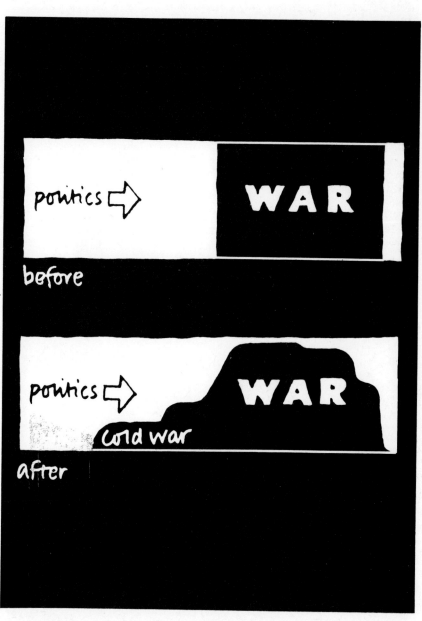

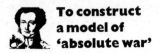

To construct a model of 'absolute war'

Not a great deal is known about Carl von Clausewitz. He was born at Burg near Magdeburg on 1 June 1780. He entered the Prussian army in 1792 as ensign and was commissioned during the Rhine campaign of 1793–4 against the French. Forced to spend the next few years on garrison duty, he devoted himself to the study of war and as a result of his efforts was admitted in 1801 to the Military School in Berlin. There he attracted the attention of the School's Director, General Scharnhorst, who introduced him at court and who in 1806 obtained for him an appointment as aide-de-camp to Prince Augustus of Prussia. Two years later, after having seen some service and having been for a time a prisoner of the French, he was appointed military instructor to Prussia's Crown Prince. Along with other German patriots, however, he resigned his commission on the eve of Napoleon's Russian expedition, and from 1812 till 1814 he served as a staff officer in the Russian army. He returned to Prussian service as chief of staff to Thielman's corps during the Waterloo campaign, and for most of the period between 1815 and his death on 16 November 1831 he was director of the Military School at which he had been educated.

Even from this brief biography it will be seen that Clausewitz's military career, although distinguished, was not in any special way important. He is of importance to the historian not because of what he did but on account of what he wrote and thought. For Clausewitz was the most important student of the phenomenon of war as it existed after Napoleon and before the tank; the first three volumes of his collected works contain the treatise *On War,* in which he examines in a rather curious way the military experience of his epoch. *On War* is a formidable piece of reading. It contains a number of essays, notes and memoranda which Clausewitz drafted during the period in which he was employed as administrative head of the Military School in Berlin. However, since he died before he could complete, far less revise, the work, his masterpiece may strike the reader as disorganized, repetitive and contradictory. Stylistically, it is certainly heavy going. On the other hand, it is important to ask what exactly was the purpose of it.

It is important to ask this question because Clausewitz is often misinterpreted. Few people bother nowadays to read his magnum opus but many are acquainted with his dictum that 'war is only a continuation of state policy by other means', so that in the popular imagination he is often represented as a warmonger. Now, to a certain extent, he has only himself to blame for this. His work is spiced with comments which invite misunderstanding. For example, 'war' he defines as 'an act of violence intended to compel our opponent to fulfil our will'; elsewhere, he states that: 'to introduce into the philosophy of war a principle of moderation would be an absurdity'; while at another point he declares: 'let us not hear of generals who conquer without bloodshed'. Yet on no account can Clausewitz be charged with militarism. The true purpose of the treatise was neither to glorify war nor to press the claims of the military. It was, rather, to put the phenomenon of war into its proper perspective and to assert the absolute need for civilian control of the war machine.

'War,' he wrote, 'is to be regarded not as an independent thing but as a political instrument.' Indeed, 'the subordination of the political point of view to the military would be contrary to common sense.' Thus politicians, in the Clausewitzian scheme of things, were to have ultimate responsibility for strategy. Clausewitz was careful to add, therefore, that they should not make wars lightly; that war would only succeed as policy if politicians first of all knew what war might realistically achieve, and if the necessary resources were available. 'Theory demands,' he wrote, 'that at the commencement of every war its character and main outline shall be

defined according to what the political conditions and relations lead us to anticipate as probable.' On the other hand, it should not be assumed that Clausewitz believed that war was too serious a business for the generals. He believed, rather, that, although war should be directed by policy, the generals should be so intimately acquainted with that policy that there should simply be no risk of military-political friction. If one examines this argument from a slightly broader perspective it can be seen that the main point of Clausewitz's treatise was to stress the *political* view of warfare. War was an instrument which statesmen might employ if and when they believed that they could get away with it. He did not see war as something inevitably rooted in class struggles or international political structures, nor indeed as something to be avoided at all costs. These attitudes were to develop only later. As far as Clausewitz was concerned, war was just a fact of political life, and one which ought to be controlled by politicians. They had the choice whether to resort to war or not. It was a choice they ought to exercise, not timidly, but calculatedly.

On War, however, did more than expound this, in Clausewitz's opinion, 'rational', way of approaching the phenomenon of war. He also attempted to show how wars in his day should be fought. As a disciple of Kant his method was to look at 'the thing in itself' and to construct a model of 'absolute war'. The student of war, he wrote, should not lose sight of this model but should: 'regard it as the natural measure of all his hopes and fears in order to approach it *where he can and where he must*.' In point of fact, however, his model was not really so abstract as is often said to be the case since Napoleon, in his opinion, had already made 'absolute war' a reality.

Thus, he wrote: [We have] seen real warfare make its appearance in ... absolute completeness in our own time.' Just what, one wonders, would he have made of the First World War?

In his analysis of 'absolute war', Clausewitz made the following points. The objectives of warfare were (a) to conquer and destroy the enemy's armed forces; (b) to get possession of his material resources; and (c) to gain the support of public opinion. These could be achieved if *all* the forces at the disposal of a commander were used with the *utmost* energy; if they were concentrated at the enemy's weakest point; and if no time were lost in doing so. 'Surprise,' he wrote, 'is the most powerful element of victory.' Clausewitz also stressed the concept of the 'centre of gravity' of the enemy's forces and the need to destroy it. The 'centre of gravity' itself he defined in various ways, since it varied from one situation to another: 'in states torn by internal dissensions, this centre generally lies in the capital; in small states dependent on greater ones, it lies generally in the army of these allies; in a confederacy, it lies in the unity of interests; in a national insurrection, in the person of the chief leader and in public opinion; against these points the blow must be directed.' It was, in fact, according to Clausewitz, the 'supreme act of strategic judgment' on the part of a commander to decide what constituted his focal point in the enemy position.

It is often argued that really all Clausewitz did was to systematize Napoleonic warfare, and he may indeed have tried to do this. On the other hand he did not fully understand what Bonaparte had done, and underestimated his achievement. The insights he had into Napoleonic warfare enabled him to draw up a set of rules, but these he applied too strictly and inflexibly when he came to judge

A page from Clausewitz's notes for his lectures at the Military School in Berlin.

Napoleon himself. Thus he was wrong, for example, in criticizing Napoleon's preference for offensive over defensive warfare, and he failed to give Napoleon his due for doggedly pursuing the British as 'the centre of gravity' of his enemies' coalitions; finally, he failed also to appreciate Napoleon's ability to divide and regroup his forces before a decisive encounter. Clausewitz, it seems, was too impressed by the numbers recruited by Napoleon and thus paid too much attention to the need to 'concentrate' armies.

So much then for Clausewitz's interpretation of his age. What influence has he had on subsequent generations? It would be difficult to deny that the man who more than any other seemed to put his theories into practice was Bismarck. Bismarck himself claimed never to have read Clausewitz, but since Moltke and others certainly did, it is not inconceivable that the ideas contained in *On War* had some kind of influence in the period of German unification. The military planning of the German general staff in the period of 1871–1914 was certainly influenced by them. With the end of the First World War, however, Clausewitz's ideas no longer seemed as useful or appropriate, except to those who recognized the value of the tank. Only those who saw the coming of mechanized as opposed to trench warfare still worked within a Clausewitzian framework. Thus it can plausibly be argued that the greatest practitioner of Clausewitzian warfare in the twentieth century was Adolf Hitler with the *Blitzkrieg*.

Once again, after Hitler's defeat, the problems of strategy appeared to have changed completely. The world had entered the epoch of atomic and nuclear warfare and was dominated by two superpowers who could not fight each other for fear of mutual self destruction. The smaller powers, on the other hand, were simply either in no position to think in Clausewitzian terms or were prevented from doing so by the superpowers when they tried. Nonetheless, there emerged in the late 1950s and 1960s, especially in the United States, a school of thought which has been labelled 'neo-Clausewitzian'. Represented by figures such as Herman Kahn and Henry Kissinger, it argued that 'rational' nuclear strategy was just as necessary as conventional military thinking and that war, despite the risk of nuclear war, should still be contemplated as an act of policy by world leaders. Its influence was appreciated most of all, perhaps, in Vietnam. However, Clausewitzian thought has also made itself felt in other areas of thought in the late twentieth century — games theory and management studies for example. It has also had a part to play in the development of peace research and conflict studies, and one can only hope that it is here rather than in any other sphere that it will make its ultimately greatest contribution.   A.S.

Darwin

With his theory of evolution through survival of the fittest Darwin provided a plausible explanation for the origin of different species. It was only a theory with no proof. But as a theory it offered an escape from the necessity of having God create each individual species. The theory was eagerly adopted by those who felt that science would in time oust God as the explanation of nature.

1809-1882

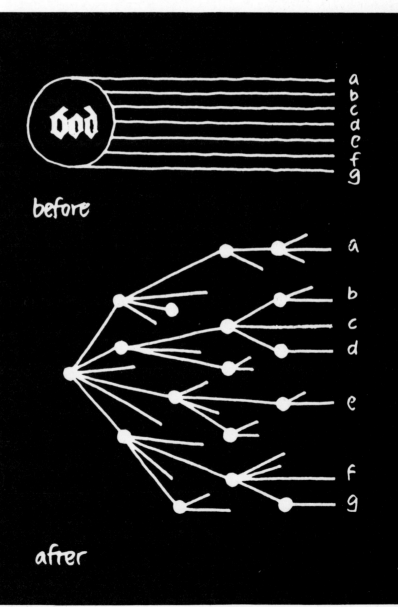

As a small boy, Charles Darwin was fond of long, solitary walks, from which he would return with fanciful tales of strange adventures. His own life contained two adventures stranger probably than any he invented, one the physical journey which he made on board the *Beagle*, the other the intellectual leap prompted by what he saw during that expedition. Perhaps because both his grandfather, that shambling polymath Erasmus Darwin, and his father had been physicians, Charles first intended to study medicine. However, the dissection of bodies horrified him and nothing in his studies seems to have roused him to enthusiasm. Such lack of success led to an inevitable conclusion — he must make his career in the Church. In 1827, therefore, he entered Cambridge University.

At university he made one friend of great significance — J. S. Henslow, the professor of botany, who reinforced Darwin's amateur interest in the natural sciences. For the young man had always been a collector, and during his medical studies had read two papers to the Plinian Society. He seems to have been excited and enthused by reading, during his Cambridge days, Humboldt's *Personal Narrative*, an account of the life and travels of that great naturalist and explorer.

He took his degree in 1831; at twenty-two, despite his interests, he was by no means a scientist, nor can really have expected to become one. At this time the Admiralty were fitting out HMS *Beagle* for a surveying expedition to South America and the Pacific, and felt, as the spirit of the times demanded, that a naturalist should accompany the captain, Robert Fitzroy, and his crew. Henslow recommended Darwin, and in December 1831 he sailed off on the voyage which would utterly change the world-picture held by all succeeding generations.

It is necessary to realize that when he left Darwin had everything to learn — not merely the facts of the sciences he was now expected to have at his fingertips, but attitudes of mind, methods of work, the day-by-day techniques of the field-naturalist. He had few instruments and very little space; he had, on the other hand, great motivating enthusiasm, a long habit of meticulous collection and all the excitements of a suddenly expanded world to sustain him. From the very beginning, he trusted to his own observations and, as a result, soon found himself disposed to believe the doctrine laid down in Charles Lyell's *Principles of Geology* — that the laws of nature are always the same, no matter what period we have under observation. It was the volcanoes on the Cape Verde Islands which first seemed to him to support this then contentious theory, and what he saw of the varied and troubled geology of South America confirmed his first opinion. This was of great importance, for it enabled him to reach backwards with some confidence into the

aeons across which his ideas were later to range. After his return, Lyell became a life-long and intellectually generous friend.

When Darwin left England, his ideas about the origins of life and the species through which it manifests itself were orthodox, as was proper in a young man still destined for the Church. He believed that all such species were immutable, having been created in their present form during some uniquely energetic beginning, presided over by a benevolent and hyperactive God. But during his long voyage, which lasted five years and brought him to Australasia, the Pacific atolls, the mountains of the Andes and the isolation of St Helena and Ascension Island, several linked questions increasingly presented themselves. They concerned the distribution of characteristics — so many creatures separated by thousands of miles

Left: Charles Darwin, c. 1855.
Below: A page from Darwin's manuscript
of *Origin of Species*.

Left: Charles Darwin, c. 1855.
Below: A page from Darwin's manuscript of *Origin of Species*.

must indeed have looked both impressively intellectual and risibly simian, a combination which, during the evolution controversy, cartoonists were not slow to fasten on. There was always in him, however, a certain sweetness, an almost naive simplicity, which kept him the friendship of many diverse people. Most of his energies were poured into his work. And initially, it was a very special energy he had, a power of concentration which allowed him to notice and not let slide away the tiny discrepancies and minute similarities through which truth is drawn from observation.

About this time Darwin read Malthus' famous *Essay on the Principle of Population*. He saw that other living creatures might well be at the mercy of such inflexible laws. For them the Malthusian formula of a geometric population-increase competing with a merely arithmetical increase in food-supply meant an existence which could only be couched in terms of struggle. During his travels Darwin had already seen how organisms, fitting sometimes uniquely into their environment, were equipped for survival. Now he understood the mainspring of the mechanism which threatened them. In the economy of nature, he wrote in his notebook on that September day in 1838, 'there is a force like a hundred thousand wedges ... forming gaps by thrusting out weaker ones.' In other words, as early as this, Darwin had realized that species were mutable and had over the millennia mutated, he understood that survival was the reason for those mutations and adaptation the manner in which they were expressed, and had worked out that what led to those adaptations was a method of natural selection weeding out those least fitted to compete. In essence his major theory was complete.

Evolution as such was not a new idea. Darwin's own grandfather had been among those to suggest it, and the great Lamarck, in particular, had drawn up a chart of evolutionary progress. But these ideas harked back to ancient notions about the inherent qualities of matter — in other words, they begged the question. It was Darwin's genius that he came to his solution by the other, the scientific route: observation. What he saw forced his ideas on him, not the other way about, and because they were based so soundly, they came complete with explanation, and with evidence. Adaptation meant survival; limited resources meant high mortality; high mortality meant that the best adapted were the most likely to survive; those which survived bred; sexual reproduction meant that desirable adaptations had the best chance of being passed on.

He began a gigantic work setting out his findings and theories. Some nine chapters of this had been completed when a manuscript appeared, posted to him by a naturalist named Alfred Wallace. It

seemed so extraordinarily similar. At the same time, however, so many creatures in many respects identical nevertheless showed significant differences, though usually very tiny ones, when separated from each other by quite short distances. It was in the Galapagos Islands that he was most struck by this: in an identical physical environment, creatures of the same species on different islands demonstrated minute yet measurable differences.

Darwin returned to England in 1836; he married his cousin, Emma Wedgwood, and in 1842 moved to a small village named Down in Kent. By now he was suffering from a periodic illness which recent research has attributed to Chagas' disease, a malady carried by a bug from the bites of which Darwin certainly suffered severely in 1835. With his tall, spare frame beginning to stoop he

The publication of *Origin of Species* provoked intense controversy and much public debate.

Right: Darwin found himself a favourite target for cartoonists: *Punch*'s fanciful evolutionary spiral leads out of chaos, through the worm, ape, anthropoid, cave-man and fop to Darwin himself.

Below: One of Darwin's most able supporters was T. H. Huxley; an illustration from Huxley's book on evolution. *Evidence as to Man's Place in Nature* (1863), showing the skeletal progression from ape to man.

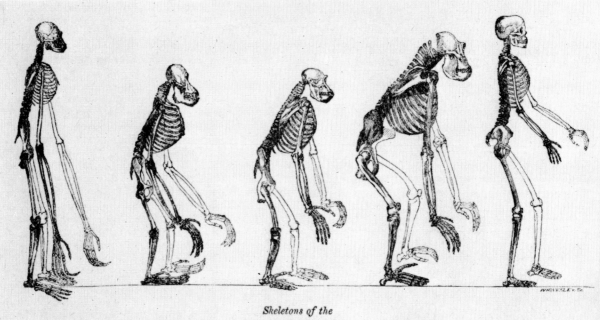

Skeletons of the

| GIBBON. | ORANG. | CHIMPANZEE. | GORILLA. | MAN. |

ffered theories of evolution and natural selection, uncannily and angerously close to Darwin's own.

Darwin abandoned the enormous book and hurried out instead hat he thought of as an abstract of it, *Origin of Species*, which ppeared in November 1869 and ran through six editions in the ext dozen years.

The uproar which followed is now well known, as is Bishop ilberforce's denunciation of the book and Huxley's devastating efence of it. Darwin had never hoped for more than the pre-ntation of an alternative view to the orthodox one; he wavered in onfidence for a long time, and never set himself in the forefront of e actual battle his book had provoked. Instead, he continued to ork with the same meticulous intensity as before. He was to write number of botanical works, but directly out of *Origin of Species* ere grew *The Variation of Animals and Plants under Domesti-tion*, where he proposed a genetic theory called pangenesis hich has had few followers; *The Descent of Man*, which to some tent renewed the old controversy by directly including *homo piens* with all his physical, mental and moral characteristics in the olutionary process; and *The Expression of Emotions in Man and nimals*, tracing the origin of all the subtlest expressions of human notions. This book too touched a nerve — well over five thousand pies were sold on the day of publication. In all his botanical orks — most notably perhaps in *Climbing Plants* — Darwin not only udied the visible phenomena with the most urgent attention, but ways placed them within his structure of ideas about survival rough adaptation.

Darwin died in April 1882; twenty MPs petitioned that he be ried in Westminster Abbey and, in a blazing cluster of dignitaries, s body was placed there on 26 April. His ideas, of course, were ot to be so easily contained.

The essence of Darwin's contribution lies not in the idea of olution itself, but rather in the fact that, having been convinced of validity through his own observations, he was able to deduce its echanism and so use it to explain what had been mysteries and omalies in the natural world. For despite the fact that evolution d been theorized about for well over a century, no one had been le to produce a satisfactory model for it. Most people — Darwin mself originally among them — had continued to believe that the orld, and all the life that it contained, had come into being at a ngle moment of divine creation.

First, Darwin pointed out the significance of something long served — that different species present very similar underlying uctures, although they may make very different use of them. us, the bone structure within a bird's wing, a horse's foreleg and a human arm have marked similarities, despite all their external and functional differences, an economy of design which argues a common ancestor. Likewise, the behaviour of a widely distributed species will show general similarities, again suggesting a common ancestor — despite some local variation. On the other hand, he was forced to ask himself why animals discovered in one area were not to be met with in another — marsupials, for example, which do not exist in Europe, Asia or Africa. This became explicable, however, if species developed in particular areas in response to particular conditions.

He was thus brought back again to the central question of variation, the differences which exist between individuals of the same species. It is this which provides the key to evolution's central process, in Darwin's opinion; natural selection. In every order there are structures common to all individuals — every bird has wings and a beak, for example. Some, however, use the former to float, others to hover, others to dart; some use the latter to dip for honey, others to tap trees for insects, others again to dredge the shallows at the water's edge. In other words, the general structure is adapted to provide for each animal its own niche in the ecology. Those best adapted survive most easily; those less well adapted die first in times of hardship. And there are always times of hardship, because not only are climates fickle — but reproduction is always threatening to run ahead of resources. Those which survive these hardships — in other words, are naturally selected — pass on their adaptations to a new generation, among whom this process is repeated. In the course of time, these adaptations become very particular indeed, giving us the enormous variety of species and sub-species, down to the most precise local variations, which the natural world displays.

There is thus a logic underlying this complexity, one which paleontologists and embryologists have been able to recognize and confirm. In demonstrating this, Darwin removed from our view of life the arbitrariness imposed on it by religious conviction, although the struggle to spread his message was long and arduous and it was only some fifty years ago that teachers were being prosecuted in some parts of the United States for attempting to do so. However, Darwin's ideas, especially when altered into 'Darwinism' and transferred into the social and political fields, have given rise to some restrictive orthodoxies of their own, demonstrating the human capacity, of uncertain evolutionary value, to search for new shackles the moment the old have been struck off.   P.B.

141

Marx felt that with the introduction of machinery in the industrial revolution labour was producing a value above its immediate needs. This surplus value was going to make the capitalists richer. In his scheme of things labour was to enjoy the full value of its efforts, setting enough aside for capital investment. Labour and capital were to change places.

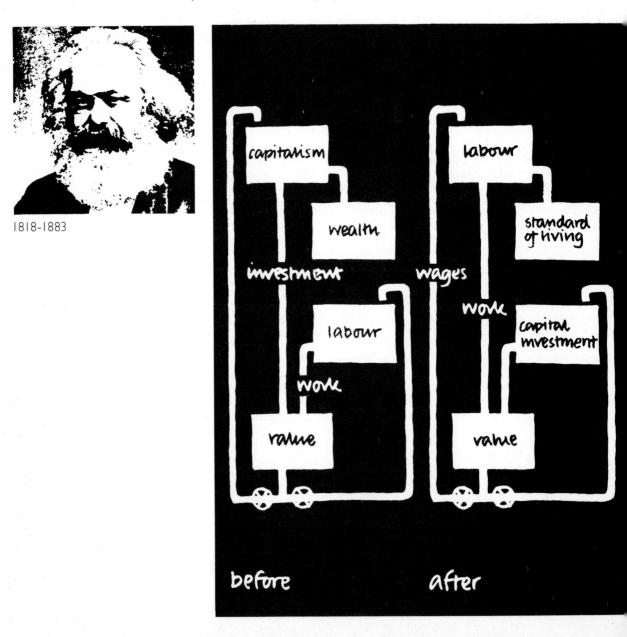

1818-1883

The Communist Manifesto, that pristine and unmodified summary of Karl Marx's revolutionary views, was published in 1848. The year was, at least potentially, a fateful one, with long-awaited uprisings erupting across the face of Europe. Nevertheless Marx's appeal — 'Workers of the World, Unite!' — attracted little attention, less interest and no response. He was thirty years old; his associate, source of some of his ideas and much of his support, Friedrich Engels, was two years younger. Marx was an exile in Brussels, already certain that he had unravelled the underlying social logic of history and that by its revealed simplicities he could accurately foretell the future of the new, industrialized Western world.

Karl Marx's father was a lawyer, a constitutionalist and a democrat, a mixture designed to summon up the hair-trigger suspicions of the authorities in his native Prussia. That he was a Jew as well will hardly have turned away their wrath, though his politic baptism a year before Karl's birth may have helped at least to confuse them. Baptized himself when he was six, Karl Marx's juvenilia display a lofty Christian idealism. In 1836 he became a student at the university of Berlin. German students of that period had lunged with unnerving enthusiasm into the billows of the Hegelian dialectic. For Hegel, attracted by that *fata morgana* which had lured so many German philosophers to destruction, the Universal World-Theory, had yet been wise enough to see that the mutability of the real world made nonsense of any once-for-all schemes. As a result, he built mutability into his World-Theory; every thesis, he said, produced its antithesis, the struggle between them resulted in a confluence, the synthesis, and in this way a new idea was born. This in turn, having altered the world, became the new thesis, to be confronted by its contrary. Although for Hegel the energy to make this machine work was provided by God, young Hegelians of Marx's day were drifting towards atheism and, more particularly, towards politics.

In the development of Marx's own ideas the publication in 1841 of Feuerbach's *The Essence of Christianity* was of great importance. It showed him the way to bring Hegel's dialectic down to earth — the dialectical struggle did not need to occur in the ethereal realms of the ideal, but might be the expression of real contradictions in the palpable world. Marx's work as editor of the radical *Rheinische Zeitung* will certainly have aided this intellectual development.

The result was, however, that the real world retaliated — the Prussian authorities exiled him. After a period in Paris, where he became involved with the proliferating Communist societies of that volatile era, he was again moved on by a careful government, settling in Brussels early in 1845. French political thinkers were very clear about the polarization of society between the workers and the bourgeoisie, and Marx reached a new clarity of vision while in Paris, calling for a proletarian uprising with conviction.

It was Engels who had introduced him to the work of the economists whose theories helped him to formulate his own; Friedrich Engels, his lifelong friend, a young man largely self-educated yet possessed of an admirable clarity of mind, member of a wealthy German family for whose small textile empire he laboured in its Manchester outpost, a man devoted to the cause of proletarian revolution, yet happy in such pleasures of the higher bourgeoisie as hunting twice a week with the Cheshire. It was Engels who introduced Marx, too, to the realities of working-class life in northern England, a picture at that period of exploitation, poverty and overwhelming ugliness. It was from the plight of the workers in the English cotton mills that Marx derived most of his ideas about the immutable lot of the proletariat in a capitalist society.

It was also Engels who introduced Marx to the German Workers' Education League, the London offshoot of a Parisian secret society called The League of the Just. From it, similar organizations derived in Brussels and Paris, and these Marx consolidated into a grandiose semi-fantasy, the Communist League. When this met for a delegate conference in London, in 1847, Marx aroused a great deal of enthusiasm by his predictions that the class war was now inevitable. He was asked to draw up the League's code of principles; thus commissioned, he hurried back to Brussels and, using as his foundation a question-and-answer outline by Engels of the ideas of Communism and borrowing from earlier books he and his friend had written, he produced the work in some six weeks.

Thus *The Communist Manifesto*, swift, trenchant and wittily dismissive of rival ideas, threw together Marx's hopes and theories in one spontaneous flurry. It disposes of all alternatives to revolution as the ultimate method of social change — though it accepts that certain stages, certain allies, may be necessary on the way — and is adamant in its conviction that the last revolution of all, that ushering in of a final just and equitable rule, would be that of the proletariat. And it defined Communists: they had 'no interests separate and apart from those of the proletariat as a whole' and their ideas could be 'summarized in the single sentence: abolition of private industry'.

In 1848 Marx made his way back again to the Rhineland but after a brief period of political activity was once more exiled. Then began the long years of English residence. Marx was a married man, the father of four children. For nearly fifteen years he struggled, sometimes scurrying in flight before his creditors, settling for a long

Right: Marx and Engels with
Marx's daughters, Jenny,
Eleanor and Laura.
Opposite: The title-page
of *The Communist Manifesto*
published in London in
February 1848.

time in two grubby rooms in Soho, sending out his children to ward off the siege of those to whom he owed money. A son and daughter died. Engels supported him as far as he could, but was himself little more than a clerk in the family factory in Manchester until, in 1864, he became a partner. From then on he was able to ease Marx's previous condition of poverty.

Marx wrote regularly for the *New York Tribune*, and it was during these years, too, that he first bent for those long hours over his books at the British Museum, hammering out the economic theories which, apart from his other writings, would later be summed up in the three volumes of *Das Kapital*. Yet there was another, less austere side to his character, a crack in the brooding facade of that monolithic revolutionary whose brow and beard glower from a million icons in the cities of his followers. For example, he expressed an occasional sidelong interest in pornography, he enjoyed a plunge into the murky waters of the Stock

Exchange, he had an illegitimate child by the family maid and allowed Engels for years to take responsibility for fathering it. In this as in other matters, he was a typical Victorian.

The main business of his life remained his political and economic analysis of society. The foundation of the International Working Men's Association in 1864 gave him both arena and function. It was he who drew up its rules (he advocated the gradual gaining of legislative power through parliamentary assemblies as the means of freeing the proletariat in such advanced industrial countries as Britain) and he became one of the stalwarts of its General Committee. This position was to give him status and a platform in 1870, when his enthusiastic support of the Paris Commune drew the attention even of the horrified bourgeoisie.

This was the apogee of his career as an activist in the revolutionary movement. Soon his position in the International was under attack from the right, where an increasingly enfranchised

English working class was drawing back from the extremism of the Paris Communards, and from the left, where the followers of Bakunin proved as impatient with the self-appointed guardians of proletarian rule as they were with any other form of authority. The International trembled away into ineffectiveness. Marx returned to *Das Kapital*, to his family, to the bastion of his opinions.

Working-class leaders from Germany, France and Britain continued to consult him; he continued his polemics against rivals, ignorance and misunderstanding. His political ideas were still two-pronged — on the one hand, such countries as Holland and England would evolve until an enfranchised proletariat could alter its oppressive institutions without violence (it was bourgeois counter-revolution which would produce the bloodshed); on the other, he continued to look for the proletarian revolution, praising the assassins of the Russian Tsar, Alexander II, and hoping for the European war which would make debris of the structures which held the working classes prisoner. With this dichotomy still unresolved, he died in 1883.

Marx was a nineteenth-century man, a believer in progress, in the upward march of the human race towards an inevitable perfection. Taking this for granted, he tried to chart the direction of that march and the nature of that perfection. Once he had begun to believe that society should be altered for the benefit of the exploited and the disenfranchised, it is clear that he became in some ways a propagandist, however much he may have thought of himself as an objective thinker. As he put it in his own famous dictum: 'Philosophers have only given varying interpretations of the world — the important thing is to change it.'

It is impossible to separate the ideas of Marx from his human compassion. He saw humanity's history as a struggle to wrest from nature what it needed. Man's creative energy provided not only the demanded solutions, but also, in the process, a new consciousness, a new awareness: humanity became, as it were, self-creating and, in that condition, free. Capitalism, however, has alienated man from his labour, from the product of his labour and from himself. In this situation humanity has arrived at its present ideas and beliefs — for 'it is not consciousness which determines existence, it is existence which determines consciousness.' This upside-down Hegelianism led Marx to his benevolent view of revolution. Human existence would have to be changed in order for human consciousness to reach towards the truth and human beings to achieve full self-awareness.

The battle lines for the coming confrontation were determined by the logic of the class struggle, and it was in the arena of industrial manufacture that its drama would be played to the finish. To this,

Manifest

der

Kommunistischen Partei.

Veröffentlicht im Februar 1848.

Proletarier aller Länder vereinigt euch

London.

Gedruckt in der Office der „Bildungs-Gesellschaft für Arbeiter" von J. E. Burghard
46. Liverpool Street, Bishopsgate.

Marx in 1875.

Marx made his central, his unique and abiding contribution — a rationale upon which revolutionary action could be based, a logic which has rescued from mere sentimentality generations of dedicated egalitarians. Marx pointed out that labour added to what it produced a value over and above that which was necessary to satisfy its own needs. A worker continued long after he had produced enough to pay for his own wages. The surplus he produced during those extra hours became the capital of the bourgeois owner of the means of production. This, made concrete in improved methods of manufacture, increased still further the value of what the worker produced — at least for a while. But increased competition would lower these profits again, and it was

labour which would bear the consequences — at least for a while. Finally, however, the contradictions in the system itself — the accumulation of surplus value, the struggle for shrinking markets — would bring it down, this collapse heralding the inevitable victory of the proletariat.

This view, however, is clearly contradictory to the purely revolutionary one he propounded elsewhere, only one of several such contradictions in his thought. It is perhaps these which have allowed so many generations of experts to produce the flood of exegesis, recapitulation, refinement, commentary and misrepresentation which now surround Marx's writings. It is clear that his work touched a nerve in modern man deeper than mere rationality.

Marx's analysis of the economic bases of social organization was to provide a theoretical foundation not merely for further critical studies of society, which he would have thought sterile and irrelevant, but for the revolutionary action which would change it. His theories were of course both codified and extended by those who came after him, most notably by Lenin, whose concerns were the practical ones of a revolutionary leader — it was he who pointed out that Marx was not a definitive authority, but had merely laid the cornerstone of the new political science. It is the amalgam of ideas known as Marxist–Leninism which today underlies much of the political activity, otherwise very various, in Eastern Europe and the Third World. Its tenets begin with an acceptance of the Hegelian dialectic, but with the reversal that Marx gave it — it was not abstract thought which modified the material world as human beings actually experienced it, but rather that world, most notably expressed in society's economic structures, which modified man and his institutions. This material world was dominated by a class struggle which was unavoidable, since the interests could not be reconciled. Only when the proletariat, having taken power, itself became the owner of the means of production would this war come to an end. Such an outcome was inevitable, since capitalism was doomed by its inherent contradictions. Revolution, however, could and must speed this process, and revolution was necessary because no other class or institution would assist the proletariat in its efforts to gain a power destructive to themselves. This revolutionary phase, and the dictatorial role of the proletariat which would have to follow it in order to consolidate the gains of the revolution, were phases of transition; eventually, a just society would be self-regulated by its own manifest perfection. The desirability of this millennium has frequently justified actions otherwise unacceptable, in the minds at least of those persuaded of its beauty.   P.B.

Process and Value

The only real break in the thinking of the West came in the nineteenth century. The Christian Church carried on the thinking of the Greek philosophers in a direct manner. The ultimate form of the 'good' of Plato was replaced by the idea of God and all else followed. It could even be said that the philosophers of the Church were more intently Greek in their thinking than the Greek philosophers themselves could ever have been. Certainly they were more consistent. The Renaissance produced no change at all in thinking, though it did produce changes in art, life and civilization. By this time what had happened was that there were two *apparently* different streams of thought. One was the pure Greek line as shown by the Greek philosophers before any admixture of Christianity. The other was the thinking of the Church. The result was that when a philosopher thought that he was breaking away from the thinking of the Church he simply turned to the non-Church Greek idiom. Since this was almost exactly the same, the change was an illusion. It was rather like someone saying that he was going to make a radical change in direction and then crossing to the other side of the road and continuing in the same direction.

Even the atheists and rationalists who had no time for Christian dogma used an essentially theological style of thinking to show their dissatisfaction. It was a bit like someone saying that he was against motorcars ... because he wanted a yellow car instead of a red one.

The change from this unified and immensely powerful idiom of thinking came in the nineteenth century. Not surprisingly it did not come with any deliberate effort or obvious break. It came about gradually and accidentally. The process is best illustrated by Charles Darwin. He had set out to join the Church. His famous five-year trip on the *Beagle* to the Galapagos islands and other places was only meant to be an interlude before he took up pastoral work. At no time did he feel that his theory of evolution was against Christian belief. He only offered it as an alternative way of looking at things, a sort of speculation. He was sure that it could be encompassed by Christian belief and a new interpretation of the book of Genesis which, after all, had never been intended as a scientific treatise. It was only the fierce opposition of Bishop Wilberforce which seemed to throw the weight of the Church against Darwin's idea.

There was nothing new in the idea of evolution. Anaximander had suggested it centuries before, and Lamarck's views on it were well known. What was new was the *process* described by Darwin: random variation and survival of the best adapted. This was only an idea, with no scientific proof for it except the poverty

There was nothing new in the idea of evolution

of our imaginations in suggesting a better one. The scientific observations put forward by Darwin certainly fitted his idea, but they did not prove it, because they could have fitted another hypothesis – if anyone had had enough imagination to come up with one. To this day there are many features of the Darwinian theory which are far from satisfactory. The theory is quite good on the 'survival of the fittest' aspect which had been suggested directly by Malthus' work on overpopulation in the face of limited food supplies. But the crucial 'random variation' aspect is not explained at all, but simply put in almost as an aspect of belief little different from Christian dogma.

But once Darwin's idea had been put forward it could never be unthought. No one really cared whether it was the only mechanism or whether it had been proved beyond doubt. It was enough that he had described a *plausible process* which could be put alongside the traditional belief that God had created all the species in one busy session. It was not necessary to attack the Genesis version or even to insist on the scientific correctness of the Darwin idea. It was enough that Darwin's plausible process could be understood. This destroyed the absolute need to accept the Genesis version as being the only possible explanation.

It is in this replacement of God by a process that the huge change in thinking takes place. There are two direct and powerful consequences. First, the world of thinking moves from being a static one to being a dynamic one, and process replaces definition. Second, the attention to process creates an entirely new value-system: process creates its own values. Darwin never intended his explanation to have more than a scientific value, but once the process was there it created social, political and philosophical values. Marx regarded Darwin as a fellow thinker, and materialists everywhere felt that his explanation had been offered solely to support their cause.

The world of thinking had been a static one. Originally it was based on Plato's idiom of *truth in being*. Thinkers devoted themselves to finding out the truth that lay below the surface. They puzzled themselves with matters of existence and essence, substance and form and all the other paraphernalia. The world was regarded as being timeless. It was somewhat like a library with the books permanently on the shelf awaiting the philosopher's examination. This static approach was strongly reinforced when God came into the picture and took over Greek thinking. Since God was infinite and omnipotent, the actual process of his activity was irrelevant. It was a sort of impertinence to wonder how God could have created things; it was enough to consider that they were created and to build up a static system of natural and dogmatic theology to explain everything and put it in its place. Static classifications and definitions were very important. Like the building blocks in an edifice they had to be solid and definite and static. It has been suggested that German philosophers were so prevalent because the German language is so very good at static classifications.

System-builders relied on static definitions because, as in the Euclidean manner, one could relate two definitions to create a third and then have three to play around with – and so on. Even mathematics was essentially static, especially when it was used to reduce motion to a series of fixed relationships. Although the planets move in their orbits, Newton's explanation of their motion is essentially static – providing the 'hooks' by which their positions are determined.

Those philosophers who followed Aristotle in the word-game approach were

This replacement of God by a process

even more committed to the static approach. In itself a word was a way of freezing experience into a parcel which could thereafter be treated as static and immutable. If words were ever allowed to be fluid and changeable in meaning then the whole basis of thinking would collapse. When a word was put, in place of an explanation, on an area of difficulty, then that word was supposed to contain that area and suppress its awkwardness. So long as this word allowed you to link up with other areas in the great static scheme of things its explanatory value did not matter. The word 'grace' for instance allowed St Augustine to build up his picture of God's action in saving man, who was predestined to damnation. Processes were arrived at by linking up static concepts.

In this static 'truth in being' world the values followed automatically. For the Greek, truth was its own value once you had found it. The unsatisfactory nature of this type of value was never really put to the test because the politicians went their own way and the people had a religion of sorts or a discipline in Sparta. The Mosaic law approach provided the simplest value system of all: obey the detail of the law and that is value. The Christian Church gave to the Platonic system a very strong value structure by placing God where the ultimate form of the good had been. Values followed automatically. The Fathers and thinkers of the Church decided what God wanted and that became a general value system. On a personal level values were determined by the quest for salvation. Anything which led towards salvation had a positive value and anything which led away a negative one. Because the structure was so solidly established, attention could be paid to individuals in terms of the salvation of souls. On a mass level Church and state were varyingly interlocked with such devices as the Divine Right of Kings, political power of the Church, the Inquisition, papal approval, the Holy Roman Empire and the control of education.

In place of this static system based on the definition of God and his intentions came a dynamic system based on process. In place of *truth in being* came *truth in action*. Truth in action did not mean that you reinforced your hold on the truth by the power with which you smote your enemy – though there are elements of this in the Marxist inheritance. Truth in action meant an attention to processes: not what things were but how they worked out. This was very closely tied up with the value system. If values were no longer going to be accepted as God-given, via theologians or Mosaic lawkeepers, there had to be some other basis. This new basis was to see whether *things worked out*. If the explained process seemed plausible and tied itself together then that could become a value. Thus Darwin's explained process of evolution, which did no more than tie itself together in a plausible fashion, offered a 'value'. In a way this is related to the mathematical basis for value: if it works out it is true. Clausewitz was not at all concerned with the morality of war. The war situation was taken for granted. Value was created if the war was fought well. Bravery, valour, strength, having God on your side, were much less important than strategy. Wars were no longer to be fought in a temper of righteous indignation but as a calculated continuation of political policy. Clausewitz considered it to be the supreme act of strategic judgment on the part of a commander to determine the enemy's 'centre of gravity' and to attack that – a policy well exemplified by the *Blitzkrieg* of the Second World War.

The Christian world had created its own universe and assigned its values within this universe. For the nineteenth-century thinkers, process created its own

In place of <u>truth in being</u> came <u>truth in action</u>

149

A poster for the 1904
Socialist Congress.

universe and the working out of that process its own values. It is difficult to argue with the basic notion. If wars are to be fought should they be fought inefficiently, haphazardly and carelessly or with the application to strategy that Clausewitz suggested? To argue that wars should not be fought at all does not answer the question. Yet to make the fighting of war more efficient must encourage its use, as may be seen by the policies of Bismarck, the German high command in 1914, and Hitler in 1939. Paradoxically it may be the application of Clausewitzian analysis that prevents the outbreak of a further war. Clausewitz was never in favour of a war that could not be won – and clearly seen to be unwinnable. He also advocated a dispassionate analysis of the situation. The neo-Clausewitzian school in the Pentagon are presumed to be making these cold assessments, and if the Russian side is matching that approach the difficulty of winning any future nuclear war should be a deterrent.

The Clausewitz approach is today probably more important outside the sphere of war than within it. His emphasis on the strategy of operations makes him the direct ancestor of management science. In a highly competitive world the comparison between management and war is a close one. In both situations the effect of thinking is immediate: success and failure are real. In both the hierarchy of power and command is similar and very different from democratic control. Resources are limited and strategic decisions of the utmost importance. Finally the morality of the situation is determined only by the value created by success. Like Clausewitz, management scientists would not query the necessity for management or competition but would concentrate on making them work.

Marx created the second major religion in the West. It is a nice twist that Jesus should have come from the Middle East but achieved success only in Western Europe and its extensions (North and South America), while Marx should have worked in Germany and England and achieved most success outside Europe, and certainly outside those two countries. In its impact on the thinking and behaviour of large sections of mankind it seems appropriate to regard Marxism as a religion. Certainly its belief-structure requires as much faith.

Marx's approach was very heavily based on process: the process of economic history and the change process of revolution. Hegel certainly had an influence on Marx, for Hegel's dialectic philosophy was, in a sense, process-based. Marxism owes much to Engels and to the active focusing of Lenin, who was to Marx what St Paul was to Jesus. Nevertheless it is wrong to see Marx only as a public relations point for the coming together of a number of ideas and the discontent of the working classes. Marx's direct attention to process was as powerful as Darwin's because he provided a plausible explanation and the values that went with it. Marx viewed government as the executive management of a political structure based on 'the conditions of production'. If the conditions of production were nomadic, agricultural or feudal the government would be in place to protect the interests of those who benefited most. According to Marx the Industrial Revolution had changed the conditions of production so that a labourer produced 'surplus value' over and above his needs and rewards. This surplus value was stolen by the capitalist as rent, profit or interest. Established institutions in society resisted the change that ought to follow these changes in conditions of production, so a revolution of the proletariat was required to realign government with the changed conditions of production. Marx's dialectical tendency also insisted that the capitalist class must produce its antithesis, which of course was the proletariat. The clash required between the two was the class struggle. Except for a brief period, Marx resisted any question of a gradual evolution of society along pink socialist lines. Like the Fathers of the Church he could see that polarization and the fierceness of struggle had a belief-reinforcing value by providing more understandable destinations than the metaphysics of God or economics. Struggle was not the final end, which was a classless Utopia in which man would cease to exploit man. Struggle was only the transitional state.

It is interesting that the 'process' basis for thinking has to deal in large masses rather than individuals. Darwin's theory dealt with overall effects. Clausewitz was not interested in a few thousand killed here or there but with the policy achieved. Marx always thought in terms of the total economic body: all workers lumped together, all capitalists lumped together, overall surplus value. All three also dealt with struggle and with survival of the fittest: in nature, in war and in social economics. That is understandable, since struggle is the most easily accessible form of process. It requires a great deal of sophistication, and a detachment from Hegel, to consider more subtle processes, and especially constructive ones.

The differences between the static idiom of thinking and the dynamic one (process) are considerable. We have examined briefly the differing creation of value in the two systems. As a final note we may consider the problems of disagreement. In the old static system you could prove something to be logically incorrect or, failing that, in disagreement with Christian belief. In process thinking it becomes much more difficult to argue with an explained process. It was impossible to prove Darwin's theory wrong, not because of its excellence but because process thinking is a description of events and one description may be as good as another. Instead of destruction one needs to show an *alternative*, even more plausible, explanation. The fight is no longer one of truth versus falsity but of likelihood versus greater likelihood. In time, however, even a process-based system like Marxism can acquire the static nature of a religion, and its treatment of schismatics.

Struggle . . . the most easily accessible form of process

Clerk Maxwell

Before Clerk Maxwell people could study the effects of light, electricity and magnetism but had no idea as to their nature. By the applied power of his thinking he deduced that they were all electromagnetic waves obeying exactly the same laws but of different wave length. He even went on to explain the behaviour of types of radiation (X-rays, radio-waves) which had not then been discovered.

1831-1879

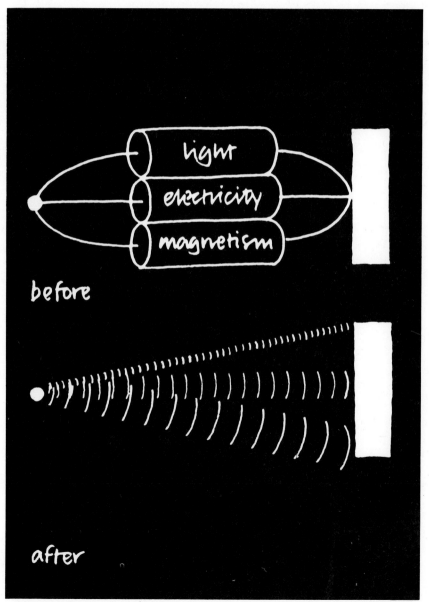

light

electricity

magnetism

before

after

**A theoretical physicist of
consummate mathematical skill
and imaginative power**

Whimsical versifier, pious Victorian, subtle philosopher, capable administrator, ingenious experimenter, James Clerk Maxwell was above all a theoretical physicist of consummate mathematical skill and imaginative power. His theory of the 'electromagnetic field' was the crowning achievement of nineteenth-century physics, uniting in one conceptual scheme a vast range of phenomena previously thought to be unrelated, and leading directly to technologies profoundly influencing life today.

He was born in 1831 into a prosperous family of Lowland Scots, and enjoyed a classical education typical of the period. Intellectual promise showed early, in intense curiosity about the workings of nature and the details of machinery. At fifteen he wrote his first paper, on a method for constructing certain geometrical curves. Thus began a dazzling career. His reputation grew, and it was soon said of him that his intuition was such that it was impossible for him to think wrongly on any physical problem.

Unlike Einstein, who was almost exclusively concerned with nature's deepest secrets in the form of her most fundamental laws, Maxwell's scientific interests were astonishingly wide. In a series of experiments on colour vision he established beyond doubt what had previously been conjecture, that normal eyes contain three different types of colour sensitive receptor, and that in colour-blind people one of these types of receptor is missing. In a paper 'On hills and dales', he gave mathematical precision to the description of features of landscapes (watersheds, river basins, etc.). In an intricate work of theoretical astronomy, he proved that the rings of Saturn must consist of vast numbers of small sparsely-distributed solid particles; any other arrangement, such as rigid solid discs or thin rings of fluid, he showed to be unstable.

He significantly advanced the development of the atomic theory. In Maxwell's day there was no direct evidence for the existence of atoms. However, John Dalton had argued that the facts of chemistry strongly supported the ancient idea that matter was built up from irreducible structural units, rather than being a 'continuum' that could be indefinitely subdivided. Therefore attempts were made to explain the large-scale behaviour of matter as the result of the microscopic motion of its atoms. Pressure, for example, arises from the impacts of vast numbers of atoms, like rain drumming on a roof. Previous theories were hampered by ignorance of the nature of atomic motion, and the crude approximation had to be made that the atoms all travelled with the same speed. Maxwell realized that this could not be true in a situation where atoms experienced frequent collisions, and by an argument of remarkable simplicity he obtained a description of the way in which different speeds are distributed among the atoms, on the average. This result enabled him to make successful predictions about matter in bulk, in particular the friction (viscosity) of flowing gases.

All this would have made him a great scientist, but what makes him a god in the physicists' pantheon is his unified theory of electric and magnetic effects, which gave precision to the concept of the 'field'. To understand this it is necessary to go back almost two centuries before Maxwell, to Newton's theory of gravitation. This is based on 'action at a distance' — instantaneously, across a vacuum, matter tugs at matter — a magical idea which Newton himself certainly found deeply mysterious. All doubts were however soon dispelled by the striking success of applications of gravitation theory to astronomy. Any theory that could explain the intricate clockwork of the heavens with such precision had to be correct,

and it was confidently expected that action at a distance would be a paradigm for the future development of physics.

And so it turned out. First electrified bodies, and then magnetized bodies were found to interact according to laws very similar to Newton's. The force between two such bodies, as measured by the mutual acceleration it produces in them, depended on the amount of electric charge and the strength of magnetization, and diminished as their distance apart increased. There was one difference: unlike gravity, electric and magnetic forces could be repulsive as well as attractive. But this did not alter the fact that here were two more substantial aspects of the physical world that could be understood in terms of action at a distance.

At first, electricity and magnetism were thought to be unrelated. Then in 1820 Hans Ørsted found that an electric current — that is, a flow of electrically charged particles — deflected the needle of a magnetic compass. Therefore electric charges could, if they were moving, produce magnetic effects. Faraday quickly discovered another connection, his 'law of induction': changing the distance between a magnet and an electric circuit caused a current to flow. This led to the developments of the electric motors and generators that dominate our technology today. The new science of electromagnetism was emerging. What were its fundamental laws? To describe the new interactions of electric charges with magnets clearly required an action at a distance more complicated than that of gravitation. The search for the new laws was beset with immense mathematical complications.

Faraday was not a mathematician, and his response to these difficulties was to develop a vivid pictorial language to describe electromagnetics. Ultimately this involved action at a distance, but it introduced the intermediate concepts of electric and magnetic 'fields'. A magnet, say, was supposed to fill the region around it with 'lines of force'. The direction of line at any point gave the direction of the force that would act on the north pole of a second magnet brought there, and the crowding of the lines would indicate the strength of the force. This pattern of lines of force in space was what Faraday called the magnetic field. He defined the electric field in a similar manner. The fields surrounding charges and magnets could be explored by measuring the forces on small 'test' charges and magnets placed at different points in the field. Although the fields were only mental crutches, auxiliary devices for calculating the mutual interactions between bodies, Faraday soon came to think of them as physically real conditions. The lines of force were tensions existing in space even when there were no 'test bodies' to measure their strength. The idea was a fruitful one. For example, Faraday's own law of induction could be stated as follows: a changing magnetic field (produced by moving a magnet) gives rise to an electric field (that urges a current round a wire placed in it).

Maxwell saw the power of Faraday's ideas and in the early 1850s set himself the task of giving them precise mathematical expression. Instead of seeking the generalized law of action at a distance, he sought the laws governing the electromagnetic field. That is, he wanted to know how from a given set of charges and magnets, moving in given ways, he could calculate the electric and magnetic fields in the surrounding space. To his surprise, he discovered that the existing laws were inconsistent with one another: to complete the logical structure of electromagnetism, there had to be some hitherto unsuspected relation between electricity and magnetism. The 'field' point of view made it possible to discover this missing link. Maxwell argued that since changing magnetic fields produce electric fields even though no charges or batteries are present, so should changing electric fields produce magnetic fields even if no magnets are present.

This is typical of the kind of argument used by theoretical physicists. It is based on the ultimately metaphysical principle that the laws of nature are as symmetrical as possible. Unfortunately the technology of the time was inadequate to test Maxwell's proposed new law directly. However, Maxwell soon found that it enabled him to write down equations for the electromagnetic field that were symmetrical and free of inconsistency. These equations had a remarkable property: electric and magnetic disturbances do not travel at infinite speed, as had been predicted on the previous 'action at a distance' theories. Instead, any change in the arrangement of a group of charges and magnets produced an 'electromagnetic wave' expanding into the surrounding space with a definite speed. This speed could be calculated using existing data from electric and magnetic measurements. It turned out to be precisely the known speed of light!

The inference was irresistible that light is an electromagnetic wave, a set of linked oscillating electric and magnetic fields travelling through space. This was a great unifying moment in physics. Such a fundamental connection between optics and electromagnetism was quite unsuspected. It had been known for half a century that light was a wave motion, and the term 'ether' had been given to the space-filling medium that was supposed to be oscillating. Now it appeared that the same ether was the medium whose tensions were described by Faraday's lines of force. Maxwell made an elaborate mathematical model of the ether as a system of cogwheels filling space. This 'represented' the ether in the same way that Faraday's fields 'represented' the laws of action at a distance. Maxwell however did not claim that his cogwheels

155

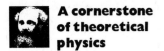

Maxwell's handwritten notes on Faraday's 'Thoughts on Ray Vibration'.

actually existed; he knew that the model was merely one of many possible models, and that his theory really depended on the truth, or otherwise, of his field equations as a description of nature. In this he was the first clear exponent of the method of modern theoretical physics: detailed models may be useful in suggesting new sets of fundamental equations, but it is the equations themselves, and not the models giving rise to them, that really count.

The wavelike fields that appeared as the solution of Maxwell's equations could have any wavelength, and it was obvious that visible light, whose wavelength is about a two-thousandth of a millimetre, is just a special case, important to us because our eyes happen to be sensitive to it. There should exist a whole gamut of radiations – the 'electromagnetic spectrum' – consisting of waves all of which travel at the same speed. Shortly after Maxwell's tragically early death in 1879, Hertz detected waves produced by purely electrical means and thus provided conclusive evidence for the correctness of the electromagnetic theory. 'Hertzian waves', centimetres to kilometres in length, form the basis of radio, television and radar communication. At the shortwave end of the spectrum, there are X-rays – the size of atoms – and gamma rays – the size of the nuclei within the atoms. The ethereal music that Maxwell produced by 'symmetrizing' the equations of electromagnetism currently encompasses about twenty octaves.

Maxwell's equations apply on cosmic scales and also within atoms. Only on the very finest scales do the effects of quantum mechanics appear, barely detectable by our most delicate instruments. Einstein showed that Maxwell's electromagnetism was inconsistent with the mechanics of Newton. This meant that no 'cogwheel' model of the ether could possibly be correct. But Maxwell's equations themselves remained valid; it was Newton's laws that needed modification. It is possible to reformulate Maxwell's theory in terms of action at a distance between bodies, but that action must be 'retarded' to allow time for the waves to travel; the resulting laws are complicated and not widely used. And so, after more than a century, Maxwell's unified theory of the electromagnetic aspects of nature is still a cornerstone of theoretical physics.   M.B.

William James

Ever since Plato the pursuit of absolute truth had led philosophers on metaphysical excursions. William James cut across these semantic indulgences and declared that truth was determined by the usefulness of a statement: by the difference that would be made in practical terms if the statement was true or false. In the place of the semantic analysis he put pragmatism.

1842-1910

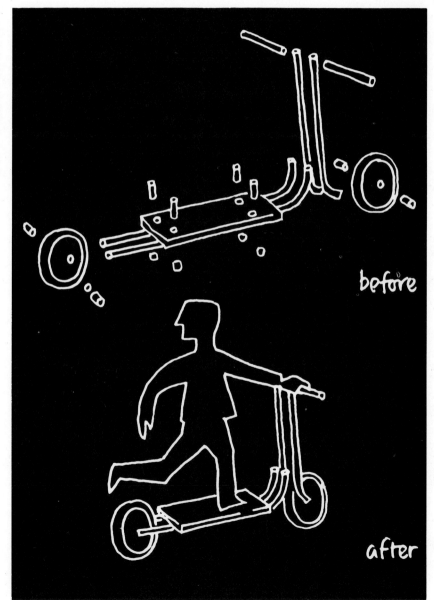

before

after

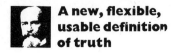
Few if any thinkers of the past century have exercised so profound and wide an influence as William James. His *Principles of Psychology* (1890) is still a classic — and a standard — book. He is a pioneer both of introspectionism and (if ironically) of behaviourism.

James was American, and distinctly so; yet his voice was predominant in European philosophy in the first quarter of the century. Although he had intellectual debts (which he scrupulously acknowledged), he anticipated or influenced both existentialism and the phenomenology from which it partly sprang. His observation of the nature of thinking and perception affected his brother Henry James, his pupil Gertrude Stein and many other writers. It

was the pragmatism of James that gave the impetus to such American pioneers of sociology as Charles Horton Cooley, George H. Mead and, later, C. Wright Mills. That many theorists accuse him of lack of rigour, philosophical inconsistency and sympathy with religious phenomena is an important clue to his contemporary relevance: he distrusted academic methodology as dry and limiting in its effect, was artistic in temperament, and would make use of whatever material lay to hand without regard for convention. In other words, he was a tolerant eclectic who paid equally careful attention to every aspect of experience. His hatred of pedantry and dullness is a peculiarly modern quality.

James's formulation of his philosophy of pragmatism came comparatively late, in 1898; but its main principles are present in all his thinking, and there is no basis for the charge that he was inconsistent as a thinker (even if he can be shown to have failed to develop a strictly philosophical system — which he did not in any case wish to do). The genesis of this pragmatism, in experience both national and personal, helps us to understand its significance and its huge appeal.

William James was born in New York in 1842, one year before his brother, the novelist Henry James. The father of these two remarkable men, Henry James Sr (1811—82), was a notable thinker in his own right. By the end of the eighteenth century, philosophy in the USA had become sterile and wholly divorced from the necessarily practical experience of a people who had been forced to *make use* of every possible resource to build up a viable nation. Henry James Sr early quarrelled with this philosophical tradition, which was narrow and Calvinistic in spirit; in due course he became a modified Swedenborgian, a believer in a 'divine-natural' humanity. He was wealthy, took his family abroad with him, and filled their childhood and youth with stimulating intellectual discussion. Though neither of his famous sons accepted his doctrines, he profoundly influenced them both — in the case of William, who edited his *Literary Remains* in 1884, probably mainly because his strong, useful personality exemplified the manner in which practicality could be combined with mysticism.

William had a restless, excitable, volatile personality. In type he was manic-depressive: his 'upward swings' led him, throughout his life, to talk too much and to think too fast, with the result that he sunk into profound depressions.

He entered the Medical School at Harvard and took his degree in 1869. But he never practised. Instead he became an instructor in physiology at Harvard in 1872. He stayed there for the following thirty-two years: first as physiologist, then as psychologist and finally as philosopher.

Left: William with his brother Henry in 1900. Opposite: William James, 1910.

James's main philosophical motive may be described in a number of ways. He felt that the idealistic philosophers' inquiries into the nature of truth were a waste of time and, worse, of useful human energy — and he wanted to dispense with them. But he found it necessary to extend the limitations of the empirical approach, exclusively scientific, which had originally attracted him. He wished to emphasize, against the abstractionism of idealists and metaphysicians, the importance of the will in experience. Above all, as a psychologist, he desired philosophy to be either something useful to people — or nothing at all. At the same time, however, he knew that when most 'people think they are thinking they are merely rearranging their prejudices'. He would not therefore reject out of hand any set of dogmas; he would instead give a new, flexible, *usable* definition of truth.

What, he asked, is the 'cash-value' of any particular claim? His question meant: 'What *difference* will it make if this or that happens to be true (or false)?' If I believe that the earth is flat, then what is really important is not whether this belief is 'true' (in the philo-sophical or even religious sense) or not, but whether good or bad consequences will result. The question we must always ask ourselves is: 'How will my belief function — for me and for others?' Our beliefs or theories are 'instruments' which we use to solve our problems.

Truth, for James, is not what such philosophers as Plato have held it to be: some entity independent of human experience. There is no such thing as purely disinterested thought. Thus: 'The ultimate test for us of what a truth means is the conduct it dictates or inspires' — this remark is James's pragmatism in a nutshell. Good things, of course, flow from such a concept: 'Faith in a fact can help create the fact.' But, if we leave it at that (as too many of James's critics do), then it is a coarse Yankee do-it-yourself kit from which bad things can also flow: the Inquisition, fascism, electric-shock 'aversion therapy' — or whatever else we recognize as evil — may very well seem to 'work' for a time ... Further, it has been charged

159

that James distorted the message of the philosopher, Charles Sanders Peirce (1839–1914), to whom he admitted he owed his formulation of pragmatism. Peirce had pointed out that our 'idea of anything is our idea of its sensible effects'; but he clearly intended this only as part of a theory of meaning, not of truth. James, it is said, unwarrantedly transformed this into a theory of truth, even causing Peirce to describe his own philosophy as 'pragmaticism' to distinguish it from James's . . .

It is correct that James did adapt Peirce to his own purposes. But this adaptation (or misunderstanding) is extremely significant. First, Peirce was a poor writer, some of whose utterances are impenetrable. Secondly, though a systematic philosopher as James was not, his influence could not be felt until his work was collected (1931–51), because he wrote only occasional papers and left much unpublished. James, on the contrary, needed to be lucid, and to publish fully and in a coherent form: he had a message: he was extending the boundaries of philosophy. 'He is so concrete, so living,' wrote Peirce in an unusually genial outburst; 'I, a mere table of contents, so abstract, a very snarl of twine.' This was true.

But James himself 'works', like his own quite deliberately limited definition of truth, precisely because he is not crude or coarse. When he used the term 'cash-value', of truths, he was simultaneously mocking the brash materialists who ran American society (it was he who coined the phrase 'the bitch-goddess success') and the over-abstract metaphysicians. It is his good qualities that have prevented his ideas being put to wrong use — for while a few bad men have praised him, it cannot possibly be argued that any of them would have been less bad had they never heard of him, which is not a statement that can truthfully be made of, to take two examples, Plato or Nietzsche.

All his other ideas may be seen in terms of his pragmatism: in terms of his concern with the practical, with what actually happens, with results, with hope. Consciousness, he early concluded, is not a series of discrete, separated 'moments': it is a flow, a flux, in which percepts are transformed into concepts. This, also put forward by Bergson, was to influence countless writers in their approach.

We cannot help, he says in *The Will to Believe* and then again in *Varieties of Religious Experience* (1902), going beyond the evidence: so, since 'our non-intellectual nature *does* influence our convictions' (my italics), and since 'all states of mind are neurally conditioned', we must judge a religion or a belief in terms of its efficacy for ourselves. There is no possibility, James insisted, of absolute knowledge — but, true to his own pragmatism, he also insisted that scepticism was tantamount to negation. What 'worked' for him was the (ultimately dualistic) notion of a strictly finite

creator fighting evil. But he did not press this on others; he was more concerned to point out that there were some 'tough-minded' people for whom a hard-headed approach to religion was acceptable — these were capable of rejecting belief on the scientific grounds of lack of evidence — and other 'tender-minded' ones who needed belief. His undogmatic notion that the matter should be studied pragmatically is the very essence of tolerance.

James propounded two further ideas that are characteristic. The first is the so-called 'James-Lange theory of emotion' (Friedrich Lange was a Dane who could not write up his excellent material convincingly). Briefly, this says that we do not strike because we are angry, but are angry because we strike: that a stimulus situation produces physical changes that are only subsequently experienced as emotion. As it was stated, the theory has been abandoned; but it is still part of the history of psychology — and it may plausibly be claimed that those who have recently answered its first critics are really only restating the original theory in the terms of sophisticated data that were not available to James . . . In any case, the notion was important to him because it reinforced his rejection of the mind—body split which still dominates metaphysics.

The second idea, of a 'pluralistic universe', goes some way towards answering James's critics. It is quite true that we cannot go to pragmatism for moral guidance: since subjective evaluation is all it allows us, how are we to judge what 'works'? Any moral framework must be thrown out of the window. But the notion of a 'pluralistic universe' partly deals with this problem: experience, says James, is not an object. Truth is not a 'thing'. Experience is the sum of the relationship between experiences of solving problems — and the process is never finished. Truth is diverse. We may be reminded of the child-psychologist Jean Piaget's explanation of truth as an 'ever-widening spiral'. Perhaps it is now most important for us to be made aware of how we function — of what 'works'. Fascism does not work. Communism does not work. Could we do better by studying ourselves, with open minds, to discover what does work? That was the noble spirit in which James made his inquiry, and his whole work breathes it. Since the wish of most men of good will today is to discover the basis of human irrationality — to find out why man does not act wholly on his unique rational faculty — it may be that James's radical empiricism, which accepted dreams or beliefs without scientific foundations as being as real as any other phenomena (on the eminently logical ground that they are phenomena), was as merciful and prophetic a contribution to thought as any in the past century.   M.S.-S.

Nietzsche

For centuries man had looked to God to provide him with the road along which he was to travel through life. Religion had provided the values that were to govern men's lives. Nietzsche found these values meek and submissive. Supermen were to arise who would restore man's moral fibre and by exercise of will and intellect determine the path he was to follow. God was dead.

1844-1900

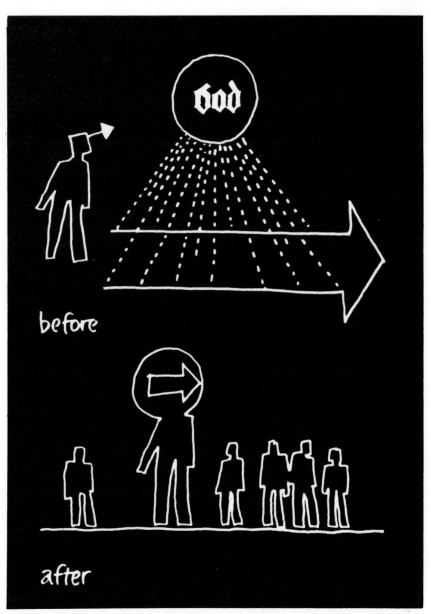

before

after

'A fine lot of scum it will be that believes in you'

'A fine lot of scum it will be that believes in you.' So wrote Elizabeth Förster-Nietzsche to her brother Friedrich in October 1888, and so in fact it turned out. The philosopher of 'the will to power' and of 'beyond good and evil' was appropriated by the supermen of fascist Europe. Hitler kept a bust of him on show for visitors, and in 1943 consoled his ally Mussolini with an elaborately-bound set of Nietzsche's collected works. God by now seemed dead indeed; the language of the German philologist had become the vocabulary of National Socialism; and Zarathustra had spoken only to pronounce a most dreadful sentence on mankind. Nietzsche — whom many already held in some way responsible for the outbreak of the First World War — was thus to acquire a share in the responsibility for the Second. More recently, however, historians have revised their verdicts.

Nietzsche was born on 15 October 1844 at Rucken in the Prussian province of Saxony. He was the son and grandson of Lutheran ministers, and in many ways this Protestant background was to be a distinguishable feature of his later thought. After his father's death, his mother moved the family home to Naumburg on the Saale in January 1850. The household there included, besides Nietzsche's mother, his younger sister Elizabeth, his maternal grandmother and two maiden aunts. Thus a possible explanation is afforded of the philosopher's later snide remarks concerning women. Nor is it a coincidence that the values against which Nietzsche later revolted were those of German provincial life.

On the other hand, provincial Germany proved a not altogether sterile environment for Nietzsche who was sent to one of Germany's most distinguished boarding-schools at nearby Pforta in 1858. There he proved an excellent scholar, received a superb classical education and graduated in 1864 before going up to the university of Bonn to study theology and classical philology. At Bonn, however, he lost interest in theology, while his love of classics grew. Thus when his classics professor, Friedrich Ritschl, moved to Leipzig in 1865, Nietzsche decided to follow him. This was a decision which must have given Ritschl much pleasure: he was later to state that in forty years of teaching he had never encountered a more promising student. Indeed, he was soon to provide most striking proof of his faith in Nietzsche's ability: not only did he publish one of Nietzsche's papers in the journal which he edited; he even recommended his, by all normal standards, unqualified disciple for the vacant chair of classical philology at Basle. Despite the fact that Nietzsche's work had so far been in the field of Greek literature rather than in philosophy, Ritschl explained: 'He will simply be able to do anything he wants to.' Thus Nietzsche in 1869 left Germany for Switzerland. He had meantime

been awarded a doctorate at Leipzig, although he had neither submitted a thesis nor undergone an examination of any kind. A most singular career was clearly in the making.

During the decade Nietzsche spent in Basle he struck up an important friendship with the composer Wagner — at that time in self-imposed exile at Lucerne — and published a number of works. The first of these was *The Birth of Tragedy*, which he published in 1872 and which, although primarily conceived as a discussion of the elements of classical Greek tragedy, also had important philosophical overtones. Nietzsche argued that, as in Greek tragedy, it was still possible to confront the future in a positive way, no matter what the fates had in store. He thus rejected the pessimism

1901 under the title *The Will to Power*, but between 1889 and his death in 1900 Nietzsche himself wrote only a few letters and some postcards. He could not will himself to health.

From the standpoint of biography it is important to remember that Nietzsche was for most of his career a lonely and a sick man. He had very few friends – most of them academic – and as far as one can tell he had very little to do with women. It is possible that he proposed marriage to the German writer Lou Salomé, but this is no more certain than the assertion that his final mental and physical collapse was the result of syphilis contracted after a rare visit to a prostitute. He injured himself seriously while riding soon after he had begun his military service in 1867; as a medical orderly in Prussian service during the Franco–Prussian War he contracted dysentery and diphtheria; finally, his eyesight was always very poor, so that the strain of reading and writing brought on migraine headaches and general physical exhaustion. All these disabilities he had to strive to overcome, and it is really no surprise that 'overcoming' was to become the watchdog of his philosophy. As the puritanism of his Protestant background was intensified by both his suffering and isolation, he became a bitter critic of the society in which he lived. He maintained that only the 'revaluation of all values' could regenerate it; or in other words, that society itself had to be overcome.

Nietzsche obviously foresaw an era of worldwide moral and political crises. Moral values, he believed had been so devitalized that man existed in a void, weighed down by the tragedy and meaninglessness of life. Christian thought and Western philosophy had so divorced man from reality that, taught to seek salvation in an eternal God or Idea, he no longer saw the possibility of changing the world through action of his own. He lacked the will to assert himself, to commit himself and to overcome his state of political and moral decadence. Thus God was 'dead'; man existed in a 'nihilistic' state; and it required a 'superman' or 'overman' to overcome this grave predicament. Nietzsche, then, was primarily a moralist. He taught men to reject the limp and lifeless values of his age and to fulfil themselves once more. Fundamentally he wanted to see created a race of men who would think and act for themselves and who would have the moral strength to withstand the forces of conformity. His *Human, All-Too-Human* bore the significant subtitle, 'A Book for Free Minds'.

But who were to be the supermen? What freedom of action were they to possess? If they rejected the values of society, just what were they to put in their place? Nietzsche himself was only too well aware of the importance of such questions, although he never answered them. Thus he wrote at one point: 'I am a dangerous

of Schopenhauer, a philosopher who had previously exercised a powerful influence on him.

His greatest works were written during the 1880s. Working relentlessly, and often in utter solitude, he published a book almost once a year. His writing often met with little or no immediate public response yet he was not deterred. He produced *Thus Spake Zarathustra, Beyond Good and Evil, On the Genealogy of Morals, The Case of Wagner, Twilight of the Idols* as well as *The Anti-Christ* and *Ecce Homo*. However, the strain he was under was immense, both physically and emotionally, while he was writing. In January 1889, therefore, he collapsed in the street in Turin and succumbed to paralysis and madness. His sister published some notes of his in

F. W. Nietzsche
1864.

Left: Nietzsche at the age of twenty.
Below: An enthusiastic soldier, Nietzsche's military career in rhe cavalry was abruptly curtailed by a riding accident.
Bottom: Nietzsche (left) with his friend, the philologist Erwin Rohde, (seated right) and members of their philological circle.

animal and do not lend myself well to adulation.' And at another: 'I decidedly do not wish to appear as a prophet, savage beast and moral monster.' Much emphasis has been given by Nietzsche interpreters, for similar reasons, to that passage in his *Thus Spake Zarathustra* in which he gave the following advice: 'You say that you believe in Zarathustra? But what does that matter?... I bid you lose me and find yourselves; and not until all of you have denied me will I return.'

But why was Zarathustra afraid to return sooner? It is at this point that we must return to the connection between Nietzsche and German nationalism. For only if Nietzsche's fear of the Germans is understood can we understand his warnings.

Nietzsche had nothing but contempt for the Germans of his day. He did not believe that they were capable of understanding him and feared what might happen if they misapplied his thought. Thus he broke with Wagner, for example, when that musical rebel joined the German establishment. 'What have I never forgiven Wagner?' he asked in *Ecce Homo*, and replied: 'That he condescended to the Germans.' Nietzsche always feared the results if he should ever do the same. He once wrote: 'As far as Germany reaches it corrupts culture'; it would appear that he foresaw a 'Germanic' corruption of his own ideas. The truth is, therefore, that far from being the voice of German nationalism, Nietzsche's was the voice that rejected it, and in view of his popular image perhaps the point is worth stressing. The Germans, Nietzsche believed, would pay dearly for achieving power because power corrupts and stupefies: *'Deutschland, Deutschland über alles . . . that I feel was the end of German philosophy,'* he said. Bismarck's triumph would turn out to be Germany's defeat — 'the defeat and even the extirpation of the German mind in favour of the German Reich'. He also rejected the antisemitism which so often accompanied the nationalism of people such as Wagner, and wrote in one of his letters to the historian Jacob Burckhardt: 'Wilhelm and Bismarck must be done away with [as well as] all antisemites. . . . Just now I am having all antisemites shot.' 'Where races are mixed,' he thought, 'there is the source of great cultures.' Modern revisionists among intellectual historians can therefore paint a picture of Nietzsche as a concerned antinationalist, fretting lest his moral concern for the individual should be perverted by some future antisemitic German leader. They can thus present a picture of him which is exactly the opposite of the traditional portrait.

The trouble is, however, that this latest portrait of the philosopher is no more a real likeness than the one it has replaced; for although it is possible to agree with the revisionists that Nietzsche was no proto-fascist, it is nonetheless plausible to argue that his philosophy indeed contained the seeds of fascism, seeds which were planted in the role he assigned to his 'supermen'.

Nietzsche, especially in his later writings, tended so much to emphasize the need to overcome that he appeared to want to give his 'overmen' despotic powers. God was to be replaced but the 'masters of the globe' who would replace him were themselves in danger of becoming tinpot gods. Zarathustra had commanded them to 'become hard', to rule and rob, to make war and to live dangerously. They were to form an elite which would distribute religions and constitutions according to rank. The supermen, therefore, were hardly meant to be a race of saintly elders; they had more in common with the Grand Inquisitor of *The Brothers Karamazov* than with any gentle prophet. Nietzsche, in fact, had fallen victim to despair. Thus if, on the one hand, he advocated the regeneration of the individual, he believed on the other that only a minority of individuals would be transformed. And to this minority he was willing to entrust the fate of all the rest.

There is, however, one final question which the critic has to pose. That is: why, if he so feared the possible consequences of his thought, did Nietzsche do nothing to revise his work? In answering this question one is immediately confronted with the paradox in Nietzsche. For just as the prophet of the affirmation of life despaired of mankind, the prosecutor of Wagner in the last resort displayed a similar desire to condescend to the Germans. Nietzsche shared with many great thinkers the desire for immortality. Thus, if he shunned society and celebrity when he was alive, he was desperate to ensure a hearing for his voice beyond the grave. The violence of his language is one proof of this; the number of his protests yet another. In fact, he protested too much: the truth appears to be that Nietzsche, once dead, did not much care who would be listening to him just so long as he secured an audience.

That the Nazis misappropriated him, therefore, was entirely his own fault; he should have had the moral strength to correct the weakness in his own philosophy. His legacy, however, was by no means mainly negative. Many found within his strange, poetic writings a vision of man's inner self which was, despite everything, inspiring. Thus Freud claimed Nietzsche as a great psychologist, while others see in him a proto-existentialist. His influence for good and bad has been immense, and nearly every German writer since his death has, at one time or other, come under his spell.   A.S.

Demystification

The definition of man as a believing animal is no better and no worse than all the other snap definitions of man. Beliefs are required to fill in the gaps between direct experiences. A child is forever asking 'why?' not in order to find the deeper explanation below surface experience but to find some way of linking a new experience to the ones he already has. Beliefs are required for the transfer of experience: the expectancy built into beliefs makes it possible to use generalizations. Finally beliefs seem to be required as a framework for action and interest.

The nineteenth century was robust and full of self-confidence. Science was on its way to explaining everything. Railways had been built with great bridges and other feats of engineering. Mechanical geniuses like Brunel had shown that there seemed no limit to man's power if something had to be done in iron or steel. The urge to make things tangible and controllable led to a certain impatience with myth and mystery. This impatience took a number of forms, and the thinking of Clerk Maxwell, James and Nietzsche illustrates the most important forms.

The mystery of 'action at a distance'

Clerk Maxwell set out to solve the mystery of 'action at a distance'. This was certainly the most mysterious aspect of nature. There was magnetism and the magnetic fields described by Faraday. There was heat, light and gravity. It was quite easy to give a name to these phenomena and to consider them explained by that name, but Clerk Maxwell wanted to go further and explain what they were. His success in explaining the electromagnetic nature of light, magnetism, and the as yet undiscovered radio-waves, X-rays and radar waves, must rank as one of the greatest intellectual feats of all time. In many ways it was superior to the feat of Newton, for Newton was dealing with the behaviour of observable bodies whereas Clerk Maxwell was dealing with unknown forces.

Clerk Maxwell's conceptual model of 'cogwheels' in space and the mathematical laws which he derived from the model are still valid today. This immensely powerful unifying theory described the behaviour and velocity of what we now call electromagnetic waves. Radio-waves were only demonstrated by Hertz after Clerk Maxwell's death, and yet they fit exactly into his calculations, as do X-rays, which were discovered even later. His theory held that the difference in the nature of the waves was simply a difference in wavelength, and that the velocity was in all cases equal to the velocity of light. The practical consequences of his explanation are immense: radio and television are simply the most obvious technologies that have depended on an understanding of electromagnetic waves.

The demystification intention of Clerk Maxwell was no different from that of any other scientist seeking for underlying mechanisms and unifying explanations. It is just that he was more successful than anyone else had ever been, and in a most difficult area. Outside a small circle of mathematicians and physicists his explanations probably had little impact, certainly much less than Darwin's explanation of the origin of species. But as an illustration of the power of man's mind to break through apparently insoluble mysteries it typifies the urge towards demystification.

William James started off in philosophy and quickly became impatient with the traditional metaphysical inquiries into the nature of truth. It seemed to him that philosophy was involved in an elaborate game of unverifiable constructions. All this was very different from the practical effectiveness of the world around. In order to escape from the mystique of traditional philosophy he created two demystification devices. The first was to separate 'psychology' from mental philosophy and to treat it as a laboratory science instead of semantic speculation. This he succeeded in doing with the publication of his book *Principles of Psychology*. His second demystification device was the extraordinarily simple concept of pragmatism. The basic notion had come from Charles Peirce, who had said that a truth is only discernible in terms of its examinable consequences. James took this much further and built on it the philosophy of pragmatism, which substituted 'usefulness' for truth. Instead of saying: 'This is true therefore it should be useful,' James suggested that we ought to say: 'The truth of this is measured by its usefulness.' He was interested in the difference that would be made if something happened to be true or false. If there was no practical difference then it could not matter whether the proposition were true or false. He insisted that truth should be measured by the conduct it inspired or dictated.

The pragmatic approach to Christian belief had been suggested at one time by Origen, who had suggested that the social utility of the belief was important. Machiavelli had been in favour of religion because it made a people more governable. Marx echoed the same sentiments when he called religion the opiate of the people. James himself could have followed this line, except that he believed in the reality of religious experience. The interesting point about James's pragmatism is that it was not a turning away from subjective beliefs to hard facts, nor the sort of materialistic doctrine that was to inspire Pavlov. On the contrary, James's pragmatism led him to accept the truth of dreams and beliefs because they obviously could dictate specific behaviour. For him subjective reality was just as valid as the objective sort. He also placed a lot of emphasis on 'will', because this seemed to play so important a part in experience.

The trouble with pragmatism is that in the hands of James himself, and of some followers, it becomes hard to distinguish between truth, value and reality. Traditionally truth and value have been closely related because truth was the ultimate value in the Platonic tradition. The demystification of truth by James seemed to suggest that the usefulness of an idea determined both its truth and its value. This creates problems because different people may have different value systems, and it becomes somewhat circular if use determines value and the value system determines the usefulness. In short, pragmatism could be used to justify any belief system at all. A government that found it useful to imprison its opponents would justify its action by the obvious usefulness of the procedure.

'The truth of this is measured by its usefulness'

Nietzsche's supermen?
Hitler receives an ovation
in the Reichstag after
the declaration of war on
Poland, 1 September 1939.

Had James been content to use the word 'reality' instead of 'truth' all would have been well. Had he said: 'The reality of an idea is measured by the effects it has,' the question of value would not have come into it, for a real idea might have a negative value as much as it might have a positive one. Unlike 'reality', truth has only a positive value in our culture. It seems that 'reality' is what Peirce intended for his pragmatism and also what James really intended. He could see, however, that to use the word 'reality' was very weak and quite useless as a demystification procedure. The mystique of philosophy was based on the search for truth. Philosophers would simply have shrugged at anyone who suggested that reality was something that had an effect. But they had to take note when someone said truth was only measured by its effect.

The demystification influence of William James was powerful because it hit at the very basis of speculative philosophy by demanding the 'cash-value' of the speculations. The demystification approach of Nietzsche was even more radical because it hit at the whole system of Christian ethics.

Nietzsche saw nothing inevitable in the Christian morality. The emphasis on humility, compassion, equality and love for one's fellow men he regarded as a slave morality which the weak had foisted on society. In particular he ascribed the origin of this slave morality to the Jews and their influence through

Christianity. He wished to awaken society to the myth of this morality, and by demystifying it to encourage the development of what he called the master morality: strength, hardness, power, health and intelligence. He attacked the myth of equality and thought that socialism was only the Gospel in modern dress. He regarded society not as an opportunity for everyone to be equal and happy but as a seedbed for the production of the supermen aristocrats who were going to have the master morality and whose task it would be to save society from its weakness and lack of will.

Instead of the myths and beliefs of Christianity, Nietzsche wanted society to be run on a basis of will and power – as exerted by the supermen. The Nazi creed and its operation was the almost perfect incarnation of Nietzsche's proposal. So too, it could be argued, was Plato's Republic. As supermen the early Christians would have qualified almost better than anyone else, even though their strength of character and will was based on the ethic which Nietzsche despised. Just as James got into trouble by using reality and truth interchangeably, so Nietzsche failed to distinguish between strength of character (and morality) and the strength of domination. Like truth and reality the two often go together – but not necessarily. The exercise of social strength often indicates a weakness of moral strength, just as those who are always talking about will are often those most conscious of its deficiency in themselves.

A religion based on will

In place of the mystique of the Christian belief, Nietzsche wished to set up a religion based on *will*. He was not alone in this. Anyone who sets out to demystify finds that one of the main functions of a belief system is to overcome the natural tendency towards selfishness and immediate gratification. Beliefs provide the needed meta-system to override the natural behaviour of the self-system. When this belief system is done away with, only the 'will' remains as a sort of internal meta-system. Even the existentialists, who recognized no overall purpose in existence, put an emphasis on the will because it was obvious that without it there could only be a sort of deterministic drift, with man being wafted along like a cork in a stream by his present circumstance and past experience.

The trouble is that will without a belief-system is like a gun without a target. Quite soon the gun comes to create its own targets with no more justification than that they shatter when shot. It has been a common fault with demystifiers that they fail to realize that the demystification only has its real value within the framework of the beliefs they are seeking to destroy. Thus Nietzsche's ideals make a great deal of sense within the framework of the Christian ethic but dangerous nonsense outside it. Similarly James's pragmatism made a great deal of sense within the framework of traditional philosophy but became weak opportunism outside of it; again, Marxism makes sense within the capitalist system and in the transitional struggle against capitalism, but outside of it must quickly adopt the clothes of totalitarianism.

As so often happens, the coherence and unity of mathematical demyst-ification, exemplified by Clerk Maxwell's feat, does not transfer to human affairs because of the interactive nature of this different universe: there is no frame-work outside of itself unless created by faith.

Pavlov

Pavlov showed that inputs into the mind could be directly related to outputs by means of the conditioned reflex. This direct linkage did away with the need for mysterious psychic phenomena. If the mind of man was no more than a complex switching system for connecting up inputs and outputs then human behaviour could be controlled and predicted without the exercise of free will.

1849-1936

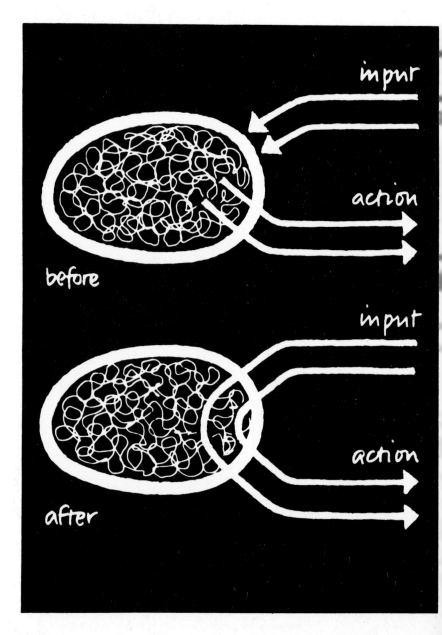

Up to the mid-nineteenth century the study of the nature of living things in general had changed little during the preceding centuries The study of behaviour, whether of man or animal, had been constrained and directed firstly and specifically by the dogma of religion, and secondly by man's unwillingness to step down from his self-appointed place at the pinnacle of nature and submit himself to scientific investigation. This dogma dictated at the outset of any philosophical or experimental inquiry that man differed from lower animals by possessing both a soul, which was immortal, and free will. It emphasized that all man's behaviour was the result of the 'free' decisions of a force or 'psyche' within himself. However, during the mid-nineteenth century the beginnings of a serious challenge to this dogma could already be discerned. Although Darwin's *Origin of Species* is popularly seen as the instigator of this challenge to man's unique place in nature, the roots of a more radical approach to the study of man and his behaviour can be traced to Russia in the period 1840–70. During this period a number of Russian physiologists, among them Herzen, Pisarev and Chernyshevsky, were establishing a 'militant materialistic approach' to the study of man which primarily advocated the application of objective physiological methods to the study of complex psychical phenomena. It was this tradition which provides a backcloth to the achievements and philosophies of I. P. Pavlov.

Ivan Petrovich Pavlov was born on 26 September 1849, the first son of a poor priest living in the central Russian town of Ryazan, and entered a theological seminary at the age of fifteen. However, with his appetite for philosophical matters sharpened, Pavlov gave up the idea of a future in the Church and in 1870 left the seminary to enter the university of St Petersburg. After studying chemistry and physiology he graduated, spending the next few years, often in desperate poverty, studying techniques of physiological investigation under the eminent physiologists of both Russia and Europe until, in 1891, he began work in the first surgical department of a physiological laboratory at the Institute of Experimental Medicine in St Petersburg.

During the intensive period of physiological experimentation that followed, Pavlov outlined a number of basic tenets which were to guide his research and become most important when his work developed naturally from the study of purely physiological factors to more psychological ones. He was profoundly influenced by the environmentalist views of I. M. Sechenov, and in particular Sechenov's assertion that 'the organism cannot exist without the external environment which supports it, hence the scientific definition of the organism must also include the environment by which it is influenced'. Pavlov adopted this approach in his interpretation of conditioning phenomena. The tradition of Russian materialism which had preceded him also engendered in Pavlov an intimate knowledge of experimental method: 'Observation collects all that which nature has to offer, whereas experiment takes from her that which it desires. And the power of biological experimentation is truly colossal.' The more complex the phenomenon, he considered, the greater was the need for experimentation – and thus the need for experimentation was greatest when studying life itself. A further factor which Pavlov held to be important in his work was the study of the physiological processes of 'normal' and 'whole' organisms, that is, animals that had fully recovered from his surgical operations. He considered that 'only he who is able to restore the disordered course of life to normal can say that he has acquired real knowledge of life'.

Although there had been many eminent Russian physiologists before Pavlov, he was perhaps the first to develop the idea of the adaptive character of physiological phenomena, and to bring together the then currently popular doctrine of associationism with reflexology. His early work centred around many observations on the responses of the glandular cells of the digestive tract to certain natural stimuli such as bread, meat or milk. After some study of this topic he began to realize that the forms of the nervous regulation of digestive gland secretion could often be conditioned not only by purely physiological factors but also by what he initially called 'psychical' factors. Firstly he found that the sight of food produced similar glandular secretions to food which had actually been placed in the mouth. The initial reaction of his contemporaries, even his close associates, was to interpret these results as a manifestation of the animal's psychical activity: the secretion of the salivary gland in these situations merely reflected a certain inner state of the organism which was inaccessible to investigation by scientific methods. However, Pavlov, true to his materialist upbringing, was convinced that the concept of 'psychical secretion' should be replaced by objective physiological concepts. So firm was this conviction that all those in his laboratory who vigorously opposed these views finally had to leave!

These studies eventually led to Pavlov's classical experiments involving the conditioning of salivary secretion in the dog. In the prototypical experiment a restrained, hungry dog was subjected to several pairings of a bell with food; firstly the bell was sounded and at its termination the dog was presented with food – normally a meat powder. Pavlov eventually observed that the animal would salivate profusely during the presentation of the bell, and the chemical constitution of the saliva was similar to that secreted when food was in the mouth. In an address delivered on the occasion of his being presented with the Nobel prize in 1904, Pavlov outlined his approach to interpreting these observations:

> We endeavoured to discipline our thoughts and our speech about these phenomena, and not concern ourselves with the imaginary mental state of the animal; and we limited our task to exact observation and description of the effect on the secretion of the salivary glands of the object acting from a distance. The results correspond to our expectations — the relations we observed between the external phenomena and the variations in the work of the salivary glands appeared quite regular, could be reproduced at will again and again as usual physiological phenomena, and were capable of being definitely systematized.

The laws which Pavlov formulated to relate the action of 'conditioned stimuli' on 'unconditioned reflexes' have since

become known collectively as Classical or 'Pavlovian' conditioning. He considered there to be two types of reflexes — inborn, or unconditioned reflexes, and individually acquired, or conditioned reflexes. These latter reflexes were acquired during the lifetime of the organism through the pairing of physiologically 'neutral' stimuli with stimuli which naturally produced responses in a reflexive manner. Prior to Pavlov's investigations, only inborn reflexes — such as the dog's salivation at the sight of food — had been recognized as the means by which organisms adapted to their environment. Pavlov's experiments demonstrated a method for creating a new reflex — the conditioned reflex — by repeatedly presenting a novel, neutral stimulus immediately prior to the occurrence of the existing unconditioned reflex. He called the originally ineffective stimulus a conditioned stimulus (CS) because the elicitation of salivation after this stimulus was conditional upon it being temporally paired with food in the past; similarly, he called food in this situation an unconditioned stimulus (US) to indicate that no other conditions were necessary for the elicitation of salivation when food was placed in the mouth.

Other examples of unconditioned stimuli with their associated unconditioned responses are electric shock to the leg producing leg flexion, or a puff of air into the corner of the eye producing blinking. Pairing a neutral stimulus such as a bell or a tone with these unconditioned stimuli will eventually lead to the bell or tone, when presented alone, eliciting leg flexion or blinking. In formulating his observations in the way he did, Pavlov had spurned the 'psychical' interpretation of his results that so many of his contemporaries were readily willing to acknowledge; he remained faithful to the materialistic teachings of the Russian school by interpreting his findings simply in terms of environment-behaviour interactions and by purposely disregarding the thoughts, desires and emotions of the animal undergoing the experiment.

Pavlov's view that the behaviour of organisms could be considered purely in terms of its interaction with the environment gave rise in the early twentieth century to the influential American school of psychology known as Behaviourism. J. B. Watson, often considered to be the founder of Behaviourism, based much of his writings on the concepts of conditioning outlined by Pavlov, and took them to their logical extreme by claiming that practically all meaningful human behaviour was the result of environmental contingencies operating through the principles of conditioning.

Despite the materialistic approach to man that Pavlov championed, he was always well aware of the possible affront to human dignity that would be sparked by the denigration of free will and removal of the control of man's destiny from his own hands and

Left: Pavlov in 1929.
Below: Pavlov at work
in his laboratory.

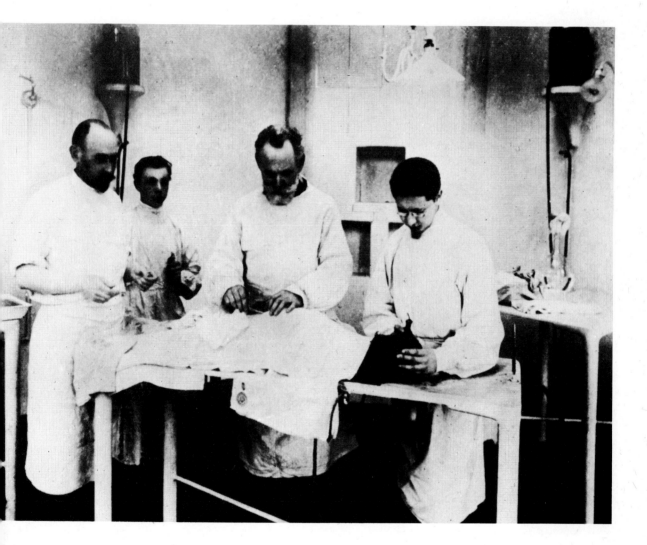

'Only science ... will deliver Man from his present gloom'

Pavlov on his return from a visit to London, 1935.

placing it in the unsympathetic hands of the environment. His reply to this accusation, written in 1932, was:

> But is it really so? For according to the view of evolution, is not man at the summit of nature ... Is not this sufficient to maintain the dignity of man, to fill him with highest satisfaction? And there still remains in life all that is also embraced in the idea of freedom of will with its personal, social, and civic responsibility; for me these still remain, and hence also the obligation for me to know myself and, constantly using this information, to maintain myself at the utmost height of my capabilities. Are not the social

and civic duties and requirements, situations which present themselves to my system, and which must lead to appropriate reactions that will promote the integrity and perfection of the system?

The final criticism of a scientific analysis of behaviour is one which is most consciously with us today: the problem of a behavioural technology. If we can formulate objective laws of behaviour which stress that behaviour is controlled by happenings in the environment, then can we not, via environmental manipulation, control the behaviour of others — not only individuals, but indeed, whole societies? Such possibilities have recently been raised by the current champion of the behaviourist tradition, B. F. Skinner, in his book *Beyond Freedom and Dignity* (1971), and the use of behaviour-modification techniques based on conditioning principles is becoming ever more widespread, both in the clinical and natural settings. However, these problems are not specific to behaviouristic psychology alone but are found in any science when technology outgrows the moral and social codes which previously constrained its application. Although reservations might currently be held at the widespread and sometimes indiscriminate application of behavioural technology, Pavlov himself was never in doubt that such a technology might one day be the salvation of mankind. He wrote: 'Only science, exact science about human nature itself, and the most sincere approach to it by the aid of the *omnipotent scientific method*, will deliver Man from his present gloom, and will purge him from his contemporary shame in the sphere of inter-human relationships.'

From this account it can probably be seen that reactions against Pavlov's analysis of behaviour are not so much criticisms of the validity of his laws of conditioning, but more reactions in defence of the sanctity of men as individuals and men as beings responsible for their own behaviour. It is unlikely that the truly mechanistic view of man which has its genesis in Pavlov's work will ever be able to encapsulate, as some would like it to, the whole spectrum of human life and achievement, but it has removed the shroud of mysticism which surrounded the causes of behaviour and it has helped man to better assess his position in nature's scheme of things. So great was Pavlov's profound concern at furthering man's understanding of himself that it was only in the last hours of his life that he ceased making scientific observations. On the day of his death, 21 February 1936, he called a neuropathologist to his bedside to discuss with him his symptoms and whether they might be of interest to science. Just hours later the 'father of modern Russian physiology' was dead.   G.D.

174

Freud

Man had prided himself on the objectivity of his conscious mind. This was the supreme tool with which he would observe and understand everything else. Freud suggested that the conscious mind far from being objective was involved in repressing and disguising the wishes of the more powerful subconscious mind. The conflicts of the subconscious mind could be seen to explain much of human behaviour.

1856-1939

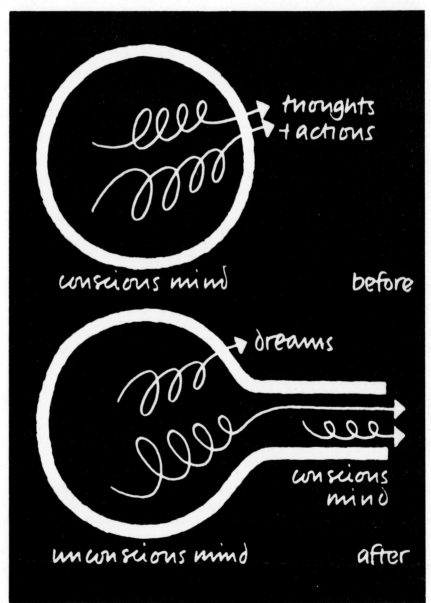

Dreams...
the 'disguised fulfilment
of a repressed wish'

Right: The laboratory at the Institute of Physiology
where Freud worked as a research student.
Below: A plan of lectures in
Freud's own hand, 1885.

Sigmund Freud was to deliver one of the next major blows to man's self-esteem and conceit of his central position as master of himself and lord of creation.

At school Freud had some leanings towards the law but: 'at the same time, the theories of Darwin, which were then of topical interest, strongly attracted me, for they held out hopes of an extraordinary advance in our understanding of the world' (Freud 1925), and on hearing Goethe's essay on nature read aloud just before he left school he decided to become a medical student.

Freud entered medical school in Vienna in 1873, but did not qualify until 1881 because he dallied particularly in Ernst von Brucke's physiology laboratory, thinking of an academic career. This was a time when the rational hope was ascendant that all ills that man is heir to would come to be understood in physical terms and yield to discoveries in the basic sciences. Brucke had pledged: 'No other forces than the common physical and chemical ones are active within the organism.' Freud shared that hope early on, and to some extent never quite abandoned it when he later predicted the more recent vogue for drug treatments in psychiatry.

In 1885 he obtained a grant to visit the great neurologist Charcot in Paris. Charcot at that time was giving grand theatrical demonstrations (sometimes attended by royalty) of neurological cases amongst which there were hysterical patients with paralysis, anaesthesia or bizarre gait. Freud noted that Charcot could create by hypnosis conditions identical to those arising spontaneously in hysterical patients and that furthermore the pattern of the disorder followed the idea in the patient's mind rather than any anatomical pathway (as seen in true neurological lesions). He therefore concluded that if hysterical disorders could be created by hypnosis perhaps they arose spontaneously by auto-suggestion, in response to an idea in the patient's mind of which he was *unconscious*.

Freud returned to Vienna and married in 1886. In his private neurological practice he found a usual proportion of hysterical cases. At first he used hypnosis as a treatment in an attempt to dispel the symptoms by suggestion. Through his association with Josef Breuer, with whom he wrote the *Studies in Hysteria* (1895), he found that by putting patients into a light hypnotic trance and encouraging them to talk freely, memories or ideas might be revived that had become repressed and unconscious because unacceptable to conscious ideals. Hence the 'talking cure' was born. Freud soon abandoned hypnosis as a direct method of intervention and not long after gave up using it even as a lubricant to talking.

Now there is nothing new in the idea of a 'talking cure'. Catharsis has relieved guilt in the Catholic confessional for centuries; and our idioms ('getting it off your chest', 'a problem shared is a problem halved') testify to its value. Nor is there anything revolutionary in the idea that we are often in conflict with our feelings or memories.

Rousseau wrote: 'There is no automatic movement of ours of which we cannot find the cause in our hearts, if we know well how to look for it there.' Writing in the 1880s, Nietzsche anticipated Freud: ' "I did that," says my memory. "I could not have done that," says my pride, and remains inexorable. Eventually the memory yields.'

The idea of the unconscious had been much discussed by nineteenth-century psychologists — in particular J. F. Herbart, who emphasized the conflict between conscious and unconscious ideas

— and its earlier origins have been traced by Whyte (1962) and Ellenberger (1970). As the authority of God declined in Europe from the Middle Ages onwards, there was a corresponding increase in human self-awareness which reached a particular intensity around 1600. The dualism of Descartes marked the high tide of the movement with its assertion that mental processes are limited to conscious awareness. The word conscious first appears in European languages in the seventeenth century. Thereafter an inevitable reaction (Whyte suggests) was the rise of the idea of unconscious mental processes which was 'conceivable around 1700, topical around 1800 and became effective around 1900'. By 1870: 'Europe was ready to discard the Cartesian view of mind as awareness.'

Freud's achievement was to address these ideas to a medical context. He thereby rescued the neurotic patient from humiliation in the public theatre of Charcot's demonstrations, where only external appearances counted, and created the private space of the analytic consulting room where hitherto unmentionable and unacknowledged aspects of man's inner world could be faced. Symptoms that had been taken for meaningless byproducts of as-yet-undiscovered somatic processes could be viewed afresh as meaningful communications about inner states of conflict.

Freud revised his own attempts to conceptualize his clinical experiences many times in his own lifetime, but only the broadest outlines of these revisions concern us here. In the 1890s he described the psychic apparatus simply in terms of conscious and unconscious levels; next (*Interpretation of Dreams*, 1900) came the topographical theory and the idea of Conscious, Preconscious and Unconscious realms; in 1923 (*The Ego and the Id*) he introduced the structural theory and the concepts of Super-Ego, Ego and Id (Ego and Id corresponding roughly to Conscious and Unconscious, and Super-Ego to conscience). Running throughout is the idea of conflict between different psychic levels.

Freud always regarded dreams as 'the royal road to the unconscious'. He drew a distinction between the often apparently absurd manifest content of a dream and the latent content behind it which could be reached by free association. Dreams were the 'disguised fulfilment of a repressed wish', the disguise being affected by condensation, displacement of effect and secondary revision. Dreams and neurotic symptoms were now seen to be constructed along similar lines, as 'compromises between the demands of a repressed impulse and the resistance of a censoring force in the Ego'. New light was similarly thrown on delinquent acts, which could no longer be dismissed as signs of moral degeneracy but as possible indications of underlying conflict. Parapraxes (slips of the tongue and pen, etc) were not mistakes in the machine but *psychically determined*.

The elements of Freud's thinking were assembled by the early

Opposite: Freud's consulting room in London.
Having fled from the Nazis, Freud spent the last
year of his life in England.
Below: Freud in 1920.

1900s: conflict over aspects of the self (thoughts, feelings, memories, instinctual drives) were unacceptable to consciousness because of the anxiety they aroused so that they were dealt with by a number of defence mechanisms — by repression, denial, projection or conversion into physical symptoms. But what aspects of the self give rise to such conflict that they must remain unconscious? A common misinterpretation of Freud is to assume he attributed all problems to sex, and thereby to dismiss psychoanalysis as culture-bound to bourgeois Vienna of the 1880s and therefore not of general relevance. Indeed Freud found that many of his female hysterical patients were suffering from sexual

conflicts, but it is instructive to quote his actual words about this (1894): 'In all the cases I have analysed it was the subject's sexual life that had given rise to a distressing effect. . . . Theoretically, it is not impossible that this affect should sometimes arise in other fields; I can only report that so far I have not come across any other origin.' This was a modest but prophetic remark. Since then we have come to recognize the immense importance of conflict over aggressive feelings which may be turned against the self in depression and suicidal attempts or converted into psychosomatic symptoms (such as migraine or high blood pressure).

Nevertheless, in the early days Freud was impressed by the frequency of sexual conflicts. To begin with he believed the stories his patients told him of sexual seduction by adults in infancy and felt it was the repression of such traumatic memories that gave rise to neurotic conflict. Before long, however, prompted by his self-analysis (from 1897) and the realization that child seduction could not be as rife as his theory required, he felt he must be mistaken. To revoke such revolutionary ideas might have unseated a lesser mind. Freud realized that what he was hearing from his patients, if not true historical accounts, were the expression of childhood fantasies of wished-for occurrences. Now he saw that *psychic reality* is often far more important than actual historical reality.

The ensuing discovery of *infantile sexuality* led to the publication of *Three Essays on the Theory of Sexuality* (1905). Until this time the polite view of the development of normal heterosexuality was that it arose *de novo* at puberty. Freud saw that this account took no note of the phenomena of homosexuality, of sexual perversions or of infantile masturbation and sexual curiosity. He came to see the sexual drive as present from birth and developing through a number of different stages (oral, anal, phallic, etc), pleasure being derived from different *erotogenic zones* at different stages. The best known of all these must be the Oedipal phase (around three to five) named by Freud (following his self-analysis) after the myth of Oedipus, who unknowingly killed his father, married his mother and then blinded (symbolically castrated) himself on discovering his crime. Freud's suggestion that Oedipal conflicts were at the centre of most neurotic disturbances has often been interpreted far too concretely and then dismissed. Obviously a child does not have exactly the same concept of either murder or sexual intercourse as an adult. Yet few would now dispute that childhood is a time of passionate love and hate, attachment and rivalry, the vicissitudes and outcome of which have a decisive effect on later character formation.

The idea of duality persists as a central characteristic of Freud's thinking whether the war is seen to be between self-preservative and sexual instincts, between self-love (narcissism) and love of

others or between life and death instincts. Whichever formulation of instinctual theory is preferred, the central characteristic of conflict over unacceptable aspects of the self, which are defended against, suppressed, denied or disowned and become more or less unconscious, remains. This view has become the theoretical core of all later forms of dynamic psychotherapy — whether psychoanalysis, group or individual psychotherapy, family or marital therapy — quite apart from the influence it has yielded in other areas such as literary and dramatic criticism, education and child-rearing practice.

Though in some of his later works (e.g. *Civilization and its Discontents*, 1930) he took a pessimistic view of the inevitable clash between the demands of instinct and the restrictions of civilization, many would now claim him as a liberator who helped free Western European thought from excessive rationalism and towards a wholeness of personality. Freud offered us new ways of understanding hitherto baffling aspects of human behaviour. His central concept of conflict over unacceptable unconscious impulses threw new light on neurotic symptoms, dreams and parapraxes. What previously seemed meaningless epiphenomena (byproducts) of a disordered nervous system could now be understood as meaningful communication of a diseased person.   J.R.P.

Einstein

Einstein shattered the traditional concepts of space, time, energy and matter. He showed that instead of moving with Newtonian motion through a neutral space, objects moved through a space-time continuum which could itself be curved. The implications of his theories led directly to the development of nuclear energy.

1879-1955

In 1895, at the age of sixteen, Albert Einstein wrote a letter to his uncle, in which he wondered what would be seen by someone travelling so fast that they could catch up with a light ray. Ten years later he solved the problem, in the first of a series of thunderbolts that exposed profound inconsistencies in the system of fundamental physical laws inherited from the nineteenth century. Meanwhile, this cosmopolitan young man (who had already lived in Germany, Italy and Switzerland) had a traditional education that left him with a lifelong hatred of all forms of authority. His university career was undistinguished, and despite boundless confidence and a constant dreamlike absorption in his subject he found himself unable to find employment as a physicist. Instead he got a job as a technical officer with the Swiss Patent Office in Berne. The work was not heavy, and he was able to devote his evenings to the deepest problems of physics and returned to the problem of that light ray.

Forty years earlier, Maxwell had shown that light was a travelling pattern of electric and magnetic fields — an 'electromagnetic wave'. Einstein thought at first that if he caught up with the light he would see a static pattern of fields, rather as a surf-rider sees a static disturbance on water while those on shore see a travelling wave. The trouble was that Maxwell's equations could not be made to yield any solution that corresponded to these static fields: the waves had always to travel at the same speed. Perhaps Maxwell's theory applied only to observers at rest relative to the 'ether' in which light was thought to travel. But A. A. Michelson and E. W. Morley, a few years before, had measured the speed of light in different directions with apparatus moving at different speeds. They found that however the observer was moving the speed of light was always the same. This was a triumph for Maxwell's theory, but a disaster for common sense. If you chase after a light ray, how can its speed fail to diminish, as measured by you?

Einstein took the Michelson-Morley result seriously, as showing that Maxwell's theory gives a valid description of light no matter how fast the observer is moving. He did not worry about contradictions with 'common sense' — after all, the speed of light was uncommonly faster than anybody had travelled at that time, and common sense was no guide in such a situation. Instead, he analyzed the logical consequences of never being able to catch up with the light. Consider two events: the emission of a flash of light and its reception after reflection from a distant mirror. Einstein showed that the time interval between these events, and the distance between them, would be different when measured by observers who were moving relative to one another, even if the observers used identically constructed clocks and rulers.

This was shattering. All of physics was thought to be consistent with Newton's laws of mechanics, and these in turn were based on the assumption that times and distances between events were absolute, that is, independent of the speeds of observers measuring them. Einstein's result showed Maxwell's electromagnetism to be inconsistent with this, and the Michelson—Morley experiment suggested that it was Newton who was wrong. Newtonian mechanics had to be replaced by something; there had to be some way of predicting how objects move in response to forces acting on them. Moreover, the old theory had been staggeringly successful for over two hundred years in astronomy and engineering, so the new theory had to give virtually the same predictions at low speeds;

only for relative motion near the speed of light could there be differences.

Einstein was able to devise a new mechanics satisfying these conditions and consistent with Maxwell's theory of light. One conclusion was that, as an object moved faster relative to an observer, it became increasingly difficult to accelerate it further — in effect the mass of the body increased with its speed, becoming infinite at the speed of light. Thus this speed is a natural limit which no material object can attain: once again, it is impossible to catch that ray of light. Another conclusion was that the mass of a body — even one at rest — must be regarded as a form of energy. In mathematical terms, the energy (E) locked up in an object is related to its mass (m) and the speed of light (c) by the famous equation:

$$E = mc^2$$

Nuclear reactions in the sun convert mass into energy at a rate governed by this equation; the energy comes to us as sunshine while the sun loses mass in proportion. Our own nuclear technologies of power generation and mass destruction are based on the same equation. All the other predictions from Einstein's mechanics, as well as the astonishing relationships between times and distances as measured by different observers, are abundantly confirmed every day by the swiftly-moving subnuclear particles produced in nuclear accelerators.

So far we have discussed what is called Einstein's 'special theory of relativity', completed in 1905. It is a theory of 'relativity' because it gives a consistent description of motions, distances etc, as measured by different observers whatever their *relative* motion. It is 'special' because it shares with Newtonian mechanics two difficulties, both connected with gravitation. Einstein spent the next ten years devising a 'general theory of relativity' which would overcome these problems. The first concerns the unique nature of the motion produced by gravity: all bodies fall with the same acceleration — a man and a motor car, pushed off a cliff together, will hit the bottom together. This was known to Galileo, and of course Newton took account of it. But other forces do not act in this way: for example a source of electric force, a charged body, may repel or attract other bodies in different ways depending on their masses and electric charges. In Newtonian mechanics and also in special relativity, however, the peculiar nature of gravity was only partially included, by making the 'inertial mass' that governs a body's resistance to motion under the action of forces the same as the 'gravitational mass' that governs its response to gravity. No explanation was given for this remarkable fact.

To appreciate the second problem, carry out the following experiment: stand outside on a starry night and look up. Let your arms hang limply by your sides. Then spin around rapidly. At once two things happen: the stars rotate, and your arms rise up almost to a horizontal position. It is impossible to believe that these effects are unconnected, but Newtonian mechanics and special relativity fail to specify the manner in which the stars' gravitation affects rotating bodies.

Einstein's bold solution to these problems was perhaps the greatest triumph ever achieved by the disciplined imagination. Imagine a laboratory falling freely under gravity (among the stars, say, or in an orbit around the sun). Within that laboratory no gravitational effects can be detected ('weightlessness') and the special theory of relativity gives a correct description of all experiments conducted there. On a larger scale the laboratory pursues a trajectory through space and time ('spacetime') in the

The Four Equations

The heart of the generalized theory of gravitation is expressed in four equations, shown in the accompanying illustration.

$$g_{ik;l} = 0; \quad \Gamma_l = 0; \quad R_{lk} = 0; \quad g_{,s}^{\underline{is}} = 0$$

German lower case G

The equations have the mathematical properties which seem to be required in order to describe the known effects, but they must be tested against observed physical facts before their validity can be absolutely established.

shortest possible time as measured by its own clock. Thus, in some sense, motion under gravity is the 'straightest' possible. In that case, why do orbits never close up on themselves, as the earth's does? Because spacetime is *curved*. The four-dimensional nature of spacetime (three for space, one for time) makes this impossible to visualize except by analogy: a 'shortest' line on a curved surface (e.g. the earth's) can bend. Strictly any such analogy is unnecessary, because Einstein's equations alone are sufficient to predict orbital motions once the cause of the curvature of spacetime is identified. It is *matter* that produces curvature — near a star, spacetime is warped, so that the shortest lines can bend. Thus on this theory gravitation emerges not as a special force but as a property of the geometry of spacetime itself, in which objects pursue the simplest possible motions.

Conceptually, 'general relativity' is completely different from Newtonian theory. Instead of absolute space and absolute time providing a passive arena in which events can happen, the very structure of spacetime is determined by the bodies in it, while at the same time it determines the trajectories of these bodies. Yet its predictions are in most cases identical to Newton's. Only for strong gravitational fields (e.g. near the sun) do the two theories differ. Einstein predicts that light should be delayed and bent when passing close to the sun, that light emitted by the sun should be slightly reddened as a result of having to climb out of the gravitational field, and that the form of the orbits of the planets closest to the sun should be slightly altered. All these effects have been observed, and the measurements favour Einstein and not Newton.

Gravitation is the dominant force in the universe on large scales, and it was natural that Einstein's theory would be applied to cosmology. The combined effect of all the galaxies is to produce an overall curvature of spacetime, and the equations show that the resulting universe cannot be static: it must either be expanding or contracting. In fact E. P. Hubble's observations of the 1920s showed that it is expanding. In recent years, under the impetus provided by radio astronomy, cosmology has become a rapidly-developing branch of science. Its principal theoretical tool remains the general theory of relativity.

The evolution of stars is governed by gravity, and the astrophysical application of Einstein's theory predicts that the ultimate fate of any star more than a few times heavier than the sun is complete collapse under its own weight. When during this collapse the star shrinks below a certain size then, although it will continue to exert gravitational effects, no light can escape from its surface and the star ceases to be visible. Such collapsed objects are called 'black holes'. At the time of writing several objects have been tentatively identified as black holes by their effects on neighbouring visible stars.

It can be convincingly argued that great theories in science 'emerge' when the intellectual climate is right. If Newton, Maxwell and Einstein had never lived, it is probable that others would have devised the theories of mechanics, electromagnetism and special relativity. But general relativity is an exception; the problem and its solution came entirely from Einstein, and if he had never lived it is possible that the theory would still not have been invented.

Einstein's scientific achievements were not confined to relativity. He also led the attempt to discover the laws governing matter on subatomic scales: the mysterious 'dual' nature of light, which behaves like waves when travelling through space and like particles ('photons') when being absorbed or emitted by matter. It was his formulation of the laws of absorption and emission that eventually led to the invention of the laser. However, the final synthesis of this part of physics, the theory of quantum mechanics, came not from Einstein but from Erwin Schrödinger and W. K. Heisenberg. According to this theory, it is impossible to predict the detailed motion of atomic systems: only statistical knowledge is possible, in the form of probabilities. Einstein never accepted that there could be such fundamental limitations to our knowledge of the world. Certainly quantum mechanics was spectacularly successful in explaining the facts of chemistry and the behaviour of solid matter, but Einstein, increasingly isolated as his fellow physicists became absorbed in applications of the new theory, maintained for the rest of his life that: 'God does not play dice with the world.'

From the success of his general theory of relativity until his death in 1955 Einstein lived in the glare of publicity. At first he was simply the eccentric genius who never wore socks. Then he became the champion of Zionism, passionate pacifist and opponent of rearmament. As the Nazis tightened their grip on Germany he saw that they could only be resisted by force, and he abandoned pacifism to the extent of advising President Roosevelt of the possibility of making atomic bombs. When the weapons were actually used on Japan he immediately advocated the establishment of a world authority which would control all weapons of mass destruction. It is hard to prove that any of these various political actions had a significant influence on the turbulent history of the times through which he lived. But even if Einstein the humanitarian may soon be forgotten, Einstein the physicist has already joined the immortals.   M.B.

Foundation Concepts

Most thinking takes place after the acceptance of certain foundation concepts. Such foundation concepts as space, time, energy and matter are so established by our senses, by tradition and by general consent that there is no need to define them every time they are discussed. Philosophers and mathematicians have spent much time discussing these concepts, but always after accepting their obvious nature. Most of our thinking about the world is based on this acceptance. Einstein's thinking led him to challenge not only our thinking about space, time, energy and matter but the very foundation concepts themselves.

Surely energy and matter are distinct? Not so, said Einstein in his special theory of relativity. Matter at rest is only a special form of energy. And if you accelerate matter towards the speed of light it gets heavier and heavier until at the speed of light it would have an infinite mass. This strange idea worked out by a human intellect could be dismissed as the mathematical ravings of a speculator – except that the theory had very practical consequences. Einstein's special theory of relativity provided the conceptual framework for the development of the atom bomb and nuclear energy. There were a lot of other people, like Rutherford, Bohr and Fermi, who did the direct developmental work; nevertheless the basic concept is provided by Einstein's theory. At present we can only use the nuclear energy provided by fission, and this is somewhat messy since there is a production of dangerous radioactive material which stays around for hundreds and thousands of years. It is very likely, however, that we shall soon be able to use the nuclear energy of fusion as in the hydrogen bomb. At this point man will have reached the ultimate in practical physics because he will be using the basic energy of nature itself – the same energy that fuels the sun and the stars. And all this became possible because a human mind found itself challenging the basic distinction between matter and energy.

In his general theory of relativity, Einstein found himself challenging the concepts of space and time and gravity. Newton's explanation of gravity had worked very well and had accounted for the orbits of the planets and other astronomical observations. There hardly seemed need for a new theory. Einstein applied his immense conceptual skills to the challenge not through dissatisfaction but through concern about the true nature of what we conveniently called gravity. The result of his thinking changed the foundation concepts of time and space as thoroughly as he had changed the concepts of energy and matter. For Newton space had been a passive arena in which bodies moved according to the forces, such as gravity, acting on them. For Einstein space and time were no

**Matter at rest is only
a special form of energy**

longer distinct but became a four-dimensional arena. Moreover this arena was not passive but was curved by the presence of matter. This curvature of spacetime by matter was what we know as gravity. In following the 'pull' of gravity objects were simply moving in a direct manner through curved spacetime. Time itself was no longer unchangeable. If the observer moved fast enough, time could be slowed down so that after such a journey the observer would have 'aged' much less than the person who stayed at home. The concepts are profound in their implication and basic in their simplicity. The difficulty in understanding them arises because we have to keep translating these new concepts back into our old, traditional concepts of space and time. It is also true that for ordinary matters in the world the Newtonian concepts work just as well. It is only when one reaches very high velocities or large gravitational masses that the Einstein theories become necessary.

Einstein also did much work on quantum theory, especially in regard to photo-electric absorption and emission. Here a surprise occurred. When W.K. Heisenberg showed that at a certain level of behaviour of the ultimate particles behaviour was no longer deterministic (the uncertainty principle), Einstein refused to accept that things could operate on a chance basis. So a mind that had successfully challenged the foundation concepts themselves was unwilling to let go of the foundation concept of determinism: that everything must have a direct cause.

No one has ever been as successful as Einstein in his challenge to our foundation concepts. But the challenge has been going on in other directions. Freud and Pavlov were led to challenge the foundation concepts of man himself.

Man has always been immensely proud of his mind and his powers of reasoning. The thinking of Einstein alone justifies this pride. The whole of our philosophy is based on man's self-consciousness and observation of his mind in action. Man was his mind. And his mind was his conscious mind. It was never necessary to talk about the conscious mind: there was no other. Of course there were memories and experiences which were not before consciousness at the moment but they were stored in the storeroom of memory. Freud's concepts shattered this complacency. After him, man could never be sure of his self-consciousness. He could never be sure of his intentions or motivation. He could never be sure that he was in control of himself. All these foundation concepts which go to make up our pride in ourselves as thinking creatures had been challenged and would never be the same again.

For Freud the conscious mind was only the shop window that we arranged for the public gaze. It was somewhat like the artificial smile that we arrange on our faces for the polite greeting we extend even to those we dislike. In fact it was even worse than that, because behind the shop window or the arranged smile is a consciousness of what is being done. But Freud insisted that behind our conscious mind was the unconscious mind, and the workings therein were not even visible to ourselves. The whole purpose of psychoanalysis was to help us become aware of what was happening in our own minds. This was a complete reversal of our pride in our minds. According to Freud, by ourselves we could never be aware of what was really going on in our minds.

The concept of conflict and repression was central to Freud's notion of the unconscious mind. We would be unaware of the conflict going on in the

**To challenge
the foundation concepts
of man himself**

Top: The International
Psychoanalytical Congress
at Weimar,
21 September 1911.
Freud and Jung were among
the delegates (above).

unconscious, and would only become aware of what was allowed through into the conscious mind. Freud insisted on the importance of sexual repression as a basis for much of the conflict because this seemed to be the case with so many of his patients. Others, like Adler and Jung, put the emphasis elsewhere. The conflict between sexual desires and the sort of thinking that could be accepted by the individual, let alone society, could clearly provide enough justification for the unconscious mind. Childhood experiences, and especially the 'Oedipal' feelings towards a parent, were seen to be important. Although these aspects became central to Freud's developing theories they were not central to his basic concept of the unconscious mind.

The foundation concepts challenged by Freud directly or indirectly were: self and self-consciousness; the conscious mind and its rational conscious decisions; motivation and intention; the neutrality of our perceptions. After Freud, if a person thought that he was acting for some reason he could never be sure that the conscious motive was not a 'sublimation' of some unconscious feeling or working out of some unseen conflict. People were encouraged to feel that they no longer knew themselves or had control over their behaviour. Moreover the insight path to self-awareness was firmly blocked.

The practical consequences of Freud's concepts were of two sorts. Psychoanalysis became established practice, especially in the United States, and there was an increased emphasis on psychotherapy, even if it did not go as far as psychoanalysis. Various techniques and group methods of encouraging self-awareness have come and gone or stayed. These are the direct practical consequences. The less direct, but more important consequences, are concerned with man's loss of confidence in himself. Freud had challenged the foundation concept of self-awareness and shown that it was impossible. On this concept had rested rational decision, motivation, choice, moral responsibility and all the other factors that had provided the basis for self-control and self-controlled behaviour. The Protestant ethic of direct responsibility was hit even harder than the Catholic, which had some provision for the dark forces of the soul in its system of confession.

An even more damaging blow to man's self-esteem was to be provided by Pavlov, whose work led unintentionally to a challenge of the foundation concepts of mind itself and of free will. If man responded to his environment by reflexes and if, through the process of conditioning, these reflexes could become attached to different features in his environment, then mind was only an illusion. Man became a cleverly adapting machine responding to, and being controlled by, his environment. The basic experiment in which the sound of a bell led to the salivation of Pavlov's dogs provided a solid base for the various theories of associationism and determinism that had for a long time been in the attic of philosophy. Suddenly they could become central, displacing the metaphysical notions about man's mind and decision. Soul, self and free will have no immediate place in Pavlov's view of things.

Soul, self and free will have no immediate place in Pavlov's view of things

The implications of Pavlov's work were seen at once. The actualization of the implications had to wait for the work of the behaviourist school of psychology, and in particular the work of Skinner. Skinner showed that behaviour could be 'shaped' by breaking down an action into small parts and rewarding the correct performance of each small section. In this way he could train pigeons to play a miniature piano. It is also the method used by animal trainers. There is no question that behaviour can be shaped in this way, completely bypassing conscious decision or learning. This applies to people as well as animals. The point at issue is no longer whether this is possible but as to how far this applies to the more complex behaviour of humans. Is it enough to say that free will is an illusion but as an illusion has subjective reality, using the pragmatism of William James?

Pavlov approached this problem by saying that our internal environment included the concepts of self, free will, religious ideals, social responsibilities and duties, and that we could become conditioned to these just as easily as to the obvious features of the external environment. In fact he saw no problem. In this view it is the duty of civilization and literature to fill our internal environment with concepts and models which, through conditioning, can control our behaviour. The problem can also be looked at in another way. If we draw the circle that is to encompass all we regard as self to include the past experiences and present motivation, then that composite self will act 'freely' in its dealings with the environment. It will do what it wants to do. But the 'it' of self will have already included the determining factors. This is close to the existentialist view that as phenomena we are a bundle of our experiences. If, on the other hand, the circle is drawn to exclude these influences then they do become determining factors or conditioning factors of the internal environment. So the illusion or actuality of free will can be maintained.

However we regard the problem of free will, the basic concept remains: that

Neither Einstein nor Freud nor Pavlov actually set out to challenge these foundation concepts

man is not rationally in control of his behaviour, which is controlled by the environment and can even be manipulated without man's consent.

In the work of Einstein, Pavlov and Freud we can see a basic challenge to the very foundation concepts of our civilization. Once these concepts have been changed it becomes impossible to treat them as unchangeable, whether or not one is convinced of the validity of the new concepts or the extent of their implications. What is interesting, in terms of thinking, is that neither Einstein nor Freud nor Pavlov actually set out to challenge these foundation concepts. Einstein started by asking himself what would happen if an observer were able to travel with the speed of light: what would such an observer see? This led him on, through a chain of concepts and mathematical reasoning, to end up with new concepts that challenged space, time, matter and energy. Freud started by observing how hypnosis, as practised by Charcot, could produce hysterical manifestations. He went on to suppose that auto-suggestion might produce similar effects in patients and so account for neuroses. Gradually this led to the concept of the unconscious mind, and this in turn to the source of the conflicts. It must be remembered that all the while Freud was practising as a therapist and needed a practical conceptual framework. Pavlov started by doing physiological work on the digestive system, and was only made aware of the effect of conditioning by accident and observation. Once he had become aware of it he worked out the principles, seeing in them a justification for the materialistic approach to psychology that he favoured.

On the whole we are rather poor at changing our concepts. And yet concept changes are more likely to lead to radically new ideas than is a re-sorting of existing concepts. It is difficult to change concepts by direct challenge and examination because when we look at a concept we see it embedded in the solid structure of its implications and consequences. Anything we try and put in its place must fill the gap caused by removing the original concept – and since it must fill the gap it cannot be significantly different. That is why concept changes tend to be oblique, and to occur when the surroundings are changed first. Or we must have the courage to think through a concept change that at first must seem inferior to what it replaces.

Keynes

It was inevitable that in time economics would become as important as politics, religion or science. Keynes was especially concerned with the economics of recession and unemployment. Conventional wisdom suggested a cutting back in wages and spending during a recession. Keynes turned this upside down and insisted on increased government spending to give people more purchasing power.

1883-1946

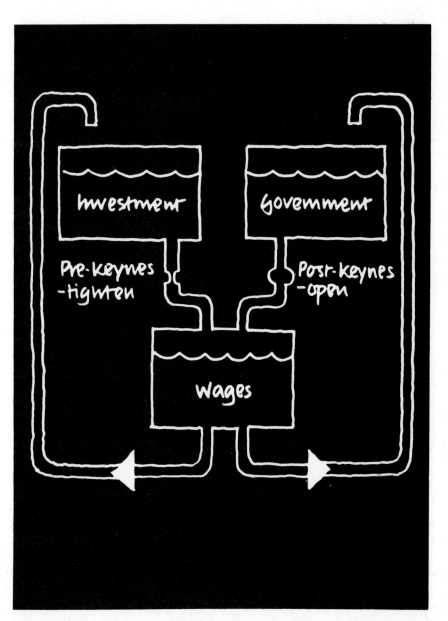

**His intellectual integrity
made him challenge
orthodox views**

John Maynard Keynes, the first and last Baron Keynes of Tilton, became the world's leading economist, both by the clarity of his thought and by the undeniable influence he had on policy. It would be necessary to go back to Adam Smith to find an economist of comparable influence.

Keynes' father, John Neville Keynes, was a Cambridge don, lecturing on logic and political economy. The intellectual stimulus of his father and of the many visitors to the Keynes' home in Harvey Road probably influenced the boy and the young man and led him to be convinced that 'a little clear thinking' or 'more lucidity' could solve most problems. After tuition from his father Keynes went to Eton, and on to King's College, Cambridge. He became a Fellow of King's in 1910, and remained one for the rest of his life, becoming Bursar and also using his skills as a practical businessman to improve his beloved college's finances. He studied economics and philosophy, and was greatly influenced by W. E. Johnson, Alfred Marshall, Henry Sidgwick and A. N. Whitehead. Joining the India Office he became, in 1913, a member of the Royal Commission on Indian currency and finance.

Although the name 'Keynes' is known and his influence recognized by many today, he came to public prominence when, at the age of thirty-five, he became the principal representative of the Treasury, with power to speak for the Chancellor of the Exchequer, at the Versailles peace conference following the First World War. Keynes found himself in strong disagreement with the proposed plan for reparations, and resigned his post to return to academic life.

The continuing influence of Keynes on the question of reparations made sure that the punishing conditions imposed on the vanquished were not repeated following the Second World War. Back at Cambridge he wrote *The Economic Consequences of Peace*, which was published in 1919 in Britain and 1920 in the USA and had considerable impact. People started discussing the basis of the Peace Treaty and the fairness of the Treaty rather than actual clauses. Adolf Hitler was not uninterested in the influence of Keynes' writing, and in subsequent speeches exploited the moral issues of the Treaty to the maximum. It has been said that it was a pity that Keynes' great economic work *The General Theory* . . . had not been written and published before *The Economic Consequences of Peace*.

Keynes was essentially a practical man, as his work as the first Chairman of the Arts Council, his position in the insurance world, his appointments as a civil servant, his editorship of the renowned *Economic Journal* show. In addition, at his death, he left a personal fortune of £400,000. His friends were not limited to academics and civil servants and his cultural interests embraced ballet, theatre, opera and painting. He belonged to the 'Bloomsbury Group' whose members included Virginia Woolf, Duncan Grant, Clive Bell and Lytton Strachey, and in 1925 he married the famous Russian dancer Lydia Lopokova.

The expression 'Keynesian theory' is partly a misnomer, and 'Keynesian theor*ies*' would be more accurate, but it is true that Keynes will be remembered mainly for his searching economic analysis aimed at the reduction of mass unemployment, which haunted the Western world between two world wars. Keynes had attacked the British government's decision in 1925 to return to the gold standard: in this action he saw something of the seeds of the economic depression of the Thirties.

In Britain unemployment never fell below ten per cent of the working population between 1921 and 1939, and in the early Thirties it was twenty per cent. In Germany in 1931 5,000,000 of the working population of 21,000,000 were without work. In the same year in the United States 12,600,000 were unemployed out of 50,400,000. The failure of the countries to recover was without precedence in the economic history of industrial society. Not only were people without work but their unemployment had lasted for anything up to four years. In this period of economic depression millions of pigs, calves, sheep and cattle were destroyed. Milk and wine were poured down drains. National newspapers in 1933 described how the sugar position was improving by the destruction of stocks, and how a hurricane in Cuba helped! But people near starvation point were unlikely to appreciate the niceties of the

Opposite: Keynes as a young man; a watercolour by Gwen Raverat.
Below: Keynes with his wife, the Russian ballet dancer
Lydia Lopokova.

economic debate going on all around them. Economists only seemed able to analyse the situation, but could not find solutions. Trade cycles had exercised many minds over the centuries, but Keynes found it difficult to accept any of the explanations and cures. When once it became evident to him that the classical theory could not explain, or give remedies for, mass unemployment, his intellectual integrity made him challenge orthodox views with ever-increasing severity and without regard to what he had taught and believed in the past.

Thousands of words have been written about the Keynesian theory, and when *The General Theory of Employment, Interest and Money* was published in 1936 it had an immediate and important influence on the teaching of economics. But by 1936 the worst of the depression was receding, and the impact of the actual publication of this book on the millions of unemployed was marginal. However Keynes had the main outline of his theory ready in 1932, and through his teaching, his conversations with Treasury officials and members of government, together with his other writings, the influence of his thought and reasoning was strongly felt. Probably more important from a chronological point of view was the publication of his *Treatise on Money* in 1930. In this book, which was a stepping stone to *The General Theory*, he shows clearly what happens when there is disparity between saving and investment. A clue to understanding Keynesian theory lies in the interpretation of these words. The layman could define 'saving' as 'not spending', and the word 'investment' could mean anything from putting spare cash into a bank to backing a horse. The Classical economists (an expression coined by Karl Marx) such as David Ricardo, James Mill, John Stuart Mill, Edgeworth and Arthur Pigou, believed that all savings made by the individual flowed through the banks to the business community, so that entrepreneurs could use these 'savings' for 'investment' purposes to purchase new machinery and plant or put up new factories. This in turn created work, and the wages paid when the new machinery was being manufactured or the factory built, flowed back again into the economic system of a country. Keynes refuted this theory and stated clearly that there was no automatic mechanism to equate the total demand and supply of productive labour.

The traditional method of dealing with the problems of the trade cycle was to aim at economies. No wonder that economics was known as the 'dismal science'. All economists preached scarcity. Economy was the theme in Britain and unemployment pay was cut and the means test introduced in 1931. Apart from the high rates of unemployment in Western industrial countries, those fortunate enough to have work found that their wages and salaries were

reduced. This might work for the individual firm or company but not for the country as a whole. Keynes admitted that a reduction in wage rates could in theory be beneficial, and if this lowered prices of goods, leaving more in the pockets of the consumer, he would have more cash to 'save'. This extra amount of savings could cause a lowering of interest rates because there were more savings available, and businessmen would be keen to take advantage of this and borrow (i.e. invest) for capital items such as new plant and machinery or new factories. This action would create new employment and the wages earned would add to total demand and the upturn of the trade cycle would come.

But it did not work out that way. Keynes believed that there exists a level of interest rate below which further increases in money supply are simply added to idle balances at the bank rather than being used to finance investment. Wage cuts or not, the economy would remain at this point of economic stagnation with chronic unemployment. Keynes revolted against the fatalism of orthodox economics in the face of mass unemployment, arguing for the control of all forms of investment, so as to combine collective direction with individual initiative and for the proper timing of public expenditure, which he argued should be increased at the onset of a recession so as to increase employment and thus through the payment of wages raise spending power and stimulate business investment. This could possibly be summed up as: if private enterprise will not invest in times of recession, the state must, even if it does not mean a balanced budget. The study that Keynes made of investment decisions, savings and general monetary theories led to the development of the National Accounts which play such an important part in the economic planning of the world today. One great advantage of the Keynes proposals was that he prescribed remedies which became obvious, were popular and pleasant. Instead of the Scrooge-like activities of government which demanded economies, Keynes was saying 'spend'. Keynes used traditional methods of analysis for problems, but when these traditional methods became inadequate he invented new ones and as a result brought about a revolution in thought in which the unthinkable became the obvious.

Socialists had been using the argument for state intervention in economic activity for a century. But this represented a permanent change in the structure of industry and was aimed at the eventual destruction of the capitalist system. Keynes was hardly advocating such drastic action. It is true that in the Thirties the Trade Union Congress in Britain had demanded an extension of public works to relieve unemployment, but something of Keynesian thought had been assimilated by the Congress.

In the United States, President Roosevelt under the 'New Deal' policy raised pay instead of reducing it and spent public money instead of saving it. The Tennessee Valley Authority which was

Left: In attacking the British government's decision to return to the gold standard in 1925, Keynes foresaw the dangers of a severe deflation and predicted mass unemployment. By 1926 the effects were already being felt and demands for wage cuts precipitated a general strike.
Below: Keynes in his study, 1940.

established in 1933 was an example of this policy. Lord Salter has said: 'In the United States the New Deal under Roosevelt and the new full employment policies in Britain owe more to Keynes than can ever be precisely assessed.' There is no proof that there was direct influence by Keynes on Roosevelt, but in the 'Brains Trust' which advised the President, Keynes had many disciples.

In Britain many economic study groups existed and these advocated a change from the orthodox economic views. Individuals such as Oswald Mosley and Harold Macmillan, to mention but two British politicians, held views which differed fundamentally from those held by their political colleagues. But all had been influenced to some extent by the writings and teaching of Keynes.

The genius of Keynes lay in his weighty contributions to the principles of economic science, which he achieved by questioning accepted assumptions; in his ability to secure public interest in the practical application of economics on critical occasions; and probably not least in his attractive prose style. These three factors made him stand head and shoulders above all others working in the same field.

Keynes challenged economic thought in much the same way that Einstein challenged Newton and Euclid. In *Keynes: Aspects of the Man and his Work* (1974), Sir Roy Harrod has said:

> Keynes was the very rare combination of a great master of eonomic theory, he was a great theorist in general, in logic and so on, with one who had at the same time a very fine understanding of what was actually happening in the world, the practical problems, the practicabilities of implementing a theory and so on. He was an intense realist in all those things, and that is an unusual combination. I think the realists are apt to be a little shaky when you take them on to pure theory, and the pure theorists are apt to be a little unpractical when you ask them what should be done in such and such a case.

So in the Thirties Keynes had the mental ability and the drive to influence people into deciding that the fatalism of the orthodox economists should be overturned in the face of mass employment.

As we move into the last decades of the twentieth century, with great economic uncertainty for the developed and developing world, the question is repeatedly asked: 'What would Keynes have thought and done in the present economic circumstances?' A study of this great man shows, with clarity, that he would not have fallen into the basic error of grafting yesterday's solutions onto today's problems.   J.P.

Wiener introduced the basic concept of cybernetics in which control of
a system is obtained by feedback from some point in the system. The perceived
error in the aim of a gun feeds back to correct the aim. The concept is
central to the understanding of complex dynamic systems and as such
is probably the key concept to our understanding of society and nature.

1894-1964

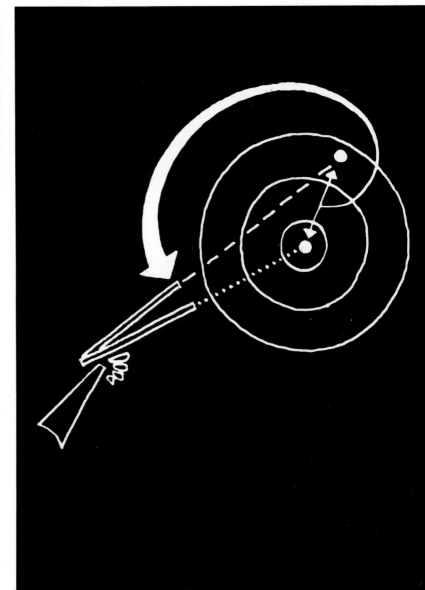

Norbert Wiener 'fathered' cybernetics (from the Greek *Kybernetes*, governor or steersman), the study of control and communication in the animal and the machine. His realization that mathematical and engineering principles could usefully be applied in order to gain a better understanding of living beings was thought by American publishers to be a concept of no importance or interest, so his book *Cybernetics* had first to be printed by a modest Parisian company. *Cybernetics* went on to become a scientific bestseller, and Wiener's ideas seeded an explosively increasing number of research investigations throughout the world.

Wiener was in his early fifties when his concepts of cybernetics reached maturity. This is very late in the life of a man who was thought a child prodigy in his own time. Born in 1894 into an academic family, he received encouragement from his father, Leo Wiener, a professor of Slavonic languages and literature in Harvard University. He was educated at Harvard and Cornell Universities, obtaining a Bachelor of Arts degree at the age of fourteen; at nineteen he was awarded a Doctor of Philosophy degree at Harvard for a thesis in which he tackled some topics in mathematical logic first developed by Whitehead and Russell. He was quick to realize and agree with Russell that logic, at that time commonly considered outside the mathematician's range of interest, was fundamental to the subject.

At the age of twenty-five he took up a professorship in mathematics at the Massachusetts Institute of Technology, where he remained for the rest of his life.

Norbert Wiener (right) at the Cybernetics Congress in Paris, 1951, playing chess on an automatic chess machine.

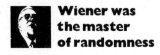

Wiener was the master of randomness

During the next twenty-five years Wiener's contribution to mathematics was sustained and imaginative. Even after the publication of *Cybernetics* (in 1948) he published two books on this major research, *The Extrapolation, Interpretation and Smoothing of Stationary Time Series* (1949) and *Non-Linear Problems in Random Theory* (1958).

Wiener was depressed by the nature of the events leading up to, and the subsequent course of, the Second World War. He felt a compelling need to apply his talent to something which would make a tangible contribution towards the defeat of Germany. He saw that an improvement in the accuracy of anti-aircraft artillery could restore the power balance to a country such as England, faced with an enemy with fast and manoeuvrable airplanes. The problem was to track an enemy plane and then to fire a shell into its flight path in a direction which would maximize the chances of hitting it. The tracking would have to be measured and the optimal

flight path calculated very rapidly. Clearly, rapid electronic computing machinery could do this task, the major difficulty being: how does one account for the fact that the pilot may be trying to avoid gunfire? The resolution of this problem was the germ which led eventually to cybernetics. In order for the computer to do its work it would be necessary to represent the pilot's actions in some rigorous way. It is easy to realize that if the pilot wishes to create as much of a surprise for his pursuers as possible, he must introduce some randomness in his manoeuvres. Wiener was the master of randomness through his interest in stochastic systems. This enabled him to create flight prediction models which would be optimal despite the possible intervention of an intelligent pilot.

The behaviour of a human being in the above system had been successfully, though fairly simply, analysed as if he were a machine. Could more complicated activities be modelled? Perhaps rather than being interested directly in such questions, Wiener was

Left: Wiener lecturing at the Massachusetts Institute of Technology. Right: Wiener's ideas on the correlations between the human nervous system and electrical circuitry led to the development of the autocorrelator, a device for analyzing electrical wave forms. Here he is watching his own autocorrelogram being computed on the correlator system for brain potentials.

passionately concerned with why one should wish to model human behaviour. First, a rigorous understanding of the human, seen as a machine, might remove some of the haphazardness found in curing human ailments, particularly informational ailments occurring in mental disorders. Second, Wiener had visions of actually being able to replace faulty human mechanisms by artificial ones, this again being dependent on a formal understanding of the former.

Wiener's concept of cybernetics has often been misquoted and misunderstood. Some will say that cybernetics advocates the replacement of human beings by machines. Wiener mentioned this only in the narrowest sense, and that is in areas where it would relieve human misery and the exploitation of human beings. In fact, he was highly conscious of the possible dangers of a misuse of fast computing machinery and in his introduction to *Cybernetics* he states:

The first revolution . . . was the devaluation of the human arm by the competition of machinery . . . The modern industrial revolution is similarly bound to devalue the human brain at least in its simpler and routine decisions . . . The answer, of course, is to have a society based on human values other than buying and selling.

What then were the distinct, new aspects of Wiener's thought? Before exploring an answer to that question it is necessary to understand the existence at the time of two traditions. First, a study of mind and brain was considered to be solely in the province of the philosopher, the psychologist, the psychiatrist, and, in the case of the brain only, the neurophysiologist. Wiener added the mathematician-communications engineer to this list for the sole reason that the brain must be an information-processing machine, and mind should be capable of being expressed in informational terms. Second, control aspects of human functioning were left entirely to the medic or the physiologist. Wiener argued that the mathematician-control engineer could have a useful contribution to make in the analysis of both function and malfunction. For

A study of the limitations of a logical machine is relevant to a study of thinking

example, he suggested that a simple act such as picking up a pencil must be the result of control signalling in the human being very similar to that required to position a gun turret. The process is called feedback, and consists of controlling the actuators, or muscles, of a mechanism (say, the hand) from a measurement of how much of the task still remains to be done (i.e. the distance of the hand from the pencil, or the gun from its desired firing position). It is well known to the engineer that if certain information regarding the rate of change of this discrepancy is not used in the control of the actuator, or if too much such information is used, the gun will overshoot the desired position and possibly enter an uncontrolled oscillation about the desired end point. Wiener was delighted to find that such oscillations were reported in human beings and labelled by medics as *ataxia* or purpose tremors. The latter is particularly true in cases of injury to a part of the brain called the cerebellum. This leads the engineer to conclude that part of the function of the cerebellum must be to compute 'rate-of-change' information, a fact probably entirely missed by the medic.

In *Cybernetics*, Wiener explains why mechanistic ideas are unpalatable to philosophers. He claims that the latter are mainly aware of Newtonian mechanisms concerned with collisions between rigid bodies, clockwork machines and so on. Ingeniously he pinpoints the cause of the trouble: Newton's concept of 'reversible' time. For example, if one were to take a cinema film of the motions of bodies such as the planets, one would, by a great deal of observation, infer the same laws of dynamics irrespectively of whether the film was being shown forwards or backwards. But a film of the evolution of living creatures shown backwards would present a very different story from that which would be seen were the film shown the right way round. Wiener firmly believed that statistical mechanics, which does not assume reversibility in its concept of time, would be far more applicable in the study of living things. (It is now known that statistical mechanics has certain inadequacies, and more abstract but less random mathematical notions are used in the modelling of living things.)

The second step in *Cybernetics* is the explanation of a formal theory of information which may be applicable to a study of the human brain as an information-processing machine. This theory was developed by Claude Shannon of the Bell Telephone Laboratories, and uses 'the probability of an event' to develop a measure of information. Wiener is quick to point to the similarity between this concept and, mathematically, an almost equivalent one in the definition of energy in statistical mechanics. He draws the parallel between energy being the lifeblood of the body where information is the lifeblood of the mind.

In *Cybernetics* Wiener also acknowledges his fascination for digital computing machines and reverts to his earlier interests in mathematics: logic and philosophy. The digital computer is entirely a logical machine. The temptation to draw a simplistic comparison between the computer as a logical machine and the human as a logical animal must have presented itself to Wiener. Nonetheless, Wiener did not fall into this trap, and his contrast between the two devices is sober and yet subtle. The study of the logical machine, he points out, is a study of the nature of logic itself, and since logic is limited by the limitations of the human mind when engaged in that activity known as thinking, a study of the limitations of a logical machine is relevant to a study of thinking. This is a long, long way from the simplistic misinterpretation of the same argument that a logical machine is a thinking machine. Indeed, in *God and Golem Inc.* Wiener writes a great deal about the stupidity of a machine when compared with the subtlety of human judgment.

In a chapter of *Cybernetics* entitled 'Gestalts and Universals', Wiener is concerned with hypothetical mechanisms which would go beyond the capabilities of a standard computer. He discusses such devices because once one has a plausible model which performs a complex activity there is no doubt that the activity itself becomes better understood. Here he examines mechanisms which have the property of recognizing similarities between perceptual events (e.g. classifying a large and a small triangle in the same way). The ideas in this chapter have only recently come under scrutiny again but in the intervening period they were abandoned because they did not lead to the exploitation of commercial digital computers.

Much has flourished under the heading of cybernetics which in some way involves a study of organizations and society. Although allowing that information is, at a theoretical level, a parameter of economics and politics, Wiener strongly disagreed with attempts to apply cybernetics to management, particularly in a capitalist system. He saw too many faults with the system itself. Later he put his view even more strongly: 'I mention this matter because of the considerable, and I think false, hopes which some of my friends have built for the social efficacy of whatever new ways of thinking this book may contain ... In this, I maintain, they show an excessive optimism and a misunderstanding of the nature of all scientific achievement.'

There is no doubt that Wiener was one of the most powerful minds of this century. In some ways, however, it is a pity that the attention which his technical thought has received has overshadowed the strong and passionate sense of moral justice for which he probably would have preferred to be remembered.   I.A.

Sartre

As the most public exponent of existentialism Sartre turned his back on the traditional concern with the essence of man and destiny and he proclaimed that man should face immediate and total reality accepting its meaninglessness instead of trying forever to analyze it. Man only existed as man when he was conscious of his rebellion against the tide of circumstance.

1905-

Jean-Paul Sartre did not invent existentialism. The term was first coined by his compatriot Gabriel Marcel as *existentialisme*, and many Germans who consider themselves as representatives of *Existenzphilosophie* vehemently deny that there are connections with French thinking. Nor is Sartre's own brand of existentialism the only one. He is an atheist humanist. Marcel was a Christian. Sartre's friend Maurice Merleau-Ponty, also an existentialist, sharply criticized his attitude to Communism – and accused him of being a concealed Cartesian dualist. The problems that Sartre's erstwhile friend Albert Camus chose to confront, in his literary works and essays, were undeniably existentialist; yet he believed in natural human rights – which means that, technically, he was not any kind of existentialist – and he, too, quarrelled (vehemently) with Sartre over Communism. But it is in Sartre's prolific work as novelist, playwright, metaphysician, critic, polemicist, political activist and editor that we may most clearly see how and why this

mode of thought has arisen, and what valid answers and what difficulties it presents. Existentialism is a trend of thought of which Sartre has been the apogee; it is not, and this must be re-emphasized, his invention. (Ancestors of the existentialist tendency of thought include St Augustine and Blaise Pascal.)

In the nineteenth century Nietzsche pronounced that God was dead. There has been argument as to exactly what he meant by this cataclysmic statement; but all that is important here is that he was certainly diagnosing what he saw as the human predicament at that time, that he advocated action based on this premiss, and that almost everyone took him literally (some were shocked, others overjoyed).

Nietzsche became incapacitated before he was able to read the works of a Dane then as obscure as himself, Sören Kierkegaard (1813–55) whose thinking is even more crucial to the formation of existentialism than is Nietzsche's. We can know nothing at all about truth, he said. There is no evidence. He relished this. He was speaking of the fundamental question: 'Why are we here?' It is a question that troubles everyone. His solution was not mystical but, simply, miraculous. Life, he stated, is horrible, meaningless and absurd. We must first accept this as a fact. We must not delude ourselves into believing – as Socrates and then Plato after him had confidently stated – that man only 'learns' what he already knows: that learning is a process of recognition by the shock which sharply dialectical discussion applies. We must take the terrible risk, admittedly a 'leap into the absurd', of faith: faith that the ridiculous notion of Jesus Christ having been an earthly incarnation of God is true. This solution is no more properly philosophical than is the pragmatism of William James. It is clearly as absurd, logically, to speak of the miracle of Jesus as it is to define truth as whatever may 'work'. But the solution brings psychology, in the sense of what actually happens in people's minds, into philosophy. We may take Kierkegaard's solution as, among other things, a description of certain kinds of subjective reality.

What the existentialists who came after Kierkegaard have in common is their conviction that existence precedes essence – our existence on earth, rather than the establishment of absolute truths, is the crucial issue; thus the commitment of Kierkegaard himself, Nietzsche, Marcel, Karl Jaspers, Merleau-Ponty and all other existentialists to immediate engagement with the world. The basis of any existentialist philosophy is that it insists upon the necessity of reflecting upon man's being in categories different from that in which the being of things is considered. For an existentialist I do not 'have' my body – I 'am' my body. I am a 'being-in-the-world'. The existentialist may or may not believe in God; he may be an

Right: 'I am not here as a politician but as an intellectual.' Sartre addressing students in the Sorbonne in May 1968. Left: Sartre, 1964.

agnostic; but he is inevitably hostile to theory, in favour of the particular and the concrete, and devoted to the non-abstract untidiness of actual life (as distinct from the unnatural neatness of philosophical theories). In existentialism the individual is supreme. For Plato and for most other philosophers individuality is inferior: man's true nature consists in his discovering his true function. But for existentialists a person can become himself only by facing the agony of choice. Existence must precede whatever may come after it (for Sartre a reified Marxism, for Marcel a community of Christians, and so on). Philosophy is emphatically not a science but a means of making being actual.

Sartre is aware of Kierkegaard, but chooses to reject his particular kind of 'leap into absurdity'. A modern man, he has transformed the nature of the 'leap'. It is directly into absurdity: into atheism. To this extent Sartre is an empiricist. There is (he is convinced) no

evidence either of a God or of a purpose directing life on earth. Very well: life itself is totally absurd, contingent, meaningless. What, then, shall we do? First and foremost we must reject all ideas of 'essence', of seeking for 'absolute truth'. He rejects Kierkegaard's 'miracle' of faith – but he does take over his notion of 'terrible risk'. Into what belief, if any, does Sartre wish himself (and us) to 'leap'? And does he believe in it and does he really expect us to believe in it? The answers are, respectively, 'Marxism', and 'No'.

Sartre has never been a member of the Communist Party; and yet his enterprise has for long appeared to be to construct a defence of its existence. Absurd? Yes; but Sartre has taken absurdity as the basic motive of his enterprise: he has had the courage to work from it as a premiss. In this, it must be admitted, he is in key with his times. Who, it may be asked, after two devastating world wars followed by a warlike, nerve-wracked and corrupt period, is any

201

Sartre and Simone de Beauvoir leaving a Paris police station after being arrested for distributing a radical student newspaper, June 1970.

longer convinced by such concepts as 'the spiritual meaningfulness of the universe'? Sartre's atheistic existentialism attempts to provide one solution – and his own evident honesty and anguish are parallel to our own. So, it must be said, are his confusions . . .

Sartre went to Germany to learn from the phenomenologist Edmund Husserl and from his pupil Martin Heidegger. He was also, at this early stage, eagerly absorbing the dialectical materialism of Karl Marx. Sartre's friend Raymond Aron – now a shrewd if reluctant critic of the left to which Sartre remains so unremittingly attached – had said to him in a Montparnasse nightclub, when he ordered an apricot brandy: 'You see, little comrade, if you are a phenomenologist, you can talk about this drink and it will be philosophy.' Sartre studied under Husserl and Heidegger – and made psychology (especially in the sense that eating, drinking, excreting, vomiting and making love are psychology) into a 'philosophy'. After the war his ideas reverberated from the Left Bank throughout Europe.

Husserl was not in the least interested in psychology; but he was interested in going 'back to the things themselves!' He meant by this that he wanted to reduce philosophy to mere notions perceived by consciousness: imaginary notions were therefore as valid, in this sense, as 'real' ones. The mind, he believed, was 'intentionalist': it passes from problem-solving to its own assertions of probabilities. Heidegger took phenomenology over: for him it was a spyglass by which we may look into the nature of being.

Sartre's father, a French naval officer, died while Jean-Paul was an infant. He does not remember him, and accepts the verdict of a psychoanalyst that he has no 'superego'. Meanwhile he regarded his mother, he remarks, as an 'elder sister', whom he 'peacefully possessed'. He became absorbed in books, and they seemed more real to him than the world: he sought, he tells us in his autobiography, the idea rather than the thing. But after he had entered adult life he reversed this. The fullest and most coherent statement of his philosophy is to be found in his first novel: *Nausea* (1938). This describes his own experiences as a young man teaching philosophy at Le Havre. His hero experiences *nausea* as he encounters Kierkegaardian meaninglessness; he also wishes to detach himself from *les salauds* ('filthy swine'), complacent middle-class people who lull themselves into a false stability by pretending that their world is 'all right'. In *The Roads to Freedom*, the trilogy of novels that appeared in the forties, Sartre further develops his notion of *mauvaise foi*, 'bad faith': he portrays a variety of people living on the edge of the crisis of the Second World War, and convincingly shows how each of them evades the central existentialist issue of *choosing* to be himself, clinging to this or that mythology and to the 'foulness' of his or her own past, rather than deciding to be what he makes himself. His hero Mathieu is aware of the problem. Sartre seemed to have killed him off at the end. Published fragments of a fourth volume make it clear that Mathieu is not dead – yet Sartre has not finished the book.

After writing some excellent plays and screen plays Sartre has gradually abandoned imaginative literature. Yet he still fails to fulfil his projects. *Being and Nothingness* (1943) is his principal philosophical work. Unlike his novels, stories and plays it is hard going; yet, often autobiographical in its descriptions of mental states, it gives phenomenological substance to Sartre's brilliantly lucid fictional analyses of motive. In it the notion of 'freedom' changes: at one time it is a will-o'-the-wisp beckoning us towards decency, at another it is merely a notion of openness (an uncreated world is at least a free one), at another it is the more difficult concept of experience correctly defined – and experience for Sartre is what man immediately is. *Being and Nothingness* was to have been followed by a work on ethics (*L'Homme*), but this never appeared. Why?

Because Sartre has always been torn between his artistic, imaginative appreciation of the nature of experience and his genuinely humanitarian impulses he has never succeeded in concluding a synthesis of them. The massive *Critique of Dialectic* (*Critique de la raison dialectique*, 1960), an attempt to give Marxism a 'human face', was pre-empted by an equally massive analysis of Flaubert's (or Sartre's?) sexuality; but the latter, too, is unfinished. What will come next?

Sartre's view of property has been criticized by Communists since his insistence that 'to possess means to unite oneself with the object possessed under the sign of appropriation' (this extends to sexuality), is not in accordance with the official Marxist line. He himself has for the most part lived with as little property as possible in hotel rooms, and neither he nor his lifelong companion Simone de Beauvoir has ever considered marriage.

Jean-Paul Sartre's greatest achievement is in the novel and the drama, in which, perhaps incomparably in our century, he can describe man's failure to do the necessary thing: to make his immediate experience into himself. Bleak though he is, he here affirms an instinct in us towards justice and decency. But his philosophy is not negligible. It contains, at its most powerful, analyses of introspective processes that are matched only in his own fiction. And in its unhappy and puzzled fumblings towards a humanist reification of Marxism it parallels, with high intelligence, a growing suspicion of capitalism that is now acknowledged even by members of the right.   M.S.-S.

Coping with Complexity

Technological improvement itself has a geometric trend

Malthus was right to fear a geometric increase in population. The geometric increase in complexity is, however, creating an even bigger problem. Technological improvement itself has a geometric trend. Until the beginning of the nineteenth century man had never travelled faster than the speed of a galloping horse. Within a century railways had been well established and were reaching relatively high speeds. The twentieth century saw the birth of the motorcar and the aeroplane. Within the experience of people still alive the aeroplane has developed from the Wright brothers' flying crate to jumbo jets seating four hundred passengers, flying thirty thousand feet up and travelling for up to five thousand miles without stopping. The technology of communication, production and destruction has increased at a parallel pace. The result of all this has been to raise the expectancies of people, to knit the world into a single economic whole and to make the old methods of reducing tension by war obsolete. The result is that thinkers have to cope with rapidly increasing complexity. Fortunately computers can cope with the information-processing side of complexity. But they cannot cope with the idea side, which still remains the duty of human thinkers.

Keynes, Wiener and Sartre were all thinkers who attempted to cope with complexity. It may be argued whether in each case history will accept their classification as great thinkers. At the moment, however, their influence and the trend of their thinking earn them this classification. In certain respects the views of Keynes may already be outmoded. Nevertheless his influence on the complexity of modern economics has been profound, and even those who now find him outmoded do so within his own framework. Ricardo and Adam Smith may possibly have been greater in stature as economists, but they were not dealing with anything like the complexity with which Keynes had to cope. Wiener is the father of cybernetics, a concept which must rank as one of the half dozen greatest of all time. Much that is now included under cybernetics was not contributed by Wiener but was already present in the field, or has come into it through the perceptions of other workers. Nevertheless Wiener deserves the credit for crystallizing the concept and giving it a solid base. Sartre is only one amongst the existentialists, and not the first, for this honour would go to Kierkegaard. Others like Marcel and Heidegger had an important contemporary influence, and an historic influence may be seen in St Augustine, William James and Nietzsche. Nevertheless Sartre has provided the focusing and communication point that has made existentialism so strong an influence.

All of a sudden, on a worldwide scale, economics has almost replaced religion and politics as the dominant influence on people's lives. Their employment, standard of living and expectancies depend as much on the economic skill of their government as on anything else. The poorer countries of the world have an even harsher dependence on the economic skill of the rest, for if this is employed skilfully but selfishly they will suffer greatly. From now on it seems that some of the greatest minds will have to apply themselves to coping with the complexities of economics. Keynes was the first of this breed.

The thinking of Keynes covered a wide range of economic fields, from the economic consequences of the Versailles treaty to the economics of running the Second World War. His *Treatise on Money* introduces new concepts and a new conceptual framework which is carried forward in his major work *The General Theory of Employment, Interest and Money*. Since unemployment and depression were so real a part of the world in which he lived, much of his most powerful thinking was directed towards these problems. He was interested in classifying the forces that determined the level of output as a whole. He disagreed profoundly with the then current economic wisdom that high unemployment meant that wage levels were refusing to descend to re-employment levels. Instead he felt that the propensity to consume must be stimulated by direct government spending aided by bank credit. If people were employed and able to consume then this would provide the incentive for investment in industry, and that in turn would create employment. For Keynes the essential point was the balance between saving and investment. Investment was equivalent to capital outlay and savings referred to money that was not yet committed as capital outlay. It was not the static balance between the two that interested Keynes. It was the disequilibrium. In his attention to this Keynes showed that he understood the processes of complex dynamic situations. If the gap between investment and savings was increasing, this would lead to a boom, but if the gap between savings and investment was widening, so that investment was falling further and further behind, then there would be depression and unemployment.

Keynes also felt that the current remedy for this situation, the adjustment of interest rates, was insufficiently sensitive since it did not take into account the 'liquidity preferences' which really determined how people invested. Although he assumed that that was dependent on the characteristics of the investment, there was also an element of psychology involved. It seems likely that in the future economists will have to pay a great deal more attention to the psychology of economics and to the complex interactions this produces. In an effort to contain the credit cycle Keynes advocated credit control and state-sponsored capital development.

It was not so much that Keynes produced a bag of tricks that were guaranteed to solve all economic problems. He did produce solutions and suggestions and a new classification of economic situations but, more importantly, he produced an attitude of mind that was willing to examine the complexity of the situation instead of applying economic dogma and wondering why it did not work.

Philosophically we have had a tradition of trying to understand the world by analysing it into separate parts and fundamental building blocks. Ever since the Greek philosophers, this has been the basis of our rational framework. The relationship of this approach to mathematics is obvious. We have endeavoured

An attitude of mind that was willing to examine the complexity

to get rid of complexity by finding the simplicity beneath it. In some areas (Newton, Maxwell, Einstein) we have been outstandingly successful; in others we have tried to achieve success by dealing with only that part of the complex situation which we could handle and ignoring the rest. This has been the approach in psychology and economics. We have rarely had the courage to deal with complexity in all its complexity.

Sartre and the existentialists had the courage to deal with the 'actuality' of complexity. They fled from rationalist frameworks and analyses which purported to make sense of the world. Instead they wanted to confront the totality of immediate experience in all its rawness. For them the moment-to-moment reality of experience was more important than the abstractions of any rationalist system. For them man was only human in his moment of decision – when he was able to indulge his mood of the moment freed from all frameworks of belief or explanation. The existentialists shied away from the traditional truth-below-the-surface seeking of the philosophers and preferred the truth of the moment: in terms of the individual, the concrete and the particular.

The existentialists treated complexity by confronting its totality without seeking to simplify or make sense of it. They were prepared to face the complexity of the moment as being meaningless but real. Reality and actuality were more important than meaning. Meaning was an abstraction and a reference to a framework. Existentialism is at the same time courageous but also self-indulgent and lazy. It is courageous because it requires man to face the world without the support of meaning and to make the decisions which confirm him as a human being. At the same time it is an abandonment of effort at understanding and a glorification of the subjective mood of the moment. In many ways existentialism has had a considerable effect on youth culture. The need for self-expression, the importance of rebellion, the sanctity of self-indulgence, the deification of the moods of the soul and a disregard for frameworks of any sort are the essential parts of the picture. The philosophy, psychology, mood or mode of life has an appeal so long as courage is involved and the framework of the rest of society remains stable enough to supply the self-indulgent with material stability and a direction for rebellion. As a philosophy for the whole of society, existentialism could never work. As an influence on existing philosophies it can have a beneficial effect in actualizing experience. As an illustration of one way to cope with complexity it is powerful. Keynes had to try to understand complexity in order to deal with it: Sartre dealt with complexity by facing it without feeling the need to understand it.

Though we do not realize it, we have come to the end of what might conveniently be called the Euclidean age of thinking. This was the age in which the universe of our thinking was assumed to be as static as the flat surfaces on which Euclid's propositions and theorems made sense. The age included the Greek philosophers and the powerful influences of Plato and Aristotle. It included the Schoolmen and all subsequent philosophers who explored concepts as static and absolute. It included all those philosophers who thought they were dealing with reality when they were really exploring the conceptual use of language. It included the mathematicians and scientists who were dealing with the stable world and determinable relationships of physics. Because we are now forced to deal with complexity we have to move out of this stable world of logic,

The 'actuality' of complexity

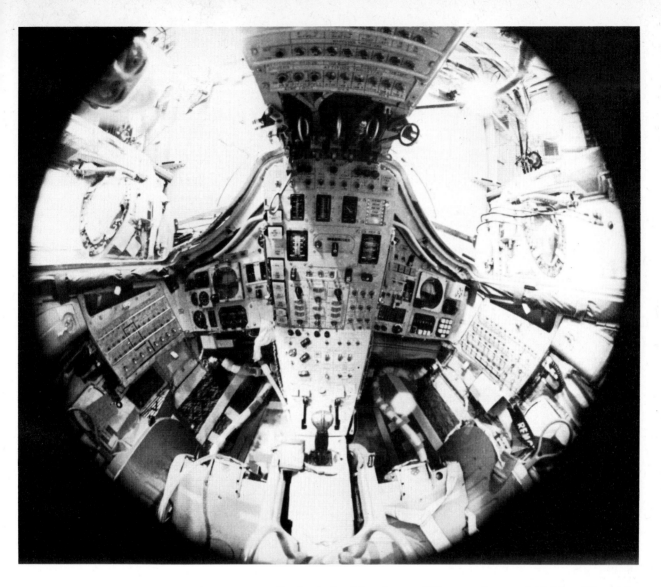

Technological complexity in
the twentieth century: America's
Apollo 9 spacecraft.

concepts, fixed relationships, into a different universe of thinking. We might
characterize the change of universe as being from the 'Euclidean' to the
'physiological'. The human body is probably the most complexly organized
organization in the world. The complexity of its organization is several orders of
magnitude greater than that of the atom.

At the moment the boundaries of science, and indeed of all our thinking, are
formed by our inability to deal with complex systems as a whole. We are unable
to deal with patterns; we still have to break them down into constituent elements
for finite measurement. We have not yet developed a conceptual framework for
dealing with complexity, with the 'physiological' as distinct from the 'Euclidean'
universe. Moreover we are very badly equipped to do so. Our educational
institutions, our media, our intelligentsia are so steeped in the Euclidean
tradition that it is difficult to see where the new thinking would come from or
how it would ever be accepted if it did emerge. Our handling of language and

concepts is still on a Euclidean basis, and language still dominates our thinking. It is possible that the new thinking may come directly from the new philosophers who are the people dealing with computers and information-processing, but they will have to develop a considerably greater conceptual depth in order to take on this new role.

Norbert Wiener was perhaps the boundary marker of this new physiological universe of complexity. In this new universe the phenomena are positive and negative feedback, rate of change sensitivity, self-stabilizing systems, self-organizing systems, self-educating systems and so on. Instead of there being an outside manipulator who places things in order and creates systems, the systems are self-creating and self-stabilizing. All is change, unless change itself is so channelled as to produce a stability in excess of what would have been the case without change. This is the world of patterns. Vast new areas of concepts are waiting to be opened up. It is the world more of the conceptualist than the mathematician. The worry is whether our concepts can develop fast enough to cope with the increase in complexity of our world. What took the slow progress of thinking and counter-thinking over centuries in the Euclidean age must now be accomplished, accepted and disseminated in little more than a quarter of a century. Wiener's Copernican revolution was more profound than that of Copernicus, but largely unnoticed outside a small world of mathematicians and system-designers. Many of the concepts had already been part of the thinking in the field of physiology, where homeostasis was an everyday concept. Wiener's work was also oriented towards control, but control and organization are but different aspects of the same thing.

We may make the mistake of looking for profound concepts when simple concepts will do. We may make the mistake of not recognizing the new concepts and explaining them in terms of the old (as so many economists did with Keynes' ideas). Our intelligentsia will be forced to make the mistake of vigorous defence of the Euclidean universe because therein lies their status and authority. But at least the Columbus trip has been made by Wiener.

The world of patterns

Postscript: the Future

What of the future? Is there any longer a need for 'great thinkers'? In what way might the great thinkers of the future contribute to society? If there are no more great thinkers, how will the thinking be done? Is there a need for thinking and new ideas, or should we just consolidate what we have?

The first question that must be answered is whether there is a need for a new ideology or 'meta-system' to guide people's values and behaviours. Many people have drifted away from strict Christian dogma, but retain the ethical and value elements of Christianity. Will a new ideology ever arise again? If so will it be a matter of slow evolutionary drift or the consequence of one man's thinking? Perhaps a new ideology can only form in opposition to what exists, rather as Marxism acquired its direction by being in opposition to capitalism. Perhaps that experiment has already been tried with fascism. Possibly the need for an overall ideology has disappeared and its place can be taken by sub-ideologies operating at practical levels. Possibly the ideologies of 'coping' will replace the ideologies of 'belief'.

On a personal level, the way man treats himself, ideologies may become as individual as fashion, with everyone trying and choosing what seems to suit them best. In place of fixed philosophies there is the beginning of a drift towards personal mysticism and non-coherent experiences. The need for self-expression, self-actualization and a sort of emotional hedonism is already apparent in the United States. It is not easy to see whether this is a new direction or merely the degeneration of the old direction. Does the failure to see a firm direction make a creed of no-direction or of such temporary directions as occur from moment to moment?

On an ethical level, the way man treats others, the basic Christian system is still operating and may actually be reinforced by the recent idealism of youth. On the other hand the Machiavellian ethic of 'what you can get away with' is becoming stronger than ever. The technically more powerful expression of dissension in terrorism does not necessarily mean a greater amount of dissension.

On a social level, the way man treats and is treated by society, the changes are likely to be much greater. Lack of a strong ideology on a personal and ethical level can only be compensated by some sort of structural·competence on a social level. The days when the social structure was taken care of by the divine appointment of a ruler were followed by the days when the rulers were appoint-ed by the divine process of head-counting, and then assumed to be competent in government simply because they would be afraid to be incompetent, since incompetence would cost them their job at the next election. We may now feel that incompetence is more than a wilful misdemeanour and that an incompetent politician is not necessarily so out of corrigible malice but out of – incompetence. It may become necessary for people to do a lot more thinking for themselves, instead of paying politicians with the currency of prejudice to do it for them. For that to happen we shall have to regard thinking as a skill that we ought to teach in schools rather than as an inevitable consequence of a high IQ acting on a knowledge education.

Perhaps the days of politics, parties, polarizations and ideologies are over, and in place of them we shall have to put competent *administration*. Perhaps instead of beliefs and dogmas we shall have to have an understanding of complex system behaviour. We shall have to pay a great deal more attention to economics, both as to its operation and as to its purpose. On the whole we may see the idiom of expansion replaced by the one of stability and even contraction to a more stable state. We may see ideologies in politics replaced by a common interest in administrative effectiveness. In place of the free-for-all we may have to see an understanding of total systems, so that our values are based on 'system-competence' rather than party flag.

Just as we should be moving out of the 'Euclidean age' of thinking into the age of dynamic interactive systems, so too we should be moving out of the 'adversary system' of logic and philosophy with its yes/no system in which truth is stacked against falsity. The new thinking will be based on a better understanding of mind, on patterns and field effects instead of the logic boxes of language.

There is certainly a bigger need than ever for new thinking and new ideas, because humanity has so filled the earth with a unified complex system that there is little room for error. Complexity has created problems which only good thinking can solve: capable drift is too slow and ideological experimentation too dangerous. The new ideas may come about through team efforts. They may come about by a succession of small contributions, just as the concern for ecology came about. They may come about through a brilliant conceptual step. For instance in the field of energy such a step may solve this problem for all time through a practical approach to nuclear fusion energy which has no con-tamination (unlike fission energy).

The drift and momentum of society is more in favour of a change in concepts by small contributed steps than by great thinking. Our media and intellectual establishments are more geared to the preservation of an obsolescent intellectual idiom than the constructive development of a new one. Our acclaim of scholarship and criticism as the currency of such establishments prevents the excesses of new fantasies and is designed, by in-built continuity, to preserve a trend even if that trend is a downward drift or a bypassed road. The advent of the computer and the understanding of complex systems may have come only just in time to aid the human mind in its difficult task. Yet computers need ideas and values which they cannot generate for themselves. It is not enough to delegate all thinking to systems technologists. The ideas have to come from individual minds – by inspired chance if we admit no more productive method. The values have to come not only from the traditional custodians of value, in literature and in the churches, but also from a people thinking with more than their votes.

Complexity has created problems which only good thinking can solve

Acknowledgments

The illustrations in this book are from the following sources:

The Bettmann Archive, 158, 159
Bibliothèque Nationale, Paris, 62
Bildarchiv Preussischer Kulturbesitz, Berlin, 122, 135, 136, 162, 163, 164 (left, right and bottom)
Bodleian Library, Oxford, 23, 39, 48
British Museum, London, 35, 57, 85 (bottom), 90, 97
Camera Press, 168
A.C. Cooper, 186
Courtauld Institute of Art, London, 95
William Gordon Davis, 181
Deutsche Fotothek, Dresden, 145, 182
General Administrative Archives, Vienna, 176
Germanisches Nationalmuseum, Nuremberg, 85 (top)
E.P. Goldschmidt & Co. Ltd, 99
Robert Harding Associates, 19
David Harris, 15
Hirmer Fotoarchiv, Munich, 46
Institute for the History of Medicine, Vienna, 177
Keystone Press Agency, 192, 201, 203
James Klugmann Collection, 144
Kunsthistorisches Museum, Vienna, 44
Peter N. Lawrence, 128
Mansell Collection, 22, 24, 34, 53, 72, 75, 118
Mary Evans Picture Library, 117
Massachusetts Institute of Technology Historical Collections, 195, 196, 197
Moro, Rome, 150
Musée National du Château de Versailles, 100
Museo Mediceo, Florence, 73
National Portrait Gallery, London, 94, 190
Joseph Needham (*Science and Civilisation in China,* Cambridge University Press), 29
Novosti Press Agency, 172, 173, 174
Österreichische Nationalbibliothek, Vienna, 178
Photo Fratelli Fabbri Editore, Milan, 82
Photographie Giraudon, 100
Popperfoto, 183, 191
Josephine Powell, 52, 56
Punch Publications Limited, 140 (top)
Radio Times Hulton Picture Library, 38, 116, 123, 126, 134, 139, 193
Ronan Picture Library, 40, 77, 99, 101, 102, 105
Royal Academy of Arts, London, 131
Royal Astronomical Society, London 41, 77
By kind permission of the President and Council of the Royal College of Surgeons of England, 138

Royal Institution, London, 155, 156
Royal Society, London, 104, 106
Science Museum, London, 154
Staatliche Museen, Berlin, 16
Uffizi Gallery, Florence, 63 (left)
Ullstein Bilderdienst, 80
University of London Library, 107, 113
Roger Viollet, 14, 58, 67, 200
Votava, 179
Weidenfeld and Nicolson Archives, 18, 36, 43, 63 (right), 78, 84, 112, 121, 127, 140 (bottom), 146, 207

The publishers would like to thank all those who have given them permission to reproduce material in this book. All possible care has been taken in tracing the ownership of copyright material used in this book and in making acknowledgment for its use. If any owner has not been acknowledged the publishers apologize and will be glad of the opportunity to rectify the error.

Picture research by Darlene Weber

ndex